HOME HARVEST

HOME HARVEST

NOTES FROM A COUNTRY KITCHEN

PAMELA WESTLAND

OCTOPUS BOOKS

NOTES

For all recipes, quantities are given in both metric and imperial measures. Follow either set but *not* a mixture of both, as they are not interchangeable.

All spoon measures are level. All eggs are sizes 3 or 4 (standard) unless otherwise indicated.

First published 1986 by
Octopus Books Limited
59 Grosvenor Street,
London W1X 9DA

© Octopus Books Limited 1986

ISBN 0 7064 2564 2
Printed in Spain by Cayfosa, Barcelona
Dep. Leg. B-7651-1986

Title page picture *Filbert shortcake: an autumn feast of hazelnut-baked shortcake filled with cream and blackberries* (recipe on page 125).

CONTENTS

INTRODUCTION

It's part of our heritage, whether we live in town or country, to want to enjoy the fruits of a cottage garden. No other potato tastes quite like the tiny new ones you unearth and cook moments later with a sprig of mint from beneath the kitchen window; no salad ever tastes as tinglingly fresh as the cool, crisp leaves picked in the garden and tossed in your own flavoured dressing; no fruit has the luxurious sun-ripened appeal of the harvest you gather through summer and autumn, and no other preserve could ever compare with the sheer delight of those you make with your own produce.

Everyone's dream garden is one that circles the house like a leafy moat, patches of welcoming scented flowers by the front door; clumps of aromatic herbs within easy reach of the kitchen; a well-established fruit tree or two – ones that have served generations and are fun for children to climb; and a netting cage of soft fruits to capture the essence of summer – without feeding the birds. There would also be, in this visionary plot, a vegetable garden to make self-sufficiency a reality, and glass tunnels or a glasshouse to bring exotic plants in need of special pampering into the realms of possibility. Hedges there would certainly be, to protect the crops from frost and winter winds and to lay an exciting treasure trail of aromatic elderflowers in the spring, followed by creamy nuts and bright berries in the autumn months.

For many of us, a garden like this is the pot of gold at the foot of the rainbow. But wherever we live, however large or small our garden or balcony, we can easily create the mood of the environment we have inherited from generations of gardeners. Herbs grown in a pot on the windowsill have all the pungency of those raised in a formal herb garden on a great estate and finger-sized courgettes raised in a growing-bag on the balcony are just as delicious in ratatouille as those flourishing on a fertile mound; the satisfaction of growing and harvesting your own crops is there, just the same.

Gardens are very personal things. What you can grow is determined to some extent by the space you have, the aspect and the soil: you can't grow main-crop potatoes to feed a family of four in a postage-stamp plot, and you can't grow much at all in tired old soil until you set about enriching it. But what you choose to grow is also dictated by what you and your family like to eat.

Walk along a row of houses with well-cared-for gardens and look over the fences – a great British pastime – and you will see that no two are alike. One of the small rectangular plots may hark back to olden days with apple trees, rhubarb, onions, runner beans, mint and marigolds growing all of a-

jumble: high on tradition, nostalgia and labour, and somewhat difficult to give each crop the soil fertilizer and dressing it needs to produce good, disease-free yields.

The next garden might be what I call the 'nail scissor' type, tiny paths and low dividing hedges neatly clipped, not a leaf out of place, with miniature beds of herbs and dwarf vegetables laid out with mathematical precision. Take a photograph of the herb and vegetable gardens when you visit one of the stately homes, scale it down and you too can have a garden of high productivity and high precision. It takes a tremendous amount of work to keep it that way, though!

Further along the road you might come across a family who go in for vegetables in a big way: rows of cloches protecting seedlings from hail, tempest and pigeons; runner beans climbing up wigwam poles in the centre of beds; herbs edging patches of brassicas – obviously a good place to get invited to supper!

And so it goes on. Another garden may appear to have nothing but flowers – but you might be surprised to find how many of them are edible and what delicious confections you can make with a handful of carnation petals or a few sprays of broom.

So, when it comes to gardening, each of us will express our personality and preferences in different ways. One person's dream is to have a no-work garden where everything grows to perfection without a row being hoed (I hate to tell you but such a utopia doesn't exist), while for many others gardening plays an important therapeutic role in their lives and is virtually the only exercise they ever get. It's more productive than jogging or aerobics, certainly!

A patchwork of ideas

Whatever kind of garden you have and whatever kind of gardener you are, I hope you will find both helpful information and inspiration throughout this book. We have divided it into sections covering herbs, fruits, vegetables, salads and flowers. In each section you will find a brief description of the range of plants you can grow, the type of soil conditions and cultivation techniques they need, when to harvest and how to store the crop.

And then there are recipes to help you make the most of your crops. Some are traditional favourites, firmly woven into our culinary heritage, while others explore new ways to prepare and cook both familiar and less familiar ingredients. One of the exciting things about gardening is that new varieties of food plants are constantly being developed: ones which are hardier and can better withstand cold northern weather conditions; ones which are more resistant to disease and will therefore crop successfully with the aid of fewer insecticides and pesticides; and ones with improved flavour. Grow your own fruit and vegetables and choose which varieties you prefer, regardless of commercial viability or restrictive regulations.

Previous pages Two versions of the cottage garden. In the oval frame on page 10, a well-trodden path divides vegetables from flowers, while on page 11 colourful aromatics rival one another, and delight honeybees, in the walled seclusion of a paved kitchen garden.

The herb garden

You may not have a patch devoted specially to herbs – but there's no need to. They fit in quite happily among the vegetables and don't look at all out of place among the flowers. Herbs are easy to grow, the annuals from seed and the perennials from small rooted cuttings, and so versatile that it's well worth extending your repertoire by a few plants each year.

Once you have fresh herbs at your fingertips, you have the key to dishes that just cannot be equalled without them. A leg of lamb spiked with garlic and snippings of rosemary, grilled fish with stalks of pungent fennel, minestrone soup with that delightful basil and pine kernel sauce called pesto – without fresh herbs these and countless other dishes through this book would never reach their full flavour potential.

That flavour can be captured to perfection by infusing fresh herbs in oil, vinegar or sugar – basil oil to dress tomato salad, marjoram vinegar to add to mayonnaise, rosemary or bay sugar to use in baking and creamy desserts – and the scents of the herb garden will linger even when snow covers the ground.

Herbal teas, self-help medicines and beauty preparations may evoke visions of your grandmother in her heyday, but we have passed the 'synthetic is beautiful' era now, and are rediscovering the pleasures of herbal preparations of all kinds. We have some delightful cottage-industry notions for you to try, so make yourself a refreshing cup of angelica tea while you browse through the pages!

The orchard

You need only one or two fruit trees – bonnets of blossom in the spring, boughs heavy with fruit in summer – to give the feeling of an orchard. And there's no better place to shelter from the heat of the sun, to sit shelling peas or stringing redcurrants.

Apples and pears, cherries and mulberries, damsons and plums, medlars and quinces – with these in your basket, turn your mind to farmhouse fare, new-style vitality drinks and old-fashioned preserves. Pheasant casseroled with slices of quince, steak in plum sauce, greengage tart and spiced apple milk shake all give a delicious hint of the versatility of fruits from your trees.

Depending on the season, even a single tree – be it a standard, half-standard, cordon or fan-trained – can give you a glut of fruits. Be thankful because that's the stuff that jams, jellies, chutneys and sauces are made of – and it will be a long year until the next harvest.

The vegetable garden

To many gardeners the vegetable crops – from the earliest tenderest broad beans through to the winter-lasting roots and brassicas – represent the height of achievement. And certainly, what with all that soil preparation, feeding, sowing, thinning, weeding and staking, there's never a dull – or an idle – moment in the vegetable garden.

The vegetable section is divided season by season according to the harvesting time of the various crops; not altogether rigid divisions, of course, for some crops are available in such variety that they can span practically the whole year. What would spring be without plump and tender shoots of asparagus and the first bright green spinach leaves; summer, without pod-popping peas, and runner beans hanging like giant green catkins; autumn, without prize-winning marrows, golden corn and the bustle of 'salting some vegetables away' for the winter; and winter itself, without all the good keepers that make soups, stews and casseroles so heartening? Some gardeners, mainly of the old school, grow little else besides vegetables, and one can easily see why.

Soft fruits

The advent of pick-your-own fruit farms up and down the country has focused many gardeners' minds anew on the joy of harvesting your own crops. Grow them at home and you choose the varieties – perhaps old favourites, perhaps recently introduced ones – that have the strongest, sweetest flavour. Home gardeners are not usually looking primarily for high yields, but for the true enjoyment of the fruits of their labours.

Think of berry fruits and currants and you think of – what? Tea in the garden, the scones piled high with strawberries and the cakes sandwiched with jam; oven-fresh dumplings and waffles glistening with blue-black berries; cranberry sauce or stuffing for a festive turkey? We have them all, these recipes, and many more; and the know-how to help you – not the birds – enjoy a fruitful harvest.

The glasshouse

Gardening is addictive. Once you experience the minor miracle – for such it surely is – of planting seeds, pitching your skill, knowledge and luck against the elements and producing succulent crops, and you get even more ambitious. You want to sow seeds even earlier, anticipating the seasons by a week or so, try your hand at tender crops that just won't flourish outdoors in our climate, and ward off the worst of winter, keeping the crops coming for another few weeks. All of which demands the installation of some protective glass.

Then you're away, the cuisine of the Mediterranean right there in your glasshouse: pipérade, grilled pepper salad, stuffed aubergines, black fig sorbet, passion fruit soufflé, glacé fruits for Christmas – and all from your own back yard.

The salad garden

Freshness is perhaps more significant in salad crops than in any other. And by growing your own you can enjoy much greater variety: a few leaves of Salad Bowl lettuce, some pak choi stalks, a chicon of chicory, a handful of spring onions, perhaps some dandelion and nasturtium leaves, a few sprigs of mint or marjoram – you can compose the salad, contrasting shape, flavour and colour, as you walk round the garden.

Gather the salad just before you need it, allowing time only for the ingredients to chill, and then toss it with a dressing just before you serve it.

But that rule of thumb is to assume that all salads are served fresh, and chilled. Many are, but some are not. Our recipes show a revised interest in *salades tièdes*, in which crisp leaves are tossed with a hot dressing, and extend to soups, terrines and delicious portable picnic fare – all from your salad garden.

The wild garden

All the countryside's a wild garden, and many of our own plots have wild corners, too. Bullace and bramble, hips and haws, nuts and nettles, flowers and leaves – there's an exciting new culinary world just the other side of the hedge.

This is the area of food for free – though of course it's only free, and indeed available, if it's on common ground. Few farmers would take kindly to a bout of scrumping on their land, no matter how irresistible the wild food recipes in this section!

Now we're really into the realms of country lore – chestnut soup, pot herbs, wild leaf salads, and drinks galore. Lime flower tea, bramble tip wine, nettle beer, sloe gin, dandelion coffee – whatever the mood or occasion there's a soothing, refreshing or exhilarating country drink to match it.

The flower garden

With all this talk of crops and yields and productivity it might seem something of an indulgence to grow flowers at all! Yet even if we didn't value them for their looks, many flowers have a surprising amount to offer the adventurous cook. You can use scented petals, just like herbs, for infusions: rose-petal water to make perfumed fondants; carnation sugar to use when you make frothy, creamy desserts; and a medley of flower waters to use both in cooking and in cosmetics.

Petals from damask, musk and other species of roses, the most romantic of flowers, have so many uses it's a crime to let them perish and fall. Four pages of 'think cooking, think roses' ideas, including old-fashioned rose posset, rose garden sorbet and eglantine sauce really should set you thinking.

Marigolds with beef? Nasturtiums in fritters? Gladiolus flowers filled with a savoury salad? Border pink rice pudding? Yes, and why not? The flower garden isn't just a pretty place!

Gifts from the garden

What *might* be indulgent would be to have a blossoming garden – all those fruits and vegetables and flowers – and keep it all to yourself! All through the book you will find recipes and ideas that are eminently suitable as gifts – preserves, flavourings, cosmetics and crafts to take to friends or sell on charity stalls. And now there's a special section, reinforcing earlier suggestions, for collections of dried herbs and flowers, fruit butters, sweet and savoury preserves, fresh-from-the-oven baking, all prettily packed for presentation.

Arrangements

Beauty is in the eye of the beholder and whatever you grow in your garden is certainly beautiful to behold. Some produce, however, is more decorative than others and we look at the garden with a critically artistic eye. The result is baskets of shiny polished fruits and vegetables, boughs of nuts and berries, sprays of herbs mingled with flowers, and posies as pretty as any a Victorian miss ever carried.

Whatever your interest in the garden – whether it is the scientific one of growing things, the creativity of cooking with fresh produce or the decorative art of composing beautiful things – I hope this book will inspire you.

THE HERB GARDEN

What varied images the term 'herb garden' conjures up! On the one hand there is the picture of the formal gardens designed for monasteries and great country estates. Here each species of herb was planted in neat rows separated by paths of brick, or stone, or low-growing, soft-to-tread-on herbs such as thyme and camomile. These formal gardens could be seen from the windows of the house in all their geometric glory, describing patterns like the spokes of a wheel, concentric circles, diamonds, squares – and always with perfect symmetry.

At the other end of the scale there were the cottage gardens, where herbs jostled for position and shafts of sunlight fell on fruit and vegetables in glorious profusion. Sage and thyme were there to flavour the sausages, and to be dried for tea in winter; elderflowers dipped down low over gooseberries – the flowers such a perfect complement to the stewed fruit; pink-flowering marjoram provided fragrant ground cover beneath the roses; and mint mingled with rows of potatoes or peas – partners already.

All of which goes to show that herbs are versatile, not only in the home, where they can be used as salads, flavourings, preservatives, garnishes, self-help medicines and beauty aids, but in the garden too. Whether your inclination is towards the neat-and-tidy approach of the formal garden or

the rough and tumble of the cottage garden, you will find herbs the most satisfying plants to grow. Just as one or two aromatic leaves can transform a dish, so the scents released by the plants, especially in the heat of summer, can transform a garden.

Most herbs have very modest requirements in terms of soil. Many of them came originally from the hot, dry regions of southern Europe, so one thing they do not like is heavy clay or damp, boggy conditions. The glossary of herbs on pages 16 and 17 gives details of individual likes and dislikes, but the general rule of thumb is that herbs don't like getting their feet wet. Planting them at the top of a piece of sloping ground could be the answer.

Decide which types of herb will be most useful to you – whether you long to grill fish on sticks of dried fennel over a barbecue, or like nothing more complicated than a snipping of chives on a tomato salad – then weigh up the space you have available. Let your imagination stray and consider low-growing herbs as edgings for flower beds and vegetable patches alike; sink pots of rampant herbs like mint (to restrain their roots) close to a door; alternate tall-growing decorative herbs such as lovage and bronze fennel with hollyhocks and foxgloves at the back of a border, and so on.

Take into account the projected height of the plants and

Conveniently to hand outside the kitchen door, fennel, sage, golden marjoram, a profusion of herbs is ready to enhance the cookery year.

whether they prefer sun – which means a south- or west-facing situation – or shade, and plan accordingly. In the early autumn, dig the ground well, work in some compost, and give the soil a final raking. Then in spring, the planting season, dig and rake the soil again and walk over it, firmly and systematically, to firm it up. Neither seeds nor roots can get a hold on life in loose, crumbly soil.

So which is it to be – seeds or roots? You can sow the seeds of most annuals in early spring, either in boxes under glass, or, once there's no danger of frost, straight into the ground. Seed packets give you the finer details of cultivation. By early summer you will be reaping a fragrant harvest.

You can buy plants or take cuttings of the perennial herbs, such as rosemary and bay (which both happen to be evergreen, too) and plant them out wherever they can grow. And if you're doubtful of your green fingers, or are short of time, you can buy annuals as container-grown plants too. Garden centres and plant shops have a wider and wider selection each year.

A herb garden is one of the easiest to manage, as most herbs come into the low-maintenance category. Thin back the straggly woody ones, like sage and thyme, water tiny seedlings and young plants assiduously in dry spells, and enjoy the plants to the full.

GETTING TO KNOW YOUR HERBS

Angelica, *Angelica archangelica* Native to northern Europe, this umbellifer likes partial shade and a rich, moist soil. It grows to a height of 2m (6ft) and so is a back-of-the-border plant. It's a biennial which, if pruned before the flowers set, becomes a perennial.

To cultivate, sow ripe seed in boxes or straight into ground in August. Trim in autumn and don't be alarmed when it dies down in winter. Use the aromatic leaves when poaching fruit or fish. Candy young stems to use as a decoration. Infuse ripe seeds to flavour milk and custard.

Basil, *Ocimum basilicum* A native herb of Greece, basil thrives in hot, dry, sunny conditions – in a pot on the windowsill especially. There are two main types of this half-hardy annual: bush, which grows to 20cm (8in), and sweet, which grows to 60cm (2ft).

Plant seed in spring, prick out seedlings into pots and plant out in summer. The bright green or purple, pointed leaves are especially good in tomato salad and sauces, with egg dishes, cream cheese, potatoes, poultry and fish.

Bay, *Laurus nobilis* Trained and trimmed in a pot or planted near the kitchen door, bay is an evergreen shrub which can reach 10m (30ft).

Grow from container-grown plants, or take cuttings in early autumn. Use the fresh or dried leaves in marinades, and infused in casseroles, stocks, sauces, milk and cream dishes.

Bergamot, *Monarda didyma* A beautiful, aromatic, bee-attracting perennial. There are crimson, pink, white and purple flowered varieties. *M. fistulosa* is the wild bergamot.

Sow seeds *in situ* in spring and surround with peat in summer to keep the roots moist. The flowers can be used as a substitute for marigolds, or crystallized, for decoration. The leaves infused in syrup work wonders on fruit salads and puddings.

Borage, *Borago officinalis* Perhaps the most attractive plant in the herb garden, it has bright blue flowers.

Sow seeds of this annual in April in a sunny spot, where they can grow to 1m (3ft) – they'll self-seed prolifically for ever more. Young leaves can be used for salad, and the flowers are candied as cake decorations or floated in drinks.

Caraway, *Carum carvi* A biennial and one of the few spices it is possible to grow in northern Europe.

Sow seeds *in situ* where they can reach 60cm (2ft). Harvest ripe seed and hang stems upside-down to dry. Caraway seeds are traditionally used to flavour cakes, biscuits and fruit pies, which they do, pungently. They're also good in pickles and with cabbage and cauliflower.

Chervil, *Anthriscus cerefolium* This biennial herb looks like a more feathery and delicate version of parsley and has the unique quality of intensifying the flavour of any accompanying herb.

Sow the seed in partial shade in succession from spring through the summer, and thin to 20cm (8in) apart. Use in a mixture of *fines herbes*, in salads, sauces, dressings, stuffings and creamy soups.

Chives, *Allium schoenoprasum* A member of the onion family, chives like sun or partial shade and even do well – if adequately fed – indoors.

Plant bulbs or divide in spring. Cut off the attractive bright mauve flowerheads – they dry well for decoration – to strengthen the plant. The more you cut the leaves, the more vigorous they will become. Use the leaves as a garnish for soups, casseroles and pâté, or chopped in salads and cheese, egg, vegetable and fish dishes.

Coriander, *Coriandrum sativum* This plant, which is an annual, grows to 45cm (18in) high. It looks much like flat-leafed parsley, but has a distinctive smell.

Sow seed *in situ* in April. Tie muslin over ripening seedheads, cut them and hang upside-down to dry. It's a dual-purpose herb: you can use the hot, spicy leaves in curries, casseroles and salads, and the dried seeds in meat dishes, stuffings, bread and biscuits.

Dill, *Anethum graveolens* Dill resembles fennel with its feathery leaves and yellow flowers. Its flavour is more subtle, with none of that hint of anise.

Sow the seed of this annual plant in a sunny, sheltered spot in spring, where it can grow to 60cm (2ft). Protect the ripening seedheads in muslin bags, then hang-dry them. The leaves are good in salads, creamy sauces, and with vegetables and fish, and the seeds are used as a preserving spice in pickles, and to flavour cabbage and root vegetables.

Fennel, *Foeniculum vulgare* Sweet fennel is the herb grown for its feathery leaves, spicy seeds and dried stalks. (It is Florence fennel that is grown for its bulbous root – see vegetable garden, p. 69.)

Sow the seed of the annual sweet fennel in April and thin to 30cm (12in) apart. It can grow to 2m (6ft) high. The leaves complement all kinds of fish and cheese dishes and are a decorative garnish. The dried seeds make a pungent, chewy topping for bread and rolls, and the dried stalks are strewn on barbecues and grills.

Lemon balm, *Melissa officinalis* A vigorous perennial which grows to a height of about 1m (3ft), the leaves of lemon balm have a strong citrus smell.

Propagate by root division in spring or autumn. The leaves are used in summer drinks, as a garnish and as a pleasant alternative to mint.

Lovage, *Levisticum officinale* This perennial herb reaches 2m (6ft) high and has a straight, thick, hollow stem.

Sow seed in boxes in autumn, and plant out about 60cm (2ft) apart in spring in a sunny position. The large, cut leaves have a 'hot' taste when they're raw and give a yeasty flavour to soups, stews and sauces.

Marjoram, *Origanum* spp One of the most versatile of herbs and, in a sunny spot, one of the easiest to grow.

Sweet or knotted marjoram (*O. majorana*) is a half-hardy annual grown from seed planted under glass in April. Wild (*O. vulvare* or **Oregano**) and pot (*O. onites*) marjorams are perennial – you can divide the plants in winter. They all bring a taste of the Mediterranean to salads, dressings, vegetables – especially potato, bean and tomato dishes – rice, pasta and stuffings.

Mint, *Mentha* spp Apple mint, Bowles mint (the ideal choice for mint sauce), curly mint, eau de cologne, peppermint, pineapple, spearmint and watermint – a catalogue of sweetly smelling herbs, each with a special characteristic. Mints are perennials that like a moist, shady spot.

Plant their roots in sunken pots if you don't want them to spread vigorously. Be adventurous – use chopped mint in cheese dishes, pasta sauces, with rice, marrow, courgettes, beans and green salad, and to flavour syrup for fruit salads and compôtes.

Oregano see **Marjoram**.

Parsley, *Carum petroselinum* Another long list of types varying from curly parsley – with tightly frilled leaves, almost like a bright green clenched fist – to flat-leafed parsley – so perfect for Greek food.

Parsley is a biennial, best bought as container-grown plants. The seed is tricky to germinate – soak it in boiling water first, then sow in shade. Use in all savoury dishes, especially with fish, and for an attractive garnish.

Rosemary, *Rosmarinus officinalis* An evergreen shrub which grows to 1.2m (4ft) and has delicate pale blue flowers.

Plant a container-grown plant or cutting in a sunny, sheltered spot – harsh winter conditions can be fatal. Chop the spiky needle-like leaves finely for stuffings and casseroles; immerse sprigs in soups, stews, sauces, dressings and milk puddings; or press small sprigs in slits in lamb for roasting or grilling. Whole sprigs make a spectacular garnish.

Sage, *Salvia officinalis* Sage is an evergreen shrub that can reach 60cm (2ft) and likes a dry, sunny position.

Sow seeds in pots in spring and set out 45cm (18in) apart. Renew plants every 4 years when they become woody and straggly. Use sage and onion stuffing to offset the richness of pork and goose, whole sage leaves tossed with tender slices of liver, chopped sage in apple pie, sage tea to ward off winter ills – this is a herb of many parts.

Salad burnet, *Sanguisorba minor* A pretty edging plant, or one to grow in tubs, salad burnet is a perennial which reaches only about 30cm (12in) high.

Sow seed in boxes in spring, harden them off under glass and plant out in summer. Use the long, slender cut leaves in salads, dressings, summer drinks, and with fish and poultry.

Savory, *Satureia hortensis* (Summer savory) and *S. montana* (Winter savory) Summer savory grows to about 45cm (18in). It has narrow green leaves and small pink flowers. The winter variety is a lower shrub with woody stems. They both thrive in a warm, sunny position.

For summer savory, sow the seeds in April and then thin out later to 20cm (8in).

Savory is known as the bean herb: the annual summer savory is traditionally added fresh to young broad beans and green beans, and the winter type, a perennial, is useful for dried bean dishes, salads, rich, warming meat casseroles and soups.

Sweet cicely, *Myrrhis odorata* An attractive 60cm (2ft) perennial with large light green leaves and umbrellas of tiny, white, sweet-smelling flowers.

Sow the seeds in early spring or propagate by root division. This is one of the few herbs used largely for desserts – infuse the leaves in syrup and fruit sauces, when stewing or poaching fruit and in salad dressings.

Tarragon, *Artemisia dracunculus* It is important to choose French tarragon and not the much more bitter-tasting Russian tarragon.

Grow from cuttings, or by root division. The long, slender leaves of this perennial are used to flavour fish, poultry and egg dishes especially. Infuse sprigs of the herb in oil and vinegar for salads, and in stock, sauces and stews.

Thyme, *Thymus* spp The plant is a low-growing perennial which likes full sun. Constant cutting back stops it from becoming woody.

Thyme is a good mixer: a couple of sprigs of the fresh herb, or a spoonful of dried thyme, are invaluable in a bouquet garni to infuse in stocks, soups, sauces and casseroles; parsley and thyme stuffing is an old favourite for game and poultry; and a little thyme also intensifies the flavour of other herbs. Not only the tiny round leaves are aromatic: harvest the purple flowers, hang them to dry, crumble them lightly and store in jars. A pinch of the dried flowers is a delicious addition to both sweet and savoury dishes. Lemon thyme, *Thymus citriodorus,* has a delicate lemon flavour and is specially good with chicken, fish and fruits.

SPRING LUNCHES

*Now there's more than a hint of warmth in the air,
and suddenly it's time to shrug off the hearty food of
winter. Celebrate the coming of spring with light
and appetizing first courses, main dishes marinated
or cooked with herbs and a traditional dessert with
an aromatic difference.*

GRAVAD LAX

*Raw salmon marinated in a herb pickle
is a Scandinavian speciality, to serve as
a first course or part of a salad buffet. It
will keep in the refrigerator for about
two weeks.*

750g (1½lb) fresh salmon, middle cut
or tail piece
dill or fennel leaves, to garnish

PICKLE
2 × 15ml spoons (2tbls) sea salt
1 × 5ml spoon (1tsp) peppercorns, crushed
2 × 15ml spoons (2tbls) dark brown sugar
3 × 15ml spoons (3tbls) gin
2 × 15ml spoons (2tbls) chopped dill leaves

1   Cut the salmon in half lengthways
and remove the bones. Leave the skin
intact.
2   Mix together the pickle
ingredients.
3   Rub the pickle well into both sides
of each piece of salmon and place the
two halves together again.
4   Wrap the salmon in foil, place it on
a flat plate or board and put a weight
on top.
5   Chill the salmon in the refrigerator
for 2-3 days, turning it once each day.
6   Skin the salmon and slice it very
thinly. Garnish it with fresh dill and
serve a vinaigrette dressing separately.
Serve with thinly sliced wholewheat
bread and butter.

SERVES 6

MAYTIME MOUSSE

*A light and appealing first course or
light luncheon dish.*

½ medium cucumber, peeled and diced
salt
6 hard-boiled eggs, peeled
1 × 450ml (15fl oz) can jellied consommé,
chilled
3 × 15ml spoons (3tbls) chopped marjoram
300ml (½ pint) double cream, chilled
freshly ground black pepper

GARNISH
½ cucumber, very thinly sliced
100g (4oz) peeled prawns
3-4 small sprigs marjoram

1   Place the diced cucumber in a
colander and sprinkle it liberally with
salt. Stand it on a plate and leave it to
drain for at least 1 hour. Rinse thoroughly under cold water. Drain the
cucumber and pat it dry with kitchen
paper.
2   Place 3 eggs, half the consommé
and half the marjoram in a blender or
food processor and blend until the
mixture is smooth. Pour it into a bowl
and blend the remaining eggs, consommé and marjoram.
3   Whip the cream until it is stiff. Fold
the cream and cucumber into the egg
mixture and season with pepper.
4   Pour the mixture into a soufflé
dish and chill in the refrigerator for
about 2 hours, until it is set.
5   Garnish the mousse with a ring of
overlapping cucumber slices around
the edge. Pile the prawns in the centre
and arrange the marjoram sprigs.

SERVES 6

LEG OF LAMB WITH ROSEMARY

*New season's lamb is traditionally
served, flavoured with sprigs of
rosemary and slivers of garlic, as a
celebration to herald spring.*

1.5kg (3¼lb) leg of lamb
rosemary oil, or olive oil, for brushing
salt
freshly ground black pepper
about 8 small sprigs rosemary
2 garlic cloves, peeled and thinly sliced

1   Trim the lamb of excess fat. Brush
it all over with oil and season it well
with salt and pepper. Make small slits
in the lamb and insert small snippings
of rosemary and slivers of garlic.
Reserve some rosemary to garnish.
2   Stand the meat on a wire rack in a
roasting pan. Cook it in the oven
preheated to 230°C, 450°F, gas 8 for 15
minutes, turning the meat once.
3   Lower the heat to 180°C, 350°F, gas
4 and roast for a further 1-1¼ hours,
until it is cooked the way you like it.
Test the meat by inserting a fine
skewer into the thickest part of the leg.
If you like your lamb on the rare side,
the juices should run slightly pink; if
you like it well done they should run
clear.
4   Skim the fat from the pan juices
and use them to make gravy.
5   Garnish the lamb with rosemary
sprigs and serve it sliced.

SERVES 6

MARINATED TURKEY KEBABS

1kg (2¼lb) boneless turkey breasts
6 button onions, peeled
12 bay leaves
6 button mushrooms, trimmed

MARINADE
3 × 15ml spoons (3tbls) sunflower oil
3 × 15ml spoons (3tbls) dry vermouth
3 × 15ml spoons (3tbls) light soy sauce
1 clove garlic, peeled and crushed
2.5cm (1in) fresh ginger, peeled and chopped
2 × 15ml spoons (2tbls) chopped coriander
salt
freshly ground black pepper

1   Cut the turkey breasts into 2.5cm (1in) squares.
2   Blanch the onions in boiling water for 3 minutes. Drain and thoroughly dry them.
3   Mix the marinade ingredients in a bowl. Add the turkey and onions. Stir, cover and set aside to marinate for several hours, or overnight.
4   Lift out the turkey and onions, reserving the marinade. Thread the meat, onions, mushrooms and bay leaves on to 6 skewers.
5   Heat the grill to medium. Grill the skewers for 10 minutes, turning them frequently and brushing them with the remaining marinade. Serve with a tomato and chive salad and rice or alternatively with Hot potato and chive salad (page 20).

SERVES 6

Variation Coriander is a good choice of herb for the marinade as it has a slight spiciness. You could ring the changes with many others, such as thyme and lovage.
If you have a 'matching' herb-flavoured oil, use it in place of the sunflower oil to complement the herb in the marinade.

A traditional spring roast perfect for Sunday lunch, the leg of lamb is studded with slivers of garlic cloves and cooked with sprigs of rosemary.

GRILLED POUSSINS WITH TARRAGON SAUCE

2 poussins
2 garlic cloves, peeled and thinly sliced
salt
freshly ground black pepper
3 × 15ml spoons (3tbls) tarragon oil
2 × 15ml spoons (2tbls) lemon juice
2-3 sprigs tarragon, to garnish

SAUCE
200ml (⅓ pint) Greek-style yoghurt
1 garlic clove, peeled and crushed
2 × 15ml spoons (2tbls) chopped tarragon

1   Split the poussins in half. Flatten them by beating firmly but gently with a rolling pin.
2   Place the poussin halves in a shallow dish. Scatter on the garlic and season with salt and pepper. Mix together the oil and lemon juice, pour over the poussins and toss to coat the poultry thoroughly. Cover and set aside in a cool place for at least 1 hour.
3   Heat the grill to high. Grill the poussins for 10 minutes on each side or until they are well cooked. Test by piercing the thickest part of the leg with a fine skewer. The juices should run clear.
4   To make the sauce, beat the yoghurt and garlic, stir in the chopped tarragon and season with salt and pepper.
5   Garnish the poussins with the tarragon sprigs. Serve with rice and serve the sauce separately.

SERVES 4

HOT POTATO & CHIVE SALAD

500g (1¼lb) potatoes, peeled and diced
salt
1 medium onion, peeled and chopped
1 × 15ml spoon (1tbls) boiling water
1 × 15ml spoon (1tbls) chive vinegar
(see p. 32)
3 × 15ml spoons (3tbls) mayonnaise
3 × 15ml spoons (3tbls) soured cream
freshly ground black pepper
1 × 15ml spoon (1tbls) finely snipped chives
3 × 15ml spoons (3tbls) walnut halves
a few chive leaves, to garnish

1   Cook the potatoes in boiling, salted water.
2   Put the onion into a bowl and pour on the boiling water and vinegar.
3   Strain the potatoes and add them to the onion.
4   Mix together the mayonnaise and soured cream, season with salt and pepper and stir in the snipped chives. Pour the dressing over the potatoes and toss to coat them thoroughly. Reheat gently if needed.
5   Stir in the walnuts. Turn the potatoes into a heated dish. Cut the chive leaves into 5cm (2in) lengths and scatter over the potatoes to garnish.

SERVES 4

TROUT ON A PARSLEY BED

A West Country way of cooking trout – fried in a pan with lots of butter and a handful of crisp parsley.

4 rainbow trout, gutted and cleaned
2 × 15ml spoons (2tbls) lemon juice
salt
freshly ground black pepper
2 garlic cloves, peeled and finely chopped
12 × 15ml spoons (12tbls) chopped parsley
75g (3oz) butter

1   Rub the fish inside and out with the lemon juice and season it with salt and pepper. Mix the garlic with 2 × 15ml spoons (2tbls) of the chopped parsley. Stuff the fish with this mixture.
2   Heat the butter in a frying pan. When it is smoking, lower in the fish and cook over moderate heat for 3-4 minutes on each side. (This method is a cross between deep- and shallow-frying.)
3   Lift out the trout on a fish slice and arrange them on a heated dish.
4   Add the remaining parsley to the butter, cook for 1 minute then pour over the fish. Serve at once.

Tiny new potatoes and steamed cauliflower and broccoli garnished with slivered almonds make good accompaniments.

SERVES 4

PARSLEY SALAD

This salad is delicious as a dressing to cream cheese and as a spread in sandwiches. It is also good tossed with pasta salad.

50g (2oz) chopped parsley
2 × 15ml spoons (2tbls) sunflower oil
1 × 15ml spoon (1tbls) lemon juice
salt
freshly ground black pepper

1   With this amount of parsley to chop, use a food processor if you have one. You can do this in advance and store the chopped parsley in a covered container in the refrigerator.
2   Just before you want to serve the salad, stir in the oil and lemon juice, and season with salt and pepper.

SERVES 4

GARDEN SALAD WITH HERB CROUTONS

½ head curly endive
1 head radicchio (red chicory)
1 head chicory
1 head celery leaves
1 handful young sorrel leaves

DRESSING
3 × 15ml spoons (3tbls) herb oil (see p. 32)
1 × 15ml spoons (1tbls) herb vinegar
(see p. 32)
salt
freshly ground black pepper
¼ × 5ml spoon (¼tsp) sugar

CROÛTONS
2 thick slices white bread
50g (2oz) butter
4 × 15ml spoons (4tbls) mixed herbs

1   Separate the endive and radicchio leaves, discarding any discoloured ones. Slice the chicory across into thin rings. Separate the celery leaves. Tear off and discard any thick stalks from the sorrel.
2   Toss all the salad ingredients in a bowl. Cover and chill in the refrigerator.
3   Mix the dressing ingredients and set aside.
4   Cut the crusts from the bread and cut the bread into cubes. Heat the butter in a pan. Fry the bread cubes over moderate heat, stirring them often until they are golden brown and dry.
5   Toss the croûtons at once in the chopped herbs. Leave them to cool.
6   Pour the dressing over the salad and toss to coat the leaves thoroughly. Scatter the croûtons on top.
SERVES 4-6

Cook's note

Try making this Greek yoghurt cheese with your own homemade yoghurt, or use Greek sheep's milk yoghurt instead of cow's milk yoghurt, for a sharper and less rich cheese.

FREEZING HERBS

You can freeze herbs on the stem, or strip off the leaves and freeze them whole. The leaves crumble at a touch when they're frozen, and don't need chopping.

Alternatively chop the fresh herbs, pack them into ice-cube trays and fill with water. Add to soups, sauces and so on as they are, or strain them through a sieve.

For summer drinks, freeze herb sprigs or flowers such as borage in ice cubes.

GREEK YOGHURT CHEESE

Strain the yoghurt the day before, then toss the cheese with fresh herbs from the garden. Close your eyes and you're on a Greek island!

600ml (1 pint) natural yoghurt
sea salt
freshly ground black pepper
2 × 5ml spoons (2tsp) olive oil
1 × 15ml spoon (1tbls) chopped thyme
1 × 15ml spoon (1tbls) sesame seeds

1   Line a colander with muslin and stand it over a bowl. Tip in the yoghurt and tie the muslin with string to enclose it. Hang the muslin bag over a bowl and leave it to drain for several hours, or overnight.
2   Tip the curds into a bowl and beat until smooth. Season with salt and pepper and beat in the olive oil. Form the cheese into a flat round shape.
3   Pound the thyme and sesame seeds together in a mortar to form a thick paste. Tip on to a piece of foil.
4   Place the cheese on the foil and turn to coat it thoroughly. Loosely wrap the cheese and chill in the refrigerator.
SERVES 4

Variation For cocktail savouries, to serve with olives and slices of cucumber, roll the curd into small balls about the size of a walnut, toss the cheese in the herb mixture and chill before serving.

Try combinations of sesame seeds and other herbs – basil, marjoram, oregano and flat-leafed parsley are all delicious in this cheese.

GOOSEBERRY & MINT FOOL

500g (1¼lb) gooseberries, topped and tailed
4 × 15ml spoons (4tbls) water
50g (2oz) sugar
2 sprigs eau de cologne mint
1 × 15ml spoon (1tbls) chopped eau de cologne mint
300ml (½ pint) double cream, whipped

1   Put the gooseberries into a pan with the water, sugar and mint sprigs. Bring to the boil and simmer for 20 minutes, or until the gooseberries are tender. Discard the mint sprigs.
2   Stir in the chopped mint and mash the gooseberries with a fork. Cool.
3   Fold in all but 2 × 15ml spoons (2tbls) of the cream.
4   Pour the dessert into a bowl and level the top. Pipe the reserved cream in rosettes to decorate. Serve chilled.
SERVES 4-6

Variation Elderflowers and gooseberries are an old country favourite, a perfect spring partnership. As a variation, tie 2 heads of elderflowers in a piece of cheesecloth and infuse them, instead of the mint sprigs, when cooking the fruit. You can still add the chopped mint leaves – it's a delicious combination.

MINT JULEP

This is a refreshing drink to serve on a warm day.

2 × 15ml spoons (2tbls) caster sugar
120ml (4fl oz) water
a strip of thinly pared lemon rind
crushed ice
120ml (4fl oz) whisky
3 × 15ml spoons (3tbls) mint leaves
4 sprigs mint, to garnish

1   Put the sugar, water and lemon rind into a pan and stir over low heat until the sugar has dissolved. Bring to the boil, remove from the heat, cool and then chill. Discard the lemon.
2   Put about 3 × 15ml spoons (3tbls) crushed ice into each of 4 tumblers. Pour on the whisky, the cooled syrup and mint leaves. Stir well and set aside for about 15 minutes to infuse. Decorate each glass with a sprig of mint.
SERVES 4

SUMMER LUNCHES

In high summer, the scents of herbs from the garden mingle with the aromas that waft from the barbecue. Ice-cold vegetable soups, chilled salads, ice-box desserts and cool drinks are all the more refreshing and delicious for the addition of a medley of leaves gathered from the herb garden.

CORIANDER & CUCUMBER SOUP

25g (1oz) butter
1 medium onion, finely chopped
½ medium cucumber, grated
600ml (1 pint) strong chicken stock
8 sprigs coriander, tied together
1 egg yolk
150ml (¼ pint) single cream
1 × 15ml (1tbls) lemon juice
salt
freshly ground black pepper
2 × 15ml spoons (2tbls) chopped coriander

1   Heat the butter and sauté the onion over moderate heat for 3 minutes. Add the cucumber, stir and cook for 3 minutes. Pour on the stock and add the bunch of coriander. Bring to the boil, cover and simmer for 25 minutes. Discard the coriander.
2   Beat the egg yolk with most of the cream – reserve 4 × 15ml spoons (4tbls) to garnish.
3   Stir in a few spoons of the soup then pour the cream mixture into the pan. Stir in the lemon juice and season with salt and pepper.
4   Remove from the heat and set aside to cool. Stir in the chopped coriander and chill.
5   Swirl the reserved cream over the soup to garnish.

SERVES 4

Variation On a cold day, or before a cold main dish, you can serve the soup hot. Stir in the chopped coriander just before serving.

TOMATO & MOZZARELLA SALAD

6 large tomatoes, thinly sliced
225g (8oz) Mozzarella cheese, thinly sliced
6 × 15ml spoons (6tbls) olive oil, or herb oil (see p. 32)
4 × 5ml spoons (4tsp) lemon juice
2 × 15ml spoons (2tbls) chopped marjoram
salt
freshly ground black pepper
4 sprigs marjoram, to garnish
8 black olives, to garnish

1   Arrange the tomatoes and cheese slices in rings on 4 individual serving plates.
2   Mix the oil, lemon juice and marjoram and season with salt and pepper.
3   Pour the dressing over the tomatoes and cheese.
4   Garnish each plate with a sprig of marjoram and the olives.

SERVES 4

Garden bunch

The rabbit dish, opposite, is a lovely recipe to flavour with a bunch of fines herbes. Tie together a sprig of chervil, chives, dill, parsley, savory, and tarragon, or any combination of 2 or 3 of these herbs.

Cool-as-a-cucumber soup is flavoured with spicy coriander. On a hot day, serve it in ice-cold dishes.

RABBIT IN FINES HERBES SAUCE

3 × 15ml spoons (3tbls) herb oil (see p. 32)
1 young rabbit, jointed
1 medium onion, peeled and chopped
1 garlic clove, peeled and crushed
350 g (12oz) tomatoes, skinned and chopped
1 × 15ml spoon (1tbls) tomato purée
150ml (¼ pint) white wine
½ × 5ml spoon (½tsp) sugar
salt
freshly ground black pepper
1 bunch fresh herbs (see note opposite)
2 × 15ml spoons (2tbls) chopped tarragon

1 Heat the oil in a flameproof casserole. Fry the rabbit joints over moderate heat, turning them to brown and seal them evenly. Remove the rabbit from the casserole and set aside.
2 Fry the onion and garlic in the casserole for 2-3 minutes, stirring once or twice.
3 Stir in the tomatoes, tomato purée, wine, sugar and seasoning. Add the bunch of herbs and return the rabbit joints to the casserole. Bring to the boil, cover and simmer for 1½ hours, or until the rabbit is tender.
4 Transfer the rabbit to a heated

Light as the day is long, a lunch menu of Rabbit in fines herbes sauce, Fruit salad with bergamot and Wine cup with borage.

dish and keep it warm. Discard the bunch of herbs. Boil the sauce for 3-4 minutes to reduce it slightly. Taste and adjust the seasoning. Stir in most of the chopped tarragon. Spoon the sauce over the rabbit and garnish with the remaining tarragon. Serve with noodles or rice.

SERVES 4

RICOTTA & DILL FLAN

75g (3oz) wholewheat flour
75g (3oz) self-raising flour
salt
75g (3oz) hard margarine
2 × 5ml spoons (2tsp) chopped dill leaves
cold water, to mix

FILLING
250g (9oz) ricotta cheese
1 × 15ml spoon (1tbls) chopped dill leaves
2 eggs, beaten
150ml (¼ pint) single cream
½ × 5ml spoon (½tsp) grated lemon rind
freshly ground black pepper

1   To make the pastry, mix together the flours and salt. Rub in the margarine until the mixture resembles fine breadcrumbs. Stir in the dill. Sprinkle on 2-3 × 15ml spoons (2-3tbls) water and mix to a soft dough. Wrap the dough in cling film or foil and chill for 30 minutes.
2   Break up the ricotta and mix it with the dill, eggs, cream and lemon rind and season with salt and pepper.
3   Roll out the dough on a lightly floured board and line a 20cm (8in) flan tin. Trim the edges and prick the base with a fork.
4   Pour in the filling.
5   Bake the flan in the oven, pre-heated to 200°C, 400°F, gas 6, for 20 minutes. Reduce the heat to 180°C, 350°F, gas 4 for a further 20 minutes. Serve cold.

   A refreshing salad is the perfect accompaniment. Try tiny courgettes and button mushrooms.

SERVES 6

FISH & HERB TERRINE

2 × 15ml spoons (2tbls) white wine
pinch of saffron powder
250g (9oz) scallops
100g (4oz) peeled prawns
salt
freshly ground black pepper
1 egg, separated
300ml (½ pint) double cream, whipped

SAUCE
12.5cm (5in) piece cucumber
4 × 15ml spoons (4tbls) basil leaves
200ml (⅓ pint) mayonnaise
2 × 5ml spoons (2tsp) grated lemon rind
pinch of grated nutmeg

1   Heat the wine, stir in the saffron and set aside to cool.
2   Put 175g (6oz) of the scallops and half the prawns into a blender or food processor. Season with salt and pepper, add the egg yolk and blend until smooth. Pour the purée into a bowl.
3   Whisk the egg white stiffly and fold it into the purée. Chill for 30 minutes.
4   Chop the remaining scallops and prawns and stir them into the wine.
5   Fold the cream and the scallop, prawn and wine liquid into the purée.
6   Pour the mixture into a greased 600ml (1 pint) soufflé dish and cover with greased foil.
7   Stand the dish in a roasting pan with cold water to come halfway up the sides of the dish. Cook in the oven, preheated to 160°C, 325°F, gas 3, for 50 minutes.
8   Leave the terrine to cool in the water, then chill it for at least 1 hour, until firm.
9   To make the sauce, peel the cucumber, remove the seeds and grate the flesh. Squeeze the grated cucumber in a piece of muslin or a clean tea towel to remove excess liquid.
10   Put the basil, mayonnaise, lemon rind and nutmeg into a liquidizer or food processor and blend until smooth. Pour the purée into a bowl, stir in the cucumber, taste and add more seasoning if needed.
11   Run a knife around the inside of the soufflé dish. Pour off any liquid and turn out the terrine onto a serving plate. Pour over a little of the sauce to garnish and serve the rest separately.

SERVES 4

GRILLED RED MULLET WITH FENNEL

4 red mullet, cleaned
8 sprigs fennel
2 × 15ml spoons (2tbls) lemon juice
salt
freshly ground black pepper
3 × 15ml spoons (3tbls) herb oil (see p. 32)
1 lemon, quartered, to garnish

1   Score the fish on each side with a sharp knife.
2   Chop the fennel leaves and stalks. Reserve 2 × 15ml spoons (2tbls) to garnish. Press some of the herb into the cavities of the fish. Sprinkle the fish inside and out with lemon juice, season with salt and pepper and press the herbs on to the skin.
3   Heat the grill to high. Sprinkle oil over the fish and grill for 3-4 minutes on each side. Reduce the heat to moderate and grill for a further 3-4 minutes on each side, basting with more oil.
4   Arrange the fish on a heated dish, scatter the chopped fennel over them and garnish with the lemon quarters.

   Serve with a green salad: one with crumbled feta cheese, Greek style, is especially good.

SERVES 4

Variation You can grill fresh sardines in the same way. Allow 2-3 per person, depending on size.

BROAD BEANS WITH SAVORY

1kg (2¼lb) fresh broad beans
salt
1 × 15ml spoon (1tbls) sunflower oil
1 small onion, peeled and finely chopped
2 garlic cloves, peeled and crushed
1 × 5ml spoon (1tsp) flour
200ml (⅓ pint) Greek-style yoghurt
freshly ground black pepper
2 × 15ml spoons (2tbls) chopped summer savory

GARNISH
4 slices lean back bacon
1 × 15ml spoon (1tbls) sunflower oil

1   Shell the beans. Cook them in boiling, salted water for 10 minutes, or until they are just tender.
2   Heat the oil and sauté the onion

and garlic over moderate heat for 3 minutes. Stir in the flour and cook for 2 minutes, still stirring. Beat in the yoghurt, season with salt and pepper and stir in the savory. Heat gently.
3   For the garnish, cut the rind from the bacon and cut the bacon into squares. Heat the oil and fry the bacon over moderate heat for 4-5 minutes until it is crisp. Lift it out with a draining spoon.
4   Drain the beans, stir them into the yoghurt sauce and toss. Turn out the beans and garnish them with the bacon. Serve hot.

SERVES 4

Variation Marjoram is a good alternative to savory in this recipe.
You can use 500g (1¼lb) frozen broad beans in place of the fresh vegetable when it is not in season.

FRUIT SALAD WITH BERGAMOT

75g (3oz) caster sugar
200ml (⅓ pint) water
1 × 15ml spoon (1tbls) lemon juice
3-4 sprigs bergamot
250g (9oz) blackcurrants
250g (9oz) strawberries, hulled
250g (9oz) raspberries, hulled
250g (9oz) cherries, pitted
small sprays herb leaves, to decorate

1   Put the sugar, water, lemon juice and bergamot into a pan. Stir over low heat to dissolve the sugar. Bring to the boil and boil for 5 minutes. Discard the bergamot.
2   Add the blackcurrants and simmer for a further 3 minutes. Stir in the cherries, raspberries and strawberries and remove from the heat.
3   Leave the salad to cool, then chill. Decorate with herb sprays just before serving.

SERVES 4-6

MINT ICE CREAM WITH CHOCOLATE SAUCE

100g (4oz) caster sugar
150ml (¼ pint) water
50g (2oz) peppermint leaves
1 × 15ml spoon (1tbls) lemon juice
300ml (½ pint) double cream, whipped
2-3 drops green food colouring (optional)
6 peppermint sprigs, to garnish

SAUCE
125g (5oz) bitter chocolate
50g (2oz) vanilla sugar
300ml (½ pint) water

1   Put the sugar and water into a pan and stir over low heat to dissolve the sugar. Add the mint leaves. Bring the syrup to the boil, and boil for 5 minutes. Remove from the heat and set aside to cool.
2   Strain the syrup through a sieve, pressing the mint with a spoon to extract the maximum flavour.
3   Stir the lemon juice into the syrup. Fold in the whipped cream, and the food colouring if using.
4   Pour the mixture into an ice-cube tray, cover with foil and freeze for about 1 hour.
5   Turn the partly frozen mixture out into a chilled bowl and whisk it to break down the ice crystals.

6   Return the mixture to the tray, cover and freeze for at least 2 hours.
7   To make the sauce, break the chocolate into squares. Put them in a bowl over a pan of hot water, or into a double boiler. Do not let the water boil, or touch the chocolate container. Stir the chocolate once or twice as it melts.
8   Put the vanilla sugar and water into a pan and stir over low heat to dissolve the sugar. Bring to the boil, then boil for 5 minutes.
9   Pour the syrup over the melted chocolate, stirring constantly. Pour the chocolate sauce back into the pan and simmer for 15 minutes, until the sauce is thick enough to coat the back of a spoon.
10   Transfer the ice cream to the main part of the refrigerator for 30 minutes before serving. Serve it in folds made with a large tablespoon. Decorate with the mint sprigs. Serve the sauce, either hot or cold, separately.

SERVES 4

WINE CUP WITH BORAGE

6 × 15ml spoons (6tbls) brandy
50g (2oz) bay sugar (see p. 33)
1 × 700ml (1¼ pint) bottle dry white wine
1 orange, thinly sliced
1 dessert apple, cored and thinly sliced
1 lemon, thinly sliced
1 × 700ml (1¼ pint) bottle sparkling rosé wine
1 litre (1¾ pints) lemonade
8 small sprigs apple mint
a few borage flowers, to decorate

1   Put the brandy and sugar into a large bowl and mix well. Pour on the white wine and stir well. Add the orange, apple and lemon slices, cover and leave for at least 30 minutes.
2   Just before serving, pour on the rosé wine and lemonade and stir well. Decorate with the apple mint sprigs and borage flowers. Serve well chilled.

SERVES 8

Keeping your cool

Have the wines and lemonade well — chilled and, on a hot day, chill the serving bowl before mixing the drink.

AUTUMN & WINTER

Evergreen herbs such as bay and rosemary, and perennials like lemon balm and thyme are all well-established favourites to enhance autumn and winter dishes. But they don't have the culinary stage to themselves! By bringing pots of annuals indoors and keeping them well trimmed throughout the winter, you can cheat the seasons. In fact it becomes a challenge to see how long you can keep them flourishing.

MINESTRONE WITH PESTO

This is a Genoese version of the popular Italian vegetable soup, made with pesto, the basil sauce which originated in Genoa.

3 × 15ml spoons (3tbls) basil oil (see p. 32), or olive oil
1 small celery stick, thinly sliced
1 small leek, trimmed and chopped
1 garlic clove, peeled and chopped
1 small carrot, scraped and chopped
1 medium courgette, coarsely chopped
75g (3oz) French beans, cut into 1cm (½in) lengths
75g (3oz) heart of green cabbage, chopped
1 small potato, peeled and chopped
900ml (1½ pints) hot chicken stock
salt
freshly ground black pepper
25g (1oz) pasta shapes, e.g. small shells

PESTO
10g (¼oz) basil leaves
25g (1oz) pine kernels
2 × 15ml spoons (2tbls) grated Parmesan cheese
2 × 15ml spoons (2tbls) olive oil

1   Heat the oil in a large flameproof casserole and fry the celery and leek over low heat for 5 minutes, stirring frequently. Add the garlic, carrot and courgette and fry for a further 3 minutes. Lastly, add the beans, cabbage and potato and fry, still stirring frequently, for 5 minutes.
2   Pour in the stock, season with salt and pepper and bring slowly to the boil. Cover and cook slowly for 1 hour, stirring occasionally. Taste and adjust the seasoning if needed.
3   Add the pasta, cover and cook for a further 15 minutes, or until the pasta is tender.

4   To make the pesto, finely chop the basil in a blender or food processor, then add the pine kernels and work to a crumb-like texture.
5   Turn the mixture into a mortar and pound to make a paste. Stir in the cheese and pound until well blended. Finally, add the oil, a few drops at a time, beating in each addition.
6   Pour the soup into a warmed tureen and stir in the pesto. Cover and leave the soup to stand for 5 minutes before serving.

SERVES 4

The Southern-Italian sauce of basil leaves, pine kernels and Parmesan cheese gives this Genoese version of Minestrone soup its characteristic flavour.

CHEESE & CHERVIL SOUFFLE

40g (1½oz) butter
2 × 15ml spoons (2tbls) flour
200ml (⅓ pint) milk
1 bay leaf
salt
freshly ground black pepper
½ × 5ml spoon (½tsp) Dijon mustard
50g (2oz) Gruyère cheese, grated
2 × 15ml spoons (2tbls) chopped chervil
3 egg yolks, lightly beaten
4 egg whites, lightly beaten
5 × 15ml spoons (5tbls) dried breadcrumbs

1   Melt the butter in a small pan, stir in the flour and cook over a low heat for 1 minute, stirring constantly.
2   Heat the milk with the bay leaf, then discard it. Gradually pour the hot milk into the pan, stirring all the time to make a smooth sauce. Simmer gently for 3 minutes.
3   Season with salt and pepper and stir in the mustard, cheese and chervil. Remove from the heat and set aside for 2-3 minutes.
4   Beat in the egg yolks and cool for 5 minutes.
5   Fold in the egg whites.
6   Grease a 900ml (1½ pint) soufflé dish and sprinkle the crumbs over the surface. Pour in the cheese mixture.
7   Bake in the oven, preheated to 200°C, 400°F, gas 6, for 20-25 minutes until the soufflé is well risen and crisp on top. Serve at once.
    A green salad with a light Herb vinaigrette (see p. 32) is an ideal accompaniment.

SERVES 4

Variation Several other herbs complement the cheese soufflé mixture well. As alternatives, try tarragon, marjoram or salad burnet in place of the chervil.

CORIANDER FISH STEW

500g (1¼ lb) white fish fillets, such as coley
100g (4oz) fresh white breadcrumbs
2 × 15ml spoons (2tbls) chopped coriander
pinch of ground mace
salt
freshly ground black pepper
sprigs of coriander, to garnish

SAUCE
2 × 15ml spoons (2tbls) herb oil (see p. 32)
or sunflower oil
1 medium onion, peeled and finely chopped
1 garlic clove, peeled and finely chopped
350g (12oz) tomatoes, skinned and sliced
150ml (¼ pint) dry white wine
1 × 15ml spoon (1tbls) tomato purée
2 × 15ml spoons (2tbls) chopped coriander
2 × 5ml spoons (2tsp) paprika
1 × 15ml spoon (1tbls) lemon juice
1 × 5ml spoon (1tsp) lemon rind, grated

1   Skin the fish and remove any bones. Mince the fish or work it to a smooth paste in a food processor. Mix in the breadcrumbs, coriander and mace, and season with salt and pepper. Knead the mixture thoroughly.
2   Shape the mixture into small balls about the size of a large walnut.
3   To make the sauce, heat the oil in a frying pan. Fry the onion and garlic over moderate heat for 3 minutes, stirring once or twice. Add all the remaining ingredients, stir well and bring to the boil. Boil the sauce, uncovered, for 10 minutes, stirring frequently.
4   Carefully place the fish balls in the sauce, shake the pan and simmer for 10 minutes. Turn the fish in the sauce once or twice so that it cooks evenly. Taste the sauce and adjust the seasoning if needed.
5   Serve the fish on a bed of rice, garnished with the coriander leaves.

SERVES 4

Variation Flat-leafed parsley is a good alternative to coriander in both the fish balls and the sauce.

If it's more convenient, you can prepare the fish balls and the sauce a day ahead of serving. Stop at the end of Step 3. Store the fish in a lidded container in the refrigerator. Cool the sauce and store that, too. To assemble the dish, reheat the sauce and then add the fish.

NEAPOLITAN BEEF

2 × 15ml spoons (2tbls) herb oil (see p. 32)
or olive oil
1.5kg (3¼lb) braising beef, very thinly sliced
2 garlic cloves, peeled and finely chopped
3 × 15ml spoons (3tbls) flat-leafed parsley
2 × 15ml spoons (2tbls) chopped oregano,
or marjoram
750g (1½lb) tomatoes, skinned and chopped
1 × 15ml spoon (1tbls) tomato purée
6 × 15ml spoons (6tbls) red wine
1 bay leaf
salt
freshly ground black pepper

1   Brush the oil over a flameproof casserole and arrange the beef slices. Sprinkle on the garlic and herbs.

Main-course variety with herbs, Meat loaf with lovage (top), and Coriander fish stew.

2   Put the tomatoes, tomato purée, wine and bay leaf into a pan, season with salt and pepper and bring to the boil. Simmer for 5 minutes, stirring frequently.
3   Pour the tomato mixture over the beef and cover the casserole.
4   Cook in the oven, preheated to 160°C, 325°F, gas 3, for 1½ hours, or until the beef is tender. Taste the sauce and adjust the seasoning if needed. Discard the bay leaf.

SERVES 6

VEAL CHOPS WITH BASIL CREAM SAUCE

If you have a pot of basil indoors, you can usually make it last until the New Year, by keeping it well trimmed.

4 loin of veal chops
50g (2oz) butter
2 dessert apples, peeled, cored and sliced
100g (4oz) button mushrooms, sliced
2 × 5ml spoons (2tsp) flour
3 × 15ml spoons (3tbls) chicken stock
3 × 15ml spoons (3tbls) brandy
2 × 15ml spoons (2tbls) chopped basil
200ml (⅓ pint) double cream
salt
freshly ground black pepper
2-3 sprigs basil, to garnish

1   Trim the chops, discarding the excess fat.
2   Melt half the butter in a frying pan and fry the apple slices over moderate heat for 2-3 minutes on each side, until they are golden brown. Lift out the apples and heat the remaining butter.
3   Fry the chops over high heat for 2 minutes on each side. Add the mushrooms, reduce the heat to moderate and cook the chops for a further 5 minutes on each side.
4   Transfer the chops to a heated serving dish and arrange the apples and mushrooms around them. Cover the dish and keep it warm.
5   Stir the flour into the fat in the pan, pour on the stock, stirring, and bring to the boil. Add the brandy, basil and cream and season with salt and pepper. Stir well and heat gently. Simmer slowly for 2-3 minutes.
6   Pour the sauce over the chops and garnish with the basil sprigs.

SERVES 4

Variation Marjoram and thyme are both good alternatives to basil, bringing completely different characteristics to the dish.

Herbs from the storeroom

To substitute dried herbs for fresh herbs in a recipe, use about one third of the quantity — that is 1 × 5 ml spoon (1 tsp) dried herbs instead of 1 × 15 ml spoon (1 tbls) of fresh herbs.

CALVES' LIVER WITH SAGE

Fresh sage leaves perfectly offset the richness of liver and give a subtle flavour to the sauce.

4 × 15ml spoons (4tbls) flour
salt
freshly ground black pepper
½ × 5ml spoon (½tsp) dried sage
12 thin slices calves' liver, about 500g (1¼lb)
50g (2oz) butter
1 × 15ml spoon (1tbls) olive oil
8-12 sage leaves
6 × 15ml spoons (6tbls) beef stock
3 × 15ml spoons (3tbls) sherry
2 × 15ml spoons (2tbls) thin cream
4 sprigs sage, to garnish

1   Mix together the flour, salt, pepper and dried sage on a plate. Toss the liver in the seasoned flour to coat it well on both sides.
2   Heat the butter and oil in a pan, add the sage leaves and fry the liver in batches over moderate heat for 30-45 seconds on each side. Keep the cooked liver warm while you cook the remainder. Remove the last batch and keep it warm.
3   Add the stock to the pan, stir well and bring to the boil. Boil to reduce the stock by half. Add the sherry and cream and simmer for 2 minutes. Taste and adjust the seasoning if needed.
4   Pour the sauce over the liver and garnish with the sage sprigs.

SERVES 4

MEAT LOAF WITH LOVAGE

2 large slices white bread
150ml (¼ pint) milk
750g (1½lb) lean minced beef
1 small onion, peeled and finely chopped
2 garlic cloves, peeled and finely chopped
1 × 15ml spoon (1tbls) olive oil
2 × 15ml spoons (2tbls) chopped lovage
½ × 5ml spoon (½tsp) ground allspice
salt
freshly ground black pepper
2 × 15ml spoons (2tbls) Greek-style yoghurt
2 sprigs lovage, to garnish

1   Cut the crusts from the bread and crumble it into a bowl. Pour on the milk, stir and leave to soak for 10 minutes. Tip into a colander; squeeze out and discard any excess milk.

2   Mix the soaked bread with the beef. Add the onion, garlic, oil, lovage and allspice and season with salt and pepper. Mix very well with a wooden spoon, or knead the mixture with your hands to make it a smooth, thick, moist paste.
3   Press the mixture into a greased 450g (1lb) loaf tin, level the top and cover with foil.
4   Bake in the oven, preheated to 180°C, 350°F, gas 4, for 1½ hours.
5   Tip out any liquid fat. Run a knife around the loaf and turn it out on to a serving dish. Blot away any fat with kitchen paper. Garnish the loaf with a swirl of yoghurt and the lovage. Serve hot.

SERVES 6-8

Variation This is a good picnic or lunch dish, served cold with salad. Leave the loaf to cool in the tin.

AUTUMN FRUIT SALAD

Sweet cicely is a lovely herb to use with fruits of all kinds, and gives a fruit salad a taste of luxury.

40g (1½oz) sugar
100ml (3½fl oz) water
3 sprigs sweet cicely leaves
1½ × 15ml spoons (1½tbls) orange juice
2 small dessert apples, cored and thinly sliced
2 small dessert pears, cored and thinly sliced
3 plums, pitted and thinly sliced
3 greengages, pitted and thinly sliced
1 small melon, peeled, seeded and diced
1½ × 15ml spoons (1½tbls) chopped sweet cicely

1   Put the sugar, water, 1 sprig of the sweet cicely leaves and the orange juice into a pan. Stir over low heat to dissolve the sugar. Bring to the boil and boil for 5 minutes. Leave to cool. Discard the sweet cicely.
2   Stir the fruits and the chopped sweet cicely into the syrup and mix well. Chill in the refrigerator.
3   Decorate the fruit salad with the reserved sweet cicely leaves.

SERVES 4

BAKING DAY

The scent of baking wafting from the kitchen is always a great temptation – but even more so when you make bread, scones, biscuits, cakes and creamy desserts flavoured with aromatic leaves. To enjoy herb breads at their very best, eat them on the day they are made, and preferably slightly warm – which is what the family will probably insist on anyway!

HERB SODA BREAD

250g (9oz) plain flour, sifted
250g (9oz) wholemeal flour
1 × 5ml spoon (1tsp) bicarbonate of soda
2 × 5ml spoons (2tsp) salt
25g (1oz) butter
1 × 15ml spoon (1tbls) chives, finely snipped
1 × 15ml spoon (1tbls) chopped chervil
or parsley
300ml (½ pint) buttermilk
a little water (if necessary)

1   Sift together the flours, soda and salt and tip in any bran remaining in the sieve. Rub in the butter until the mixture is like fine breadcrumbs. Stir in the herbs. Pour on the buttermilk and mix to a soft dough. Add a little water if needed.
2   Knead the dough until it is smooth. Shape it into a round about 20cm (8in) across. Place the loaf on a greased baking sheet and cut a cross in the top.
3   Bake the loaf in the oven, preheated to 200°C, 400°F, gas 6, for 35-40 minutes, until it is well risen and firm. The bread should sound hollow when tapped underneath.
4   Stand the bread on a wire rack to cool slightly.

MAKES 1 LOAF

Variation You can ring the changes with the herbs you use to flavour the quick-to-make and irresistible-to-eat bread. Or spice it up by substituting 2 × 5ml spoons (2 tsp) dill, fennel or caraway seeds for the chopped herbs.

WHOLEMEAL HERB BREAD

This bread, flavoured with fennel, is delicious to serve with fish soup, mussels in garlic butter and smoked fish.

1 litre (1¾ pints) hand-hot water
1 × 15ml spoon (1tbls) malt extract
1 × 15ml spoon (1tbls) dried yeast
1.5kg (3¼lb) wholemeal flour
3 × 15ml spoons (3tbls) salt
50g (2oz) lard
2 × 15ml spoons (2tbls) chopped
fennel leaves
2 × 15ml spoons (2tbls) fennel seeds,
for topping

1   Put 300ml (½ pint) of the warm water in a bowl. Stir in the malt until nearly dissolved and sprinkle the yeast on top. Leave in a warm place for about 10 minutes, until frothy.
2   Put the flour and salt into a large bowl. Rub in the lard until the mixture resembles breadcrumbs. Stir in the chopped fennel seeds.

3   Add the yeast liquid and the rest of the warm water and mix until the dough leaves the sides of the bowl.
4   Turn on to a floured board and knead for about 10 minutes until the dough is smooth and elastic. Alternatively, use an electric mixer.
5   Divide the dough into 3 equal portions. Divide one portion into 2 halves for the 2 smaller loaves.
6   Grease two 1kg (2¼lb) loaf tins and two 450g (1lb) loaf tins with lard. Knead each portion of the dough then press or roll out to an oblong as wide as the long side of the tin, and as long as 3 times the short side of the tin. Fold into 3 and turn over so the joins are underneath. Put the shaped dough into the tins.
7   Cover with oiled cling film, or put each tin into a large polythene bag. Leave to prove in a warm place for 1-1½ hours or until risen to the tops of the tins.
8   Brush the tops of each loaf lightly with water and sprinkle with fennel seeds.
9   Bake in the oven, preheated to 220°C, 425°F, gas 7, for about 40 minutes or until the bread is browned and hollow-sounding when tapped on the underside.
   Turn out and cool on a wire tray.

MAKES TWO × 1KG (2¼LB) AND TWO × 450G (1LB) LOAVES.

Variation To make a batch of bread with varied herb flavours, divide up the mixture at Step 1. Allow 1 × 15ml spoon (1tbls) chopped herb for each one-third of the recipe. Dill, marjoram, chives, parsley and mint are all tasty alternatives.

HERB & POTATO SCONES

65g (2½oz) butter
250ml (8fl oz) water
175g (6oz) flour
2 large eggs
275g (10oz) hot mashed potato
salt
freshly ground black pepper
1 × 15ml spoon (1tbls) each chopped chervil, chives, dill and parsley

1   Boil the butter and water in a large pan. Tip in the flour all at once and stir quickly to form a thick paste. Break in the eggs one at a time, beating until the mixture is smooth. Beat in the hot mashed potato. Season the mixture with salt and pepper and stir in the chopped herbs. Set aside to cool.
2   Heat a griddle iron or a heavy-based frying pan over high heat and grease it lightly. Using wetted hands, shape the cold mixture into flat, round cakes. Cook them, a few at a time, for 3-4 minutes on each side, until golden brown. Keep warm while you make the remainder.
3   Serve the scones hot, with butter and cheese or to accompany ham.

MAKES ABOUT 16 SCONES

ONION & CHIVES TWIST

150g (5oz) medium oatmeal
150ml (¼ pint) milk
175g (6oz) self-raising flour
1 × 5ml spoon (1tsp) baking powder
½ × 5ml spoon (½tsp) sugar
salt
1 × 15ml spoon (1tbls) herb oil (see p. 32), or sunflower oil
1 medium onion, peeled and grated
2 × 15ml spoons (2tbls) chives, finely snipped
pinch of ground mace

1   Put 100g (4oz) of the oatmeal in a bowl, pour on the milk and set aside to soak for 20 minutes.
2   Sift together the flour, baking powder, sugar and salt. Stir in the oil, grated onion, chives and mace, and add the oatmeal and milk. Mix to form a dough.
3   Knead the dough until it is smooth.
4   Break the dough into 2 halves and roll each one into a long strip about 30cm (12in) long. Pinch 1 end of each strip together and criss-cross the strips to simulate a plait. Pinch the other ends together.
5   Place the loaf on a baking sheet, brush the top with milk and sprinkle on the remaining oatmeal.
6   Bake the loaf in the oven, pre-heated to 230°C, 450°F, gas 8, for 15 minutes. Reduce the heat to 200°C, 400°F, gas 6 and continue baking for 15 minutes, or until the loaf sounds hollow when tapped on the underside.
7   Cool the loaf on a wire rack.
   It is delicious served with cheese and a green salad or tomato salad.

MAKES 1 LOAF

ROSEMARY CREAM

4 egg yolks
1 × 15ml spoon (1tbls) caster sugar
300ml (½ pint) milk or single cream
300ml (½ pint) double cream
2 sprigs rosemary
75g (3oz) demerara sugar

1   Beat the egg yolks and caster sugar until they are thick and creamy.
2   Put the milk or single cream, the double cream and the rosemary into a bowl over a pan of simmering water or the top of a double boiler and heat it.
3   Strain the heated cream on to the egg yolks and sugar and beat well.
4   Return the mixture to the bowl and cook, stirring constantly until the custard is thick enough to coat the back of the spoon. Do not allow the water to boil, or touch the container; the eggs would scramble.
5   Strain the custard into a flameproof dish – a glass one looks attractive. Set aside to cool.
6   Sprinkle the demerara sugar over to cover the surface completely.
7   Preheat the grill to high and grill the dessert until the sugar caramel-izes. Set aside to cool.
8   Crack the caramel topping with the back of a spoon before serving – it will look like a spider's web.
   Soft fruits such as raspberries and strawberries are lovely with this.

SERVES 4-6

BAY TREE SPONGE CAKE

175g (6oz) wheatmeal self-raising flour
1 × 5ml spoon (1tsp) baking powder
175g (6oz) soft margarine
175g (6oz) caster sugar flavoured with bay (see p. 33)
2 × 5ml spoons (2tsp) grated lemon rind
3 eggs
1 × 15ml spoon (1tbls) lemon juice

FROSTING
75g (3oz) butter, softened
75g (3oz) full-fat soft cheese
100g (4oz) icing sugar flavoured with bay (see p. 33), sifted
1 × 5ml spoon (1tsp) lemon juice
2 × 15ml spoons (2tbls) clear honey
175g (6oz) gooseberry or greengage jam
crystallized herb leaves, to decorate

1   Sift the flour and baking powder and tip in any bran in the sieve. Add the margarine, sugar, lemon rind and eggs, and beat until the mixture is smooth. Beat in the lemon juice.
2   Divide the mixture between 2 greased 19cm (7½in) sandwich tins and level the tops.
3   Bake the sponge cake layers in the oven, pre-heated to 160°C, 325°F, gas 3, for 25-30 minutes, until they are firm but springy to the touch. Stand the tins on a wire rack to cool. Turn out the layers.
4   Beat the butter, cheese, icing sugar, lemon juice and honey until it is smooth.
5   Spread 1 cake layer with jam and cover it with half of the frosting. Place the other layer on top and cover it with the remaining frosting. Decorate the top with crystallized herb leaves such as sweet cicely or angelica.

MAKES ONE 19CM (7½IN) CAKE

A good morning's work! From left to right: Bay tree sponge cake, Wholemeal herb bread with Herb butter (basil), Onion and chives twist, Herb and potato scones.

A TASTE OF HERBS

Gather fresh herbs from the garden to flavour oils, vinegars, and mayonnaise. Herb-flavoured butters transform grills and sandwiches and herb sugar makes a subtle difference to desserts and baking. The scents of spring and summer can be captured in clear refreshing herb jellies which perfectly offset the richness of game, poultry and meat and add flavour and colour to any dish.

HERB OILS

Herb-flavoured oils have a long list of talents. Use them not only for salad dressings and sauces but for stir-frying meat and vegetables, for starting off meat dishes, in ragoûts and soups, in marinades and to add a last-minute sparkle to pizzas. Try, among others, basil, tarragon and oregano, or a blend of several herbs.

4 × 15ml spoons (4tbls) chopped fresh herb
450ml (¾ pint) olive oil
1-2 sprigs of the fresh herb

1   Put the chopped leaves in a mortar and pound them until they are crushed almost to a paste. Add a few drops of oil, pound the leaves again, and gradually add more oil.
2   Mix in the remaining oil and pour into a jar. Stir well, cover the jar and keep for 2 weeks, shaking occasionally.
3   Strain the oil into sterilized bottles, pressing the leaves to extract the maximum flavour. Push a sprig of herb into each bottle. Cover and store.

MAKES ABOUT 450ML (¾ PINT) OIL

TO MAKE A BOUQUET GARNI

Mix together equal quantities of dried chervil, parsley, tarragon and chives. Put ½ × 5ml spoon (½tsp) of each on to a small square of muslin and tie up before storing in a lidded container in a cool, dry, dark place. These little herb bags can then be used to flavour soups, sauces, stocks and casseroles.

HERB VINEGARS

Whether you use only a few drops of vinegar in salad dressing or sauce, or you use it as a preservative for pickles and chutneys, the flavour of herbs makes all the difference.

10 × 15ml spoons (10tbls) chopped fresh sage or other herb
450ml (¾ pint) white wine vinegar
1-2 sprigs of the fresh herb

1   Put the chopped leaves in a mortar and pound them until they are crushed and almost like a paste. Transfer them to a heatproof jug.
2   Bring the vinegar to boiling point and pour over the herb leaves. Mix well. Set aside to cool.
3   Pour the vinegar and herbs into a jar. Cover and keep for 2 weeks.
4   Strain the vinegar into sterilized bottles, pressing the herb to extract the maximum flavour. Push a sprig of the fresh herb into each bottle. Cover and store.

MAKES ABOUT 450ML (¾ PINT) VINEGAR

Variation Tarragon vinegar is perhaps the best known, but if you have a herb garden of your own, the sky's the limit in the variations you can make. Try, for example, salad burnet vinegar, which is especially good for fish sauces, and basil vinegar, for making a salad dressing to use with tomatoes.

AROMATIC VINAIGRETTE

This is a mixed herb dressing to toss with salads of all kinds, to serve as a dip for fresh vegetables, and to sprinkle over cold cooked leeks, celery and celeriac as an appetizer. Use other combinations of herbs as available.

sea salt
freshly ground black pepper
½ × 5ml spoon (½tsp) Dijon mustard
½ × 5ml spoon (½tsp) sugar
2 × 15ml spoons (2tbls) white wine vinegar
8 × 15ml spoons (8tbls) olive oil
2 × 5ml spoons (2tsp) lemon juice
1 garlic clove, peeled and crushed
1 × 5ml spoon (1tsp) chopped flat-leafed parsley
1 × 5ml spoon (1tsp) chopped chervil
1 × 5ml spoon (1tsp) chopped chives
1 × 5ml spoon (1tsp) chopped coriander
1 × 5ml spoon (1tsp) chopped tarragon

1   Pound the salt and pepper in a mortar. Stir in the mustard and sugar, then gradually stir in the vinegar.
2   Add the oil gradually, still stirring, until it is all blended with the other ingredients. Stir in the lemon juice, garlic and herbs.
3   Store the dressing in a covered jar in a cool place – but not in the refrigerator – for up to 3-4 days.

MAKES ABOUT 200ML (⅓ PINT) DRESSING

HERB BUTTERS

Glistening butter, speckled with herbs and gliding over grilled steak, chops, gammon or fish both looks appetizing and adds instant flavour. Use the butters in sandwiches and filled rolls too.

75g (3oz) unsalted butter, softened
1-3 × 15ml spoons (1-3tbls) chopped fresh herb (see below)
1 garlic clove, peeled and crushed
1 × 15ml spoon (1tbls) lemon juice
salt
freshly ground black pepper

1 Cream the butter until it is soft and 'workable'.
2 Beat in the herb, garlic and lemon juice and season with salt and pepper. Shape the butter into a roll about 2.5cm (1in) across.
3 Wrap in cling film and chill in the refrigerator for about 45 minutes, until it is hard. Or wrap the butter in polythene and store in the freezer.
4 Serve the butter cut into pats.

MAKES ABOUT 75G (3OZ) BUTTER

Mint and chive butters are good with new potatoes, peas, broad beans and to garnish pasta and rice dishes. Use 2 × 15ml spoons (2tbls) chopped mint – and try peppermint or spearmint as a refreshing change – or very finely snipped chives. Also use as a spread in cheese sandwiches.
  Sage butter (delicious with pork, duck and goose), use only 1-1½ × 15ml spoons (1-1½tbls) of the chopped herb. Purple sage is especially effective.
  Tarragon butter is lovely with grilled or poached salmon and trout; *dill butter* goes well with white fish of all kinds; and both *chervil* and *parsley butter* (made with curly or flat-leafed types) have almost limitless uses with poultry, meat and fish. Use 3 × 15ml spoons (3tbls) of all these herbs.
  'Bouquet garni' butter can be made by mixing ½ × 15ml spoon (½tbls) each of chopped fresh parsley, chervil, tarragon and chives with 75g (3oz) butter.

IN PRAISE OF OIL

Good quality olive oil is a perfect preservative and will keep herbs 'fresh' for months. Chop fresh herb leaves, pack them into wide-necked jars and pour on oil to cover.
  Goat's cheese, such as feta, is particularly delicious stored in oil. Cut the cheese into cubes or round slices and pack them in jars. Push a few sprigs of herb – basil, marjoram or thyme, for example – in each one. Then top up the jars with herb-flavoured oil. Cover the jars tightly and store in a cool, dark place. Serve the cheese as a dressing on green salad, or with rye bread.

GOOSEBERRY & LEMON BALM JELLY

Serve this lovely fruit and herb jelly with poultry, meat and oily fish – especially mackerel – or spread it on toast or teacakes.

1kg (2¼lb) gooseberries
2 × 15ml spoons (2tbls) lemon juice
750ml (1¼ pints) water
about 4 sprigs lemon balm
about 750g (1½lb) sugar (see note, p. 35)
4 × 15ml spoons (4tbls) chopped lemon balm

1 Put the gooseberries in a large pan with the lemon juice, water and lemon balm. Simmer for 30 minutes.
2 Pour the fruit and liquid into a jelly bag and drain for several hours.
3 Measure the strained fruit juice and weigh out the sugar. Warm the sugar in a low oven.
4 Put the fruit juice and sugar into a pan and stir over low heat until the sugar dissolves. Increase the heat, bring to the boil, and boil rapidly for 10 minutes, then test for set (see setting note, p. 34).
5 When setting point has been reached, stir in the chopped lemon balm and leave for about 5 minutes.
6 Stir the jelly well then pour it into warmed, sterilized jars. Cover with waxed paper discs and paper covers or non-corrosive lids.
7 Leave to cool, then label and store.

MAKES ABOUT 1.5KG (3¼LB)

FINES HERBES MAYONNAISE

Here's a sauce with a difference – a lovely pale green colour and the aroma of the herb garden. Serve it as a dip with crudités, with cold poached salmon and trout, with aspic dishes, and with hard-boiled eggs. A little stirred into fish soups works wonders.

2 egg yolks
salt
½ × 5ml spoon (½tsp) Dijon mustard
300ml (½ pint) olive oil
2 × 15ml spoons (2tbls) white wine vinegar
1 × 5ml spoon (1tsp) lemon juice
4 × 15ml spoons (4tbls) chopped fines herbes
– a mixture of chervil, chives, dill, mint, parsley, savory and tarragon

1 Beat the egg yolks and salt, then beat in the mustard. Gradually pour on the oil drop by drop, beating constantly. When the oil has emulsified, add the oil in a thin, steady stream.
2 Gradually add the vinegar and lemon juice, beating all the time. Stir in the herbs. Taste the sauce and add a little more salt if needed.
3 Store the sauce in a lidded container in the refrigerator or in a cool place.

MAKES ABOUT 300ML (½ PINT) SAUCE

HERB SUGARS

A vanilla pod isn't the only way to flavour jars of sugar. Herb-flavoured sugars make a subtle but exciting difference to custards, fruit mousses, fruit salads and compôtes. Use them for baking biscuits and sponge cakes too.

3 sprigs rosemary or bay, 10cm (4in) long
500g (1¼lb) caster, granulated or icing sugar

1 Wash and thoroughly dry the herb sprigs and pick off any discoloured leaves.
2 Stand the herb upright in a storage jar, pour the sugar over and close the jar. Store as usual.
3 Top up the jar with more sugar as you use it, and replace the herb after about 6 months.

MAKES ABOUT 500G (1¼LB) HERB SUGAR

ROSEMARY JELLY

Lamb and rosemary are long-standing partners but this jelly is equally good with other meats – pork and ham especially. Stir a little into meat casseroles, soups and sauces.

1kg (2¼lb) cooking apples, prepared weight
4 × 15ml spoons (4tbls) lemon juice
1 litre (1¾ pints) water
about 16 sprigs rosemary
about 750g (1½lb) sugar (see note, p. 35)
2-3 drops green food colouring (optional)

1   Follow the general directions for making Sage and cider jelly. Strain the peeled, cored and chopped apples from the water acidulated with 15ml (1tbls) lemon juice. Put them with the remaining 3 × 15ml spoons (3tbls) of lemon juice and the water. Add about 12 sprigs of rosemary.
2   Bring to the boil and simmer for 30 minutes, or until the apples are tender.
3   Pour the apples and liquid into a jelly bag and leave to drain for several hours.
4   Measure the fruit juice and weigh the sugar. Warm the sugar in a low oven.
5   Pour the fruit juice and the warmed sugar into a pan and stir over low heat until the sugar dissolves. Increase the heat, bring to the boil and skim off any scum from the surface. Boil rapidly for 10 minutes, then test that setting point has been reached (see boxed note). Stir in the green food colouring if you use it.
6   Pour the preserve into warmed, sterilized jars and add a sprig of rosemary to each. Cover the jars and leave them to cool.
7   Label the jars and store.

MAKES ABOUT 1.5KG (3¼LB)

SETTING POINT

To test when a preserve jelly has reached setting point, and is ready to pour into pots, take the pan from the heat, spoon a little on to a cold saucer and leave it to cool. Push a finger across the surface – the jelly will wrinkle, like ripples in sand, if it has reached setting point. If it is not ready, bring it back to the boil and fast-boil for a few minutes more.

ROSEMARY

Sweet-smelling rosemary – for remembrance – a herbal 'must' for every garden. The leaves have a variety of culinary, medicinal and cosmetic uses.

APPLE & MINT CHUTNEY

The addition of chopped mint to this fruit chutney gives it a refreshingly tangy flavour.

900ml (1½ pints) malt vinegar
1 × 15ml spoon (1tbls) mixed pickling spice
2 blades mace
1.5kg (3¼lb) cooking apples, prepared weight
500g (1¼lb) light Muscovado sugar
2 × 5ml spoons (2tsp) salt
40g (1½oz) sultanas
4 × 15ml spoons (4tbls) chopped apple mint

1   Put the vinegar, pickling spice and mace into a suitable pan and bring slowly to the boil. Boil for 5 minutes.
2   Peel, core and chop the apples. Add them to the pan with the sugar, salt and sultanas. Bring slowly to the boil, stirring occasionally until the sugar dissolves. Simmer for 1 hour, or until the liquid has evaporated and the preserve has thickened. Stir in the mint.
3   Spoon the chutney into warmed, sterilized jars. Cover with waxed paper discs and non-corrosive lids. Leave the jars to cool.
4   Label the jars and store in a cool, dark, dry place.

MAKES ABOUT 2.5KG (3¼LB)

PARSLEY & LEMON JELLY

Use either curly or flat-leafed parsley (which has a 'hotter' flavour) for this preserve, which is particularly delicious with grilled fish and pork.

6-8 large sprigs parsley
250ml (8fl oz) boiling water
250ml (8fl oz) lemon juice
500g (1¼lb) sugar
2-3 drops yellow food colouring (optional)
250ml (8fl oz) liquid pectin
6 × 15ml spoons (6tbls) finely chopped parsley

1   Put the parsley sprigs into a bowl and pour on the boiling water. Leave to infuse for 15 minutes.
2   Strain the liquid through a sieve into a pan, pressing the parsley to extract the maximum flavour.
3   Add the lemon juice and sugar and stir over low heat until the sugar dissolves. Increase the heat, bring to the boil and stir in the food colouring if you use it. Stir in the pectin, bring to the boil and boil rapidly for 1 minute. Skim off any foam that rises to the surface.
4   Remove the pan from the heat and stir in the chopped parsley. Leave the jelly to settle for about 5 minutes.
5   Stir the preserve and pour it into small, warmed sterilized jars. Cover with waxed discs and then with non-corrosive screw-on lids. Leave to cool.
6   Label the jars then store in a cool, dark place and leave to set.

MAKES ABOUT 900ML (1½ PINTS)

Variation You can use grapefruit juice instead of all but 2 × 15ml spoons (2tbls) of the lemon juice.

DRYING HERBS

To dry herbs, cut them on a dry day and hang them upside-down in bunches in a warm, dark place. Crumble the leaves and store them in lidded jars in a cool, dark place.

Leave herb seeds – dill, fennel and coriander, for example – to ripen and go brown on the plant. Tie bags over the seedheads and hang them up to dry.

SAGE & CIDER JELLY

This strongly flavoured preserve is especially good with goose, duck and pork and can be brushed over roast poultry, meat and ham as a glaze.

1kg (2¼lb) cooking apples, prepared weight
1 × 15ml spoon (1tbls) lemon juice
750ml (1¼ pints) water
750ml (1¼ pints) medium cider
5 sprigs sage
about 750g (1½lb) sugar (see note, below)
5 × 15ml spoons (5tbls) chopped sage

1 Peel, core and chop the apples and drop them straight into a bowl of water, acidulated with the lemon juice. This will stop them from going brown. You can use windfall or damaged apples – just discard the affected parts.
2 Strain the apples, put them in a large pan and pour on the water and cider. Add 2 sprigs of sage. Bring to the boil and simmer for 30 minutes, or until the apples are tender.

3 Wring out a jelly bag – it can be muslin, thick cotton or traditional flannel – in hot water and hang it over a bowl. Pour in the fruit and liquid and leave to drain overnight or for several hours. Do not try to hasten the process by pressing the liquid through the bag; this will make the jelly cloudy.
4 Measure the strained fruit juice and weigh out the appropriate amount of sugar.
5 Spread the sugar on baking trays and warm it in the oven at 110°C, 225°F, gas ¼.
6 Pour the fruit juice into a pan and add the warmed sugar. Stir over low heat until the sugar dissolves, then increase the heat and bring to the boil. Skim off any scum as it rises, using a perforated spoon. Boil rapidly for 10 minutes, then test the preserve for set (see setting note, p. 34).
7 When it is ready, stir in the chopped sage and leave it to settle for about 5 minutes.
8 Stir the jelly well, then pour it into

warmed sterilized jars and push a sprig of sage into each. Cover the jars with waxed paper discs and paper covers or non-corrosive screw-on lids (such as plastic coffee-jar lids).
9 Leave the jars to cool, then label and store in a cool, dark, dry place.
MAKES ABOUT 1.5KG (3¼LB)

Variation Try substituting one of the mints, tarragon, thyme, dill and so on for the sage.

How much sugar

For jellies made with a high-pectin fruit juice, such as apple or gooseberry, you should allow 800g of sugar to each 1 litre (1lb sugar to each 1 pint) of fruit juice.

Clear as a shaft of sunlight, a batch of herb jellies. Left to right: Sage and cider jelly, with thyme variation; Rosemary jellies; Parsley and lemon jelly.

HERBAL TEAS

Whether you feel like a refreshing pick-me-up or a soothing drink to hasten sleep, there's a tisane to fill the bill. Natural curiosity might urge you to try these infusions of herb leaves, seeds and roots which people relied on for centuries as simple medicinal remedies. You can drink the tisanes hot or cold, with or without milk, and sweetened (or not) with honey or sugar.

ANGELICA LEAF TEA

Ladies used to sip angelica tea to help banish headaches and to cure exhaustion.

3 × 15ml spoons (3tbls) chopped
angelica leaves
450 ml (¾ pint) boiling water
2 thin slices lemon, to serve

1   Put the angelica leaves into a small teapot, pour on the boiling water. Stir.
2   Cover the pot and leave to infuse for 3-4 minutes.
3   Pour the tea through a strainer and serve hot, with a slice of lemon.

MAKES 2 CUPS

COMFREY LEAF & ROOT TEA

The leaves and dried roots of comfrey were held to have particularly soothing properties, to aid digestion and help with chest complaints.

2 × 15ml spoons (2tbls) grated dried
comfrey root
450ml (¾ pint) water
3 × 15ml spoons (3tbls) chopped
comfrey leaves
2 × 5ml spoons (2tsp) lemon juice
2 thin slices lemon, to serve

1   Put the grated comfrey root and water into a pan, bring to the boil and simmer for 10 minutes.
2   Put the comfrey leaves into a teapot, strain on the liquid and stir in the lemon juice.
3   Cover and leave to infuse for 3-4 minutes.
4   Pour the tea through a strainer and serve hot, with a slice of lemon.

MAKES 2 CUPS

FENNEL SEED TEA

Spicy fennel tea acts as a pick-me-up, especially on a chilly day.

1 × 15ml spoon (1tbls) dried fennel seeds
450ml (¾ pint) boiling water
1 thin slice orange, halved, to serve

1   Pound the seeds in a mortar to crush them, but do not grind them to a powder.
2   Put the crushed seeds into a teapot, pour on the boiling water and stir.
3   Cover the pot and leave to infuse for 3-4 minutes.
4   Pour the tea through a strainer and serve hot, with a half slice of orange.

MAKES 2 CUPS

Variation Follow this method to make caraway seed tea, which was said to relieve headaches, and dill seed tea, which is especially refreshing on a hot day.

HERBAL LEAF TISANES

You can follow the Angelica leaf tea method using many other herb leaves. For guidance, here's a list of countrylore remedies accredited to these tisanes.

Basil	For gastric troubles and catarrh
Bergamot	To induce sleep
Borage	To help with catarrh and as a tonic
Dandelion	As a blood purifier and general tonic
Lovage	As a cleansing and refreshing drink
Mint	To relieve colds, headaches, sickness and heartburn
Parsley	As a general tonic and diuretic
Rosemary	For headaches and insomnia
Sage	As a general tonic
Thyme	To relieve colds, sinus troubles and bronchial attacks

HERBAL BEAUTY PREPARATIONS

The pendulum of popular demand is swinging away from artificial and chemical-based cosmetics and back to natural ingredients with the gentle cleansing and toning properties of herbs. These preparations are surprisingly simple and quick to make at home.

CUCUMBER & PARSLEY MILK

Use this milk morning and evening, after deep-cleansing your skin. It will remove any traces of dust and, at the same time, act as a light moisturizer.

5cm (2in) piece cucumber
3 × 15ml spoons (3tbls) chopped parsley
300ml (½ pint) milk

1   Peel the cucumber. Chop the peel and the flesh finely and put it into a jar. Add the parsley and milk.
2   Cover the jar, shake well and leave overnight in the refrigerator.
3   Strain the milk, pressing the sieve to extract the maximum juices from the cucumber and parsley.
4   Pour the milk into a bottle, cover with a screw-on cap and label. Store in the refrigerator.

MAKES 300ML (½ PINT)

APPLE MINT TONER

This gentle herbal preparation, said to be good for skins with enlarged pores, is soothing and relaxing.

2 × 15ml spoons (2tbls) chopped apple mint
3 × 15ml spoons (3tbls) cider vinegar
300ml (½ pint) soft water

1   Put the mint and vinegar into a jar, mix well and close. Leave to infuse for 7-8 days, shaking occasionally.
2   Strain the liquid through a sieve, pressing the mint to extract the maximum moisture.
3   Pour the water on to the vinegar, mix thoroughly and leave to cool.
4   Pour into a bottle, cover with a screw-on cap and label.

MAKES 300ML (½ PINT)

LEMON BALM HAIR RINSE

This rinse is especially good for fair hair which has a tendency to greasiness.

4 lemons
3 × 15ml spoons (3tbls) lemon balm
1 litre (1¾ pints) water

1   Peel the lemons and squeeze the juice.
2   Put the lemon peel, lemon balm and water into a pan, bring to the boil, cover and simmer for 15 minutes.
3   Remove from the heat and leave to infuse for 2 hours.
4   Strain through a sieve and press to extract the maximum moisture from the lemon peel and lemon balm.
5   Stir in the lemon juice and leave to cool.
6   Pour into a bottle, cover with a screw-on cap and label.

MAKES 1 LITRE (1¾ PINTS)

ROSEMARY & SAGE HAIR RINSE

In this old country recipe, rosemary is used to prevent dandruff and sage to bring out the natural tints in dark hair.

3 × 15ml spoons (3tbls) rosemary
2 × 15ml spoons (2tbls) sage
1 litre (1¾ pints) boiling water
150ml (¼ pint) cider vinegar
1 × 5ml spoon (1tsp) lemon juice

1   Put the herbs and water into a pan, bring to the boil, cover and simmer for 15 minutes.
2   Remove from the heat and leave to infuse for 2 hours.

3   Strain through a sieve, pressing the herbs to extract the maximum moisture.
4   Stir in the vinegar and lemon juice. Leave to cool.
5   Pour into a bottle, cover with a screw-on cap, and label.
   Pour 4-5 × 15ml spoons (4-5tbls) of the hair rinse on the hair after washing and rub it well into the scalp.

MAKES 300ML (½ PINT)

SAGE & EGG SHAMPOO

This is a mild shampoo, particularly good for medium and dark-coloured hair.

2 × 15ml spoons (2tbls) sage
1 litre (1¾ pints) water
4 × 15ml spoons (4tbls) grated Castile soap
2 eggs, beaten

1   Put the sage and water into a pan, bring to the boil, cover and simmer for 15 minutes.
2   Strain through a sieve, pressing the sage to extract the maximum moisture.
3   Stir the soap into the hot liquid to dissolve it. Set aside to cool.
4   Beat in the eggs and whisk well.
5   Pour the shampoo into a bottle, cover with a screw-on cap and label. Leave for at least 1 day before using.
   Add a little cider vinegar – about 2 × 15ml spoons (2tbls) – to the final rinsing water to remove all traces of shampoo and leave the hair soft and smooth.

MAKES 1 LITRE (1¾ PINTS)

THE ORCHARD

Even a single fruit tree in a garden provides the stuff that memories are made of: picnics under a shower of confetti-like petals; hot afternoons spent on top of the world, reading a book or shelling peas in a tree house; the thrill of harvest and the satisfaction of turning all that home-grown produce into pies, puddings and preserves. Memories from way back are usually of massive fruit trees dominating the garden – perhaps a single apple tree, a bumper cropper, in the centre of a pocket handkerchief lawn.

But times have changed and the large, spreading apple – or any other type of fruit – tree is rapidly being superseded by forms much more suited to the restricted space of small town gardens. The message is clear: you don't need a large garden to become an enthusiastic fruit grower.

It isn't the growing habit of your choice of fruit variety – Cox's Orange Pippin apple, Conference pear, Cambridge Gage plum – that determines the height and growing habit of the tree you plant: it's the root stock on to which the buds are grafted. Professional growers select the root and stem stock of fruit trees – some may be wild ones – according to their known vigour, root processes and so on; this draws the outlines, so to speak, of your tree. The variety that is budded or grafted on to it gives you the icing on the cake – the individual type, flavour, colour and texture of the fruit.

Assess the space you have available, you can be sure there's a fruit tree tailor-made to suit it. Choose the aspect carefully too. You have to balance the pros of a good south-facing spot, which would mean plenty of sun and good-quality fruit, with the frost problem. The earlier a tree flowers the more chance there is of the fruit being nipped in the bud by frost. If the obvious place for fruit trees is a notorious frost pocket, hedge your bets by choosing late-flowering varieties, or ones which have some degree of built-in frost resistance.

There's certainly more to growing tree fruit than at first meets the eye – which is why it is such a fascinating and rewarding branch (if you'll forgive the pun) of gardening. You can't just decide to plant a tree and then settle back and wait for it to bear fruit. Some fruit trees will never bear fruit at all, or not in any quantity, unless compatible pollen is carried by bees from another fruit tree nearby.

If all your neighbours are into tree fruit growing, then the insects will buzz productively from one garden to another and everyone will eventually have a bountiful harvest. Otherwise, you will need to make sure that the tree you choose is self-pollinating or, alternatively, buy two compatible trees. It sounds complicated, but the possible permutations and the rota of flowering times trip off the tongue of every grower; just remember to ask before you buy.

Perhaps the most desirable of all home-grown summer fruits, cherries can easily be grown, fan-trained or cordon-style against a fence, and that way they're easier to protect from birds!

Get talking to anyone about tree fruits – apples, pears, plums or whatever – and you'll come to the same conclusion: fruit that you buy just doesn't have the flavour that it used to. There isn't the variety in the shops any more. Some fruits are virtually unobtainable unless you happen to live in the country and there's a little roadside table selling crops from someone's garden. Things definitely, you get the strong impression, ain't what they used to be.

If you grow your own, you can change all that. You can plant varieties of fruit that may not be commercially viable (who cares?); that have only minority appeal; or that do not conform to some regulation or grading system – maybe it's just that the skin is freckled and doesn't present well on the shelves. In other words, you can grow what *you* like.

With careful selection, and by quizzing the grower before you buy, you can have fruit that crops early in the season (and tends to have a shortish storage life) and late-cropping varieties that will last almost the year around. These fruits, the ones you harvest last of all, are the ones to wrap gently in waxed paper or newspaper and put on to racks – a cool, dry room is what they like best. You can bring them out with pride months later, just before the early croppers are ready to harvest.

You can branch out into the more unusual fruits: damsons for fabulous damson cheese; medlars and quinces that scent a room as they ripen like some garden of Eden pot-pourri; or mulberries that stain your fingers a tell-tale black as you gather them. These are the stuff memories are made of.

GROWING FOR VARIETY

Fruit trees, like the fruits themselves, come in all shapes and sizes. Choose the form best suited to the space you have available and to your needs.

For growing in open ground, choose from pyramid trees, which have branches radiating out from just over 30cm (1ft) up the stem; bush trees, which have stems of 60cm-1 metre (2-3ft) in height, half-standards, in which the trunk is restricted to 1.2 metres (4ft) high; and standard trees, with trunks upwards of 2 metres (6ft) in height.

Never waste a south- or west-facing wall. It's crying out for a trained fruit tree, and serves a double purpose. The wall protects the tree from frost and wind and retains any vestige of heat. Other vertical surfaces, though they may lack the thermal properties, play a good supporting role – fences, sheds and even purpose-built wire frames.

Fan-trained trees (as the term implies) have branches trained outwards and upwards from the base. There are few more wonderful sights in a well-established garden or glasshouse than a fan-trained cherry, plum, apricot, peach or fig tree. Apples and pears, for some reason, are less often seen in this form, but are equally successful.

Espalier trees have a main central stem with one or more pairs of horizontal branches growing at right angles on each side – like a long thin body with its arms outstretched – and cordon trees consist of a single straight stem with fruit spurs along the whole length. According to the width available, the cordon, or row of cordons, can be trained horizontally or vertically. Cordons are particularly useful in small gardens, allowing you to grow a good choice of varieties.

Skilled gardeners, or those confident of pulling off an element of beginner's luck, may choose to buy one-year fruit trees (known as maidens) and train and prune them to the required shape. The rest of us are probably best advised to buy three- or four-year-old trees which are already shaped.

You can plant fruit trees at any time between November and March. Often it's a question of waiting on the weather – you obviously can't plant when the ground is rock hard with frost, and shouldn't do so when it's heavy and soggy.

What happens if your precious trees arrive when the conditions are foul? Keep them in their packing in a frost-free place if there's ice and snow outside. Otherwise dig a trench, sprinkle in dry peat or sand if it's water-logged, and bury the roots – what's known as heeling them in – until you can perform the official planting ceremony.

Don't be afraid to trim the roots before planting – you really don't need every last shred and whisker. Cut off any that are growing vigorously straight down and damaged ones, making diagonal cuts with really sharp secateurs. Measure the span and depth of the roots and dig a hole that won't cramp their style. On the other hand, it mustn't be over-deep. It's very important, when all is said and planted, that the union – that's the join between the root stock and the fruit variety you chose – should be a comfortable 7.5cm (3in) above soil level.

Firm the soil well in around the roots – remember they act as an anchor as well as a feeding tube – and tread the soil firmly when the hole is filled in. There's a great deal of satisfaction in stamping about in your wellingtons when you've just planted a tree.

All free-standing trees benefit from the extra support a strong stake gives them. Drive in a stout stake 30-60cm (1-2ft) from the stem, and tie the two uprights together with the purpose-made adjustable plastic ties you can get from most garden centres and shops.

Take special care of young trees in a dry spell. Until the roots are long enough to find a deep-down source of water, they're very vulnerable. Water all around them really thoroughly, then pack a thick layer of grass cuttings or other moisture-holding material – called mulch – around them. Don't expect the nutrients in the soil and water alone to produce miracle crops – all fruit trees need feeding at least once a year with garden compost, manure or chemical preparations.

Cutting them back

Pruning is not just a cosmetic operation to establish and maintain the size and shape of a tree. It's essential to ensure healthy growth and hearty crops. The two main principles are to help nature along by arranging the shape of the trees so that the main branches and their fruiting spurs get as much light and air as possible, and to encourage the development of those all-important fruiting spurs. The golden rule is that 'hard pruning' (removing a lot of wood, which takes courage to implement at first) encourages growth, while lighter pruning discourages it.

PICKING YOUR FRUIT TREES

Apple By hook or by crook, taste an apple before you plant a tree – flavour is such a personal judgement.

Prune apple trees in their dormant stage, mid-November to mid-March. Some varieties, such as Cox's Orange Pippin, start growth close to the branch. Others, like Worcester Pearmain and Bramley's Seedling, produce fruit buds near the tips of long growth. It's a trap for the unwary! Be sure to leave enough tip-bearing shoots to give you a bumper harvest.

You do have to try to keep one jump ahead of fruit tree predators. Tie bands of sacking or carpet underfelt close to the ground around trunks in early July to prevent Codling moth caterpillars doing a climb-the-greasy-pole act, then burn the protective bands together with the caterpillars in the autumn. Spray the trees against an invasion of aphids in winter, with an oil wash.

Dessert varieties (in approximate flowering order): Discovery; George Cave; Tydeman's Early; Worcester Pearmain; James Grieve; Fortune; Jester; Cox's Orange Pippin; Jupiter; St Edmunds Russet; Egremont Russet; Ashmead's Kernel.

Culinary varieties: Bramley's Seedling; Lord Derby; Edward VII; Monarch; Lane's Prince Albert; Howgate Wonder.

Crab apple These were the first wild apples; great flavours have been bred from these small beginnings. 'Crabs' have a high pectin content, make superb jelly and are good in a spicy pickle. John Downey is a good variety.

Cherry There are quite simply two types of cherry, sweet and sour.

Both give best results in a sheltered site on well-drained medium soil with a good lime content, and least favourable crops on sandy soil.

Sweet cherries form fruiting spurs on old wood. Prune 'cosmetically' – to remove overcrowded branches – in June and August, and paint over the wounds to avoid the danger of silver leaf infection.

Sour varieties, such as Morello, bear fruit mainly on the previous season's wood, the tips of branches. To avoid straggly trees with an excessive number of bare branches, cut back several older ones hard in April each year.

Among the sweet dessert varieties are Early Rivers, which has large dark crimson fruit, Stella, with black fruit, Merchant and Merpet. The best-known acid variety, ideal for jam-making, is Morello which has dark red and very juicy fruit.

Unfortunately, birds aren't discriminating – they like them all. Protect fruit with netting or bird-scaring fibre – when you pull this out it looks like a spider's web.

Damson A type of bullace, damson trees are so hardy that they are often used as a windbreak for more tender subjects. They like a damp site and should be given a dressing of nitrogen in spring. Most varieties are self-fertile. The small plum-like fruits make excellent preserves.

Medlar Like quinces, medlar trees like damp, heavy soil, a sunny spot and protection from cold winds. Prune them like apple trees. Harvest the russet-brown fruit in December – they need a touch of frost first – and eat them as soon as they are ripe. They are traditionally served with port.

Mulberry These trees like a rich, well-drained soil in a sunny position. The roots must not be pruned (they would bleed) and the trees need little pruning. For maximum cropping, restrict each shoot to four buds. The fruit, like a large loganberry, can be either black (which is to say dark red) or white (pale green). And yes, these are the leaves you use to feed silkworms.

Pear There are few fruits more luscious than a fully ripe dessert pear; or, come to that, less compromising than a tough old cooking pear!

Pears blossom earlier in the season than apples and are more prone to frost damage, so choose a sheltered site. They are usually grafted on to quince root stock, which means that they cannot tolerate dryness.

Give the trees a mulch of compost or well-rotted manure each spring all around – but never touching – the trunk. (If this were covered it would encourage subsidiary growth from the union.) Prune like apples, but less heavily in the early years.

Few varieties of pear are self-pollinating, so it's not usually a question of which *one* to choose, but which two or three are compatible. Or you can solve the problem by using a 'family tree' which has three or more varieties on the one root stock.

Pears, like apples, are highly prone to disease. If scab blisters appear on shoots remove them at once, before they spread to leaves and fruits, and burn them. Protect fruit from birds, even to the extent of tying paper bags over prize specimens.

Varieties to consider: Conference; Beurre Hardy; Dr. Jewel Guyot; Doyenne du Comice; Beth; Glou Morceau, and a culinary variety, Catillac.

Plum and Gage These do best grown as fan-trained trees against a wall and must be kept moist and well mulched throughout the growing season. Most of the fruit is carried on new wood, so the only pruning you have to do is to remove dead wood in winter and 'cosmetic' pruning to keep the tree in shape in summer. As the trees are in flower for only 10 days and not all varieties are self-pollinating, you have some careful matchmaking to do.

Some available varieties: Czar; Giant Prune; Marjorie's Seedling; Victoria; Oullins Golden Gage; Cambridge Gage; Yellow Pershore; the small, early Cherry Plum.

Quince Here's a tree to plant for future generations. Plant it in moist, heavy soil and it will live to a ripe – and gnarled – old age. Quince trees need little pruning, just remove dead wood in winter. Harvest the golden fruit from late October and some can be stored until February. Portugal is a good variety which has been going strong since 1610.

VITALITY DRINKS

They're up-to-the-minute versions of milk shakes and hot toddies, made with buttermilk, yoghurt, wine, honey and mineral waters. They come in all colours of the rainbow – just as fruits in the orchard do – and one is even candy-striped. And they're just the thing to refresh you on long, lazy days in the garden, or on chilly evenings round the fire.

CANDY STRIPER

Here's a stunning drink to serve at a young teenage party – it can take the place of dessert. It looks its best with fat, bendy, striped drinking straws. The secret is to have tubs of fruit purée ready made, when the drink can be assembled in moments. It's also a fun way to use small stocks of purée in the freezer.

1 litre (1¾ pints) natural yoghurt
300ml (½ pint) sweetened greengage purée
300ml (½ pint) sweetened cherry purée
300ml (½ pint) sweetened apple purée
pinch of ground cinnamon
300ml (½ pint) cream soda
10 small scoops vanilla ice cream

1   Beat one-third of the yoghurt into the greengage purée, one-third into the cherry purée and one-third into the apple purée lightly spiced with cinnamon.
2   Make layers of each purée in turn in 10 glasses, to give a candy-striped effect. Just before serving, pour on the soda and top with ice cream. The guests give the drink a good stir with the bendy straws!

MAKES 10 GLASSES

Colour variety

You can go for traffic~light colour contrasts with plum, quince and greengage purée, or subtle, summery combinations of peach, apricot and nectarine from the glasshouse. They're all delicious and pretty.

SPICED APPLE SHAKE

Fruit purée whizzed with buttermilk or yoghurt in the blender makes instant full-of-goodness drinks.

1 dessert apple, halved
1 × 15ml spoon (1tbls) lemon juice
150ml (¼ pint) apple purée
300ml (½ pint) natural yoghurt
1 × 15ml spoon (1tbls) clear honey
pinch of ground cinnamon
40g (1½oz) hazelnuts, chopped
2 sprigs apple mint, to decorate

1   Peel, core and chop one half of the apple. Core and thinly slice the other half and toss the slices in lemon juice.
2   Put the apple purée, yoghurt, honey, cinnamon and chopped apple into a blender or food processor and blend until smooth. Stir in the hazelnuts.
3   Pour the drink into 2 glasses.
4   Thread the apple slices and balance them on top of the glass. Decorate with apple mint sprigs and serve chilled.

MAKES 2 GLASSES

PLUM COOLER

This is delicious on a very hot day, with a scoop of vanilla ice cream stirred into each glass.

300ml (½ pint) plum purée
4 × 15ml spoons (4tbls) blanched almonds
2 × 15ml spoons (2tbls) wheatgerm
450ml (¾ pint) buttermilk
2 × 15ml spoons (2tbls) set honey
2 drops almond essence (optional)
2 × 15ml spoons (2tbls) almond slivers, toasted

1   Put the plum purée, blanched almonds, wheatgerm, buttermilk, honey and almond essence, if you like it, into a blender or food processor. Blend until smooth.
2   Pour the drink into 3 glasses and sprinkle the toasted almonds on top.

MAKES 3 GLASSES

Drink your health with a trio of cool fruity drinks. Left to right, *Greengage and mint fizz, Candy striper and Plum cooler.*

GREENAGE & MINT FIZZ

The tanginess of stone fruits makes an unusual and refreshing drink when mixed with sparkling mineral water or soda.

500g (1¼lb) greengages
1 × 15ml spoon (1tbls) mint
4 × 15ml spoons (4tbls) water
600ml (1 pint) ice cream soda, chilled
4 × 15ml spoons (4tbls) soured cream
4 pinches of grated nutmeg
4 sprigs mint, to decorate

1   Put the greengages in a pan with the mint and water. Bring slowly to the boil and simmer for 10-15 minutes, stirring often, until the fruit is cooked.
2   Rub the fruit through a sieve. Set aside to cool, then chill.
3   Just before serving, pour the ice cream soda on to the purée, whisking all the time.
4   Pour the drink into 4 glasses. Top each one with a swirl of soured cream, a pinch of nutmeg and a sprig of mint.

MAKES 4 GLASSES

PEAR & BANANA MALTIE

This is just the thing to give someone who feels in need of a tonic. It's also a good breakfast-in-a-glass.

4 × 15ml spoons (4tbls) malted milk powder
150ml (¼ pint) hot milk
300ml (½ pint) natural yoghurt
1 banana
2 pears, peeled, cored and chopped
50g (2oz) rolled oats

1   Put the malted milk powder into a bowl and pour on the hot milk, stirring constantly. Leave to cool.
2   Put the milk paste, yoghurt, banana and pears into a blender or food processor and blend until smooth. Stir in half the rolled oats.
3   Pour the drink into 2 glasses and sprinkle the remaining oats on top. Serve chilled.

MAKES 2 GLASSES

PEAR MULL

Some of the tastiest recipes are those discovered by chance. I came upon this when I had some left-over pears poached in red wine. I liquidized them in the blender – and got hooked on the result. It's perfect on a cold evening.

350ml (12fl oz) red wine
50g (2oz) light Muscovado sugar
1 strip thinly pared orange rind
juice of ½ orange
1 strip thinly pared lemon rind
juice of 1 lemon
2 cloves
½ × 5ml spoon (½tsp) ground cinnamon
2 pears, peeled, cored and sliced
2 thin slices orange, to decorate

1   Put all the ingredients, except the orange slices, into a pan and slowly bring to the boil. Simmer for 10 minutes.
2   Lift out the pears with a draining spoon and put them into a blender. Strain on the wine, discarding the flavourings. Blend until smooth.
3   Pour the hot wine into 4 warmed heatproof glasses. Decorate each with half an orange slice. Serve hot.

MAKES 4 GLASSES

ORCHARD PRESERVES

A bumper harvest from the tree fruits in the orchard means a busy time in the kitchen. Freezing fruit is undeniably quicker, but it doesn't have the charm of pots of golden apple butter, slices of purple damson cheese, jars of spiced crab apples and little squares of sweetmeats made from that cottage garden favourite – the quince.

ORCHARD JAM

500g (1lb) dessert apples
500g (1lb) cooking pears
500g (1lb) plums or greengages
5cm (2in) piece cinnamon stick
2 × 15ml spoons (2tbls) lemon juice
300ml (½ pint) water
1.25kg (2¾lb) sugar

1　Peel, core and chop the apples and pears. Stone the plums and cut them into quarters.
2　Put the apple and pear peelings and cores, the plum stones and the cinnamon on to a piece of muslin and tie it to make a bag.
3　Put the fruit, lemon juice and trimmings into a pan, pour on the water and bring slowly to the boil. Simmer for 25 minutes, or until the fruit is soft. Remove the bag of trimmings.
4　Spread the sugar on baking trays and warm it in a low oven.
5　Tip the sugar into the pan, stir over low heat until it dissolves, then increase the heat.
6　Bring the preserve quickly to the boil, and fast-boil until setting point is reached (see below). Skim off any foam as it rises to the top.
7　Cool the jam slightly in the pan, then stir it well.
8　Pour it into warm, sterilized jars. Cover the surface with waxed paper discs, then cover the jars with paper jam-pot covers or screw-on lids.
9　Cool, label and store in a cool, dry dark place.

MAKES ABOUT 1.75KG (4LB)

Setting point

Test jam for set in the same way as for preserve jelly. (See page 34)

DAMSON CHEESE

This preserve is particularly good with cold poultry and game.

1kg (2¼lb) damsons
150ml (¼ pint) water
about 900g (2lb) sugar
glycerine, for brushing

1　Put the damsons and water into a pan. Bring to the boil, cover the pan and simmer for 25 minutes, or until the fruit is very soft.
2　Weigh a pan. Rub the fruit and liquid through a sieve into the pan and note the total weight. Deduct the weight of the pan. Crack some of the stones and add the kernels to the fruit pulp.
3　Weigh out an equal amount of sugar to fruit pulp.
4　Add the sugar to the fruit pulp and stir over low heat until it has dissolved.
5　Bring to the boil, then cook the pulp over moderate heat, stirring frequently until it is so stiff that drawing a wooden spoon through it leaves a deep channel. Depending on the moisture content of the fruit and the exact level of heat, this will take about 1¼-1½ hours.
6　Brush moulds lightly with glycerine – small wide-necked yoghurt pots or mousse cases are ideal.
7　Spoon in the preserve. Cover the surface with waxed paper discs, then with jam-pot covers or greaseproof paper. Label and leave to cool.
8　Store the fruit cheese in a cool, dry, dark place – the closest equivalent you have to a cool larder. Leave it to mature for 3 months before serving.

MAKES ABOUT 1KG (2¼LB)

QUINCE SWEETMEAT

Like the pasta de membrillo of Spain, this quince paste is cooked until almost all the moisture has evaporated. It is cut in squares, tossed in icing sugar and served with coffee. Delicious!

1kg (2¼lb) quinces
1 litre (1¾ pints) water
1kg (2¼lb) sugar
icing sugar, to serve

1　Roughly chop the quinces and put them in a pan with the water. Bring to the boil and simmer for 30-35 minutes until the fruit is really tender.
2　Press the fruit through a coarse sieve or pass it through a vegetable mill.
3　Return the purée to the pan and cook it over a very low heat, until it is dry and thick, stirring frequently.
4　Spread the sugar on a baking tray and warm it in a low oven.
5　Add the sugar to the pan and stir over low heat until it dissolves. Continue cooking for 2-3 hours, stirring frequently, until the paste is so dry that it is quite an effort to draw a spoon through it. Another method is to put the paste in a covered casserole dish and cook it in a low oven overnight.
6　Spoon the paste into an oiled Swiss roll tin and spread it evenly. Leave it to cool and set. Cut into squares, it will keep almost indefinitely in an airtight container, in a cool dry place.
7　Toss the paste in icing sugar to serve.

MAKES ABOUT 750G (1½LB)

APPLE BUTTER

Making apple butter used to be a community project along America's East coast. The apples from the orchard and the task of preparing them was shared, and the butter was made in huge vats in the cookhouses.

1.5kg (3¼lb) cooking apples
600ml (1 pint) water
600ml (1 pint) dry cider
½ × 5ml spoon (½tsp) ground cinnamon
pinch of grated nutmeg
grated rind and juice of 1 lemon
about 1.25kg (2¾lb) sugar

1   Roughly chop the apples. Put them in a pan with the water and cider. Bring to the boil and simmer for 15-20 minutes until the apples are soft, stirring frequently.
2   Put the fruit through a sieve or pass it through a vegetable mill.
3   Weigh the fruit pulp, stir in the spices, lemon rind and lemon juice.
4   Weigh out 350g (12oz) sugar to each 450g (1lb) fruit pulp.
5   Spread the sugar on baking trays and warm it in the oven. This will prevent it from lowering the temperature of the fruit pulp too much when it is added.
6   Return the fruit pulp to the pan and simmer it, stirring frequently, until it is dry. Add the warmed sugar and stir over low heat until it has dissolved.
7   Simmer the preserve very slowly, stirring almost constantly, until it is thick enough to coat the back of a spoon.
8   Pour into warm, sterilized jars, cover the surface with waxed paper discs then cover the jars with paper jam-pot covers. Leave to cool, then label.
9   Store the fruit in a cool, dry place for no more than about 6 months.

MAKES ABOUT 1.5KG (3¼LB)

Variation Use crab apples instead of apples, or mix other fruits – blackberries or plums for example – with the apples.

SET PIECES

Fruit cheeses and fruit butters both evoke the nostalgia of farmhouse teas. You make cheeses in small moulds to turn out and serve with cold meats and salads, or sliced and spread on toasted buns and teacakes.

You can use any strong-flavoured fruit – damsons, plums and blackcurrants are old favourites. But why cheese? The boiled fruit is sieved, then cooked to a thick pulp with an equal weight of sugar until it's thick enough to set in a mould: almost as firm as a slice of cheese, in fact.

Fruit butter is spreadable and about the same consistency as softened butter. With a lower ratio of sugar to fruit than either fruit jelly preserves or fruit cheeses, it doesn't keep so long. Use it for a filling for sponge cakes, in tartlets and on bread and scones. Apple butter is a good straight-from-the-jar sauce to serve with pork and goose.

Set fruit cheeses and butters in decorative shapes to make attractive and unusual gifts. Fruit butters made from brightly coloured soft fruits are especially good as individual portions in small heart-shaped moulds.

SPICED CRAB APPLES

Crab apples are fiddly to peel and core, but there's actually no need to: pickling softens the pips and cores so that the whole fruit is edible. Serve this fruit pickle with ham, pork, game or poultry.

1kg (2¼lb) light Muscovado sugar
600ml (1 pint) vinegar
40g (1½oz) pickling spice
strip of thinly pared lemon rind
1kg (2¼lb) crab apples

1   Put the sugar and vinegar into a pan. Tie the spices in a muslin bag and add this and the lemon rind to the pan.
2   Stir over low heat to dissolve the sugar.
3   Prick the crab apples all over with a darning needle. Add them to the vinegar mixture, bring to the boil and simmer until they are tender – about 30 minutes.
4   Lift out the apples with a draining spoon and pack them into warm jars. Keep the jars warm in a low oven.
5   Fast-boil the vinegar until it has reduced in volume by about one half. Discard the bag of spices.
6   Pour the syrupy vinegar over the crab apples to cover them. Cover the jars with vinegar-proof (non-corrosive) lids, such as the plastic-lined ones on coffee jars. Cool and label.
7   Store the pickled apples in a cool, dry, dark place for at least 3 months before serving.

MAKES ABOUT 1.5KG (3¼LB)

FARMHOUSE FARE

Traditional country food – the kind that makes the most of home-grown fruits and home-raised meat – has stood the test of time. Many regional dishes are not only delicious but also make good nutritional sense. The acid in stone fruits, whether it's apples with pork, quinces with game, or plums with beef, goes a long way towards offsetting the richness of the meat.

PEAR CORIANDER SOUP

Use cooking or dessert pears, even windfalls, and offer a prize for guessing the ingredients.

25g (1oz) butter
1 medium onion, peeled and chopped
½ × 5ml spoon (½tsp) lightly crushed coriander seed
1 × 15ml spoon (1tbls) flour
600ml (1 pint) chicken stock
500g (1¼lb) pears, peeled, cored and chopped
2 × 5ml spoons (2tsp) lemon juice
300ml (½ pint) single cream
salt
freshly ground black pepper
coriander sprigs, to garnish

1   Melt the butter and fry the onion over moderate heat for 3-4 minutes. Stir in the coriander seeds and the flour and cook for 1 minute.
2   Pour on the stock, stirring all the time and bring to the boil. Add the pears and lemon juice and simmer for 15 minutes, or until the fruit is tender.
3   Purée the soup in a blender or food processor.
4   Return the purée to the pan and stir in the cream. Season with salt and pepper, and heat gently.
5   Serve the soup garnished with coriander leaves.

SERVES 4

PEARS WITH BRIE SAUCE

This is a delicious first course with a delicate flavour.

4 large dessert or cooking pears
1 bay leaf
1 × 5ml spoon (1tsp) lemon juice
250 ml (8fl oz) Greek-style yoghurt
75g (3oz) Brie, chopped
2 × 5ml spoons (2tsp) flat-leafed parsley, chopped
freshly ground black pepper
salad leaves, to serve
4 × 15ml spoons (4tbls) walnut halves

1   Peel and halve the pears and scoop out the cores.
2   Poach the pears in boiling water with the bay leaf and lemon juice until they are really tender – 5-25 minutes, depending on the type.
3   Lift out the pears with a draining spoon and pat them dry. Set aside to cool.
4   Put the yoghurt and Brie into a blender or food processor and work to a smooth purée. Stir in the parsley and season the sauce with pepper.
5   Line 4 serving plates with salad leaves – spinach, endive or decorative ones like vine leaves. Place 2 pear halves on each, pour the sauce over and garnish with the walnuts.

SERVES 4

Left, a perfect farmhouse combination, sausage, sage and apple plait served with tangy red cabbage with plums.

Right, a single vine leaf makes a natural garnish for pears with Brie sauce.

PHEASANT WITH QUINCE

Slices of quince give a bitter-sweet flavour to this creamy sauce. You can use cooking pears or apples instead.

2 young oven-ready pheasants
40g (1½oz) butter
salt
freshly ground black pepper
12 button onions, peeled
120ml (4fl oz) dry white wine
2 quinces, peeled, cored and sliced

SAUCE
120ml (4fl oz) dry white wine
1 × 15ml spoon (1tbls) flour
250ml (8fl oz) soured cream

1   Put a small walnut-sized knob of butter inside each pheasant and season the birds inside and out with salt and pepper.
2   Heat the remaining butter in a flameproof casserole and sauté the pheasants on all sides over moderate heat until browned.
3   Add the button onions and wine, cover and simmer for 30 minutes. Turn the birds, add the quince slices, cover and simmer for a further 20-25 minutes, until the birds are tender. Pour off and reserve the liquid.
4   To make the sauce, simmer the wine to reduce it in volume by half.
5   Skim the fat that rises to the top of the cooking liquid. Put it into a small pan, stir in the flour over moderate heat and pour on the cooking liquid and reduced wine, stirring constantly. Bring the sauce to the boil and simmer until it thickens. Stir in the soured cream and heat gently. Season with salt and pepper.
6   Carve the pheasants, arrange the onions and quince slices and pour on a little of the sauce to garnish. Serve the remainder separately.

SERVES 4-6

CHICKEN & CHERRY TURNOVERS

225g (8oz) shortcrust pastry
20g (¾oz) butter
2 spring onions, trimmed and thinly sliced
1 × 15ml spoon (1tbls) flour
150ml (¼ pint) milk
salt
freshly ground black pepper
a pinch of grated nutmeg
225g (8oz) cooked chicken breast
225g (8oz) cherries, pitted
1 egg, beaten, to glaze
2 × 15ml spoons (2tbls) sesame seeds

1   Divide the pastry into 4 equal pieces. Roll each one out to an 18cm (7in) circle.
2   Melt the butter in a small pan and sauté the onion over moderate heat for 2 minutes. Stir in the flour and pour on the milk, stirring constantly. Simmer for 2 minutes. Season with salt, pepper and nutmeg. Set aside to cool.
3   Dice the chicken and stir it into the sauce with the cherries.
4   Divide the filling between the 4 pastry circles, putting it on one half only. Dampen the pastry edges and fold one half over the other, to enclose the filling. Pinch the cut edges all round to seal them.
5   Place the pasties on a baking sheet and brush the tops with egg. Sprinkle them with sesame seeds and prick them with a fork.
6   Bake the pasties in the oven, preheated to 200°C, 400°F, gas 6, for 25-30 minutes, until the pastry is golden brown. Serve hot or cold.

MAKES 4 PASTIES

Choosing your bird

If you buy your pheasants unprepared, choose the younger ones by their soft beaks and soft, even, v-shaped feathers. Hen pheasants are always the tastiest.

MR COX'S PORK CHOPS

Pork and apples make a very successful partnership. It's a strange thing, but dessert apples are often a better choice than cooking apples when you want to cook them in slices or rings, as here, because they hold their shape more. And they're better still if you don't peel them.

4 large pork loin chops
40g (1½oz) butter
1 large onion, peeled and sliced
2 garlic cloves, peeled and crushed
2 dessert apples, cored and sliced into rings
1 × 15ml spoon (1tbls) lemon thyme
250ml (8fl oz) dry cider
2 × 15ml spoons (2tbls) calvados (optional)
salt
freshly ground black pepper
4 × 15ml spoons (4tbls) double cream
sprigs of lemon thyme, to garnish

1   Trim the excess fat from the chops. Melt one-third of the butter in a frying pan. Fry the chops over high heat for 2 minutes on each side. Transfer them to a baking dish.
2   Melt the remaining butter and fry the onion and garlic over moderate heat for 3 minutes, stirring once or twice. Transfer the vegetables to the casserole.
3   Fry the apple rings for 1 minute on each side, add them to the chops and sprinkle on the herb.
4   Heat the cider and, if you like it, the calvados. Pour it over the casserole and season with salt and pepper.
5   Cook in the oven, preheated to 180°C, 350°F, gas 4, for 40 minutes, or until the meat is cooked.
6   Stir in the cream and garnish with the sprigs of thyme.

SERVES 4

Apple glaze

Make an aromatic golden glaze, lovely to melt over grilled pork chops, with apple purée and butter — an apple butter of a different kind. Beat 4 × 15ml spoons (4 tbls) firm apple purée and ½ × 5ml (½tsp) chopped sage into 50g (2oz) softened butter. Shape in a roll, wrap in foil and chill. Serve in slices.

STEAK IN PLUM SAUCE

7 dessert plums
2 × 15ml spoons (2tbls) water
750g (1½lb) rump steak
2 × 15ml spoons (2tbls) sunflower oil
20g (¾oz) butter
1½ × 5ml spoons (1½tsp) flour
1½ × 5ml spoons (1½tsp) lemon juice
½ × 5ml spoon (½tsp) Worcestershire sauce
1½ × 15ml spoons (1½tbls) brandy
1½ × 15ml spoons (1½tbls) double cream
salt
freshly ground black pepper
flat-leafed parsley, to garnish

1   Simmer 5 of the plums in the water for 5-10 minutes until they are soft. Rub them through a sieve.
2   Trim excess fat from the meat and cut it into serving pieces.
3   Heat the oil in a frying pan over high heat, and when it is very hot sear the meat for 2 minutes on each side, according to how you like it.
4   Lift out the meat and keep it warm. Melt the butter in the pan, stir in the flour and then add the lemon juice, plum purée and Worcestershire sauce. Stir well and bring to the boil. Simmer for 2 minutes. Stir in the brandy and cream, season with salt and pepper and heat gently without boiling.
5   Pour the sauce over the steak, cut the reserved plums into quarters. Garnish the dish with the plums and parsley.

SERVES 4

CASSOULET

This is a version of a French country dish, ideal to serve for lunch on a cold, winter's day.

350g (12oz) dried flageolets, soaked and drained
1kg (2¼lb) lean lamb
500g (1¼lb) belly of pork
250g (9oz) chorizo sausage, skinned and thickly sliced
2 large onions, peeled and sliced
4 garlic cloves, peeled and sliced
2 quinces or medlars, peeled, cored and sliced
a few stalks parsley, thyme and chervil
2 bay leaves
1 litre (1¾ pints) hot chicken stock
salt
freshly ground black pepper
150g (5oz) white breadcrumbs
1 × 5ml spoon (1tsp) chopped sage

1   Cook the beans in fast-boiling unsalted water for 30 minutes. Drain them.
2   Cut the excess fat from the lamb and cut it into very thick slices. Cut the rind from the pork and snip it finely. Thickly slice the pork.
3   In a large, flameproof casserole, make layers of the beans, lamb, pork, pork rind and sausage, the onions and garlic, and the quinces or medlars. Add the sprigs of herbs and bay leaves tied together.
4   Pour on the hot stock, season with salt and pepper, cover the dish and bring to the boil. Mix half the breadcrumbs with the sage and sprinkle on top.
5   Cover the dish and cook in the oven, preheated to 160°C, 325°F, gas 3, for 2 hours.
6   Stir in the layer of sage and breadcrumbs, taste the stock and add more seasoning if needed. Discard the herbs.
7   Sprinkle on the remaining breadcrumbs. Cover the dish and cook for 30 minutes. Remove the lid and continue cooking for a further 30 minutes.

SERVES 6

Variation If you don't have quinces or medlars, substitute 2 cored and sliced dessert apples. Stir them into the casserole with the first layer of breadcrumbs.

SAUSAGE, SAGE & APPLE PLAIT

This is a good combination of flavours in any form, brought together here in a supper dish.

250g (9oz) puff pastry
250g (9oz) sausagemeat
1 small onion, peeled and finely chopped
2 × 5ml spoons (2tsp) chopped sage
2 small cooking apples, peeled,
cored and chopped
2 hard-boiled eggs, chopped
salt
freshly ground black pepper
1 egg, beaten, to glaze

1   Roll out the pastry on a lightly floured board to an oblong 30 × 25cm (12 × 10in). Transfer the pastry to a baking sheet.
2   Mix together the sausagemeat, onion, sage, apple and chopped eggs and season with salt and pepper.
3   Shape the mixture into a roll and place it along the centre of the pastry.
4   Cut the pastry on each side of the filling into 1cm (½in) wide strips, making diagonal cuts. Brush the strips with beaten egg.
5   Wrap the pastry strips over the filling to enclose it and brush the top with egg.
6   Bake the plait in the oven, pre-heated to 200°C, 400°F, gas 6, for 35 minutes, or until the top is golden brown.
  Serve hot with a tomato sauce (p. 59), or cold with herb mayonnaise, (p. 33).

SERVES 4-6

RED CABBAGE WITH PLUMS

This is a hearty vegetable dish which is most at home with beef and pork dishes.

1 small red cabbage, cored and shredded
1 large onion, peeled and chopped
4 × 15ml spoons (4tbls) red wine
2 × 15ml spoons (2tbls) red wine vinegar
225g (8oz) plums, halved
salt
freshly ground black pepper
1 × 15ml spoon (1tbls) redcurrant jelly

1   Put the cabbage, onion, red wine and vinegar into a flameproof casserole, cover and heat slowly, stirring frequently.
2   Simmer for 30 minutes.
3   Add the plums, season with salt and pepper, cover and simmer for a further 30 minutes, or until the cabbage is tender.
4   Stir in the redcurrant jelly.

SERVES 4-6

Variation Apples have a longer storage life than plums. Use the same quantity of peeled, cored and sliced cooking apples instead, and add another 1 × 15ml spoon (1tbls) redcurrant jelly.

FENNEL & APPLE SALAD

2 medium bulbs fennel
3 dessert apples, cored and thinly sliced
2 × 15ml spoons (2tbls) orange juice
2 spring onions, peeled and sliced
2 × 15ml spoons (2tbls) seedless raisins
2 × 15ml spoons (2tbls) walnut halves
50g (2oz) stoned dates, sliced
½ bunch watercress sprigs

DRESSING
4 × 15ml spoons (4tbls) sunflower oil
2 × 15ml spoons (2tbls) orange juice
1 × 5ml spoon (1tsp) grated orange rind
3 × 15ml spoons (3tbls) natural yoghurt
1 garlic clove, crushed
salt
freshly ground black pepper

1   Trim the fennel and discard any tough or discoloured outer leaves. Slice thinly into rings.
2   Toss the apple slices into the orange juice.
3   Mix the dressing ingredients together.
4   Toss together the fennel, apple, spring onions, raisins, walnuts and dates. Pour on the dressing and mix well.
5   Pile the salad into a dish and arrange the watercress sprigs around the outside.
  The salad is good with cold roast poultry and meats and with cold meat pies. It can also be served as a first course.

SERVES 4

Special arrangements

Salads look even more appetizing, as a first course, arranged on individual plates. To serve the apple and fennel salad in this way, toss the apple slices in the orange juice and arrange them in a fan shape on each plate. Mix the spring onions, raisins, walnuts and dates and then spoon into a mound at the base of the fan. Scatter the fennel rings over and garnish with the watercress. Pour the dressing over just before serving.

ORCHARD PUDDINGS

A glut of fruit in the orchard is the cue for a return to traditional puddings. Fruit tarts, turnovers and flans, batter puddings and pancakes, creamy moulds and jellies have enriched that satisfying harvest feeling for generations. All these puddings will be firm family favourites, but be generous – guests will love them too!

MULBERRY SUMMER PUDDING

7-8 thin slices white bread
750g (1½lb) mulberries
2 × 15ml spoons (2tbls) water
125g (5oz) caster sugar
2 scented geranium leaves

1   Cut the crusts from the bread and line the base and sides of a 900ml (1½ pint) soufflé dish or straight-sided cake tin. Trim the bread to fit so that there are no gaps.
2   Put the mulberries, water, sugar and leaves into a pan. Stir over low heat to dissolve the sugar, then simmer for 10 minutes, or until the fruit is soft. Discard the leaves.
3   Pour the fruit into the dish and cover the top with more bread.
4   Place a saucer or plate to fit inside the dish and put a weight on top.
5   Leave the dish in the refrigerator overnight.
6   Run a knife around the outside of the pudding. Invert it on to a serving plate. Serve chilled.

Small scented geranium leaves, especially the cream and green variegated ones, make a lovely decoration for this deep purple-coloured pudding. Make a ring of them around the plate and a cluster or spray on top.

SERVES 4-6

Did you know?

Summer pudding was once called hydropathic pudding because it used to be served in hospitals to patients who couldn't eat pastry.

QUINCE MOULD

A bowl of golden quinces scents the room so superbly that there could be an understandable reluctance to cook them!

75g (3oz) sugar
300ml (½ pint) water
1 lemon
500g (1¼ lb) ripe quinces
750g (1½lb) cooking apples
20g (¾oz) powdered gelatine
4 × 15ml spoons (4tbls) double cream

1   Stir the sugar and water over low heat until the sugar has dissolved. Thinly pare a strip of lemon rind and add it to the syrup. Bring to the boil and fast-boil for 5 minutes.
2   Peel, core and thinly slice the quinces. Poach them in the syrup for 20-25 minutes, until they are soft.
3   Lift out the quinces with a draining spoon. Rinse a 1 litre (2¼ pint) mould with cold water. Arrange the quince slices in a pattern.
4   Fast-boil the syrup for a further 5 minutes. Stir in the juice from the lemon.
5   Peel, core and chop the apples and simmer them for 10 minutes, or until they are soft. Discard the lemon rind. Sieve the apples or liquidize them with the syrup in a blender.
6   Dissolve the gelatine in hot water and stir it into the apple purée. Set aside to cool.
7   Spoon the apple purée over the quinces. Leave in the refrigerator for 3 hours to set.
8   Turn out the mould on to a serving plate. Pour the cream over the top, to dribble down the sides.

SERVES 6-8

Two desserts to be proud of, especially when the fruit is home-grown, Plum strudel, an Austrian speciality with more than a hint of almonds, left and Greengage tart (recipe on page 53).

PEAR CLAFOUTI

50g (2oz) flour
salt
40g (1½oz) caster sugar flavoured with bay (see p. 33)
1 × 15ml spoon (1tbls) sunflower oil
2 eggs
1 egg yolk
300ml (½ pint) milk or single cream
500g (1¼lb) dessert pears
25g (1oz) butter, grated
3 × 15ml spoons (3tbls) icing sugar

1   Sift together the flour and salt and stir in the caster sugar. Beat in the oil, eggs and milk (or cream) and beat until the batter is smooth.
2   Peel, core and slice the pears. Arrange them in a greased baking dish. Pour on the batter and dot the top with butter.
3   Bake the pudding in the oven, preheated to 180°C, 350°F, gas 4, for 40-45 minutes, until the batter is well risen and crisp on top.
4   Sift the icing sugar over the pudding and serve at once.

SERVES 4

Variation Other orchard fruits are delicious cooked in this way. Use peeled, cored and sliced apples, pitted cherries, or halved and stoned plums or greengages.

PLUM STRUDEL

175g (6oz) flour
salt
1 egg, beaten
2-3 × 15ml spoons (2-3tbls) warm water
icing sugar, to sift

FILLING
1kg (2¼lb) plums
150g (5oz) butter
75g (3oz) white breadcrumbs
50g (2oz) blanched almonds, chopped
50g (2oz) caster sugar (optional)

1   Sift the flour and salt. Make a well in the centre, pour in the egg and mix well. Sprinkle on just enough water to make a soft dough.
2   Knead the dough until it is smooth and pliable and no longer sticky – this will take about 15 minutes.
3   Roll out the dough to cover a lightly floured tea cloth stretched over a table. Leave it for 10 minutes to rest.
4   Quarter the plums, removing the stones. Melt the butter and set aside 2 × 15ml spoons (2tbls). Mix the melted butter with the breadcrumbs and almonds.
5   Sprinkle the crumb mixture over two-thirds of the length of the pastry, arrange the plums on top and sprinkle on the sugar, if using.
6   Brush the uncovered pastry with butter. Lift the cloth and roll up the pastry, starting from the covered side.
7   Place the roll on a greased baking sheet, with the end of the roll underneath. Brush the top with butter.
8   Bake the strudel in the oven, preheated to 200°C, 400°F, gas 6, for 40 minutes, until the pastry is well browned and crisp.
9   Transfer the strudel to a wire rack. Sprinkle the top with icing sugar. Serve warm. Ice cream is a delicious accompaniment.

SERVES 6-8

Variation This light, crisp pastry can be used to enclose other tree fruits too. Apple strudel with walnuts, cherry strudel with almonds, pear strudel spiced with a pinch of ground cinnamon and the fruit tossed with hazelnuts – they are all delightful.

APPLE RING MOULD

*Bramley apples have the best flavour
for this dish. Other suitable varieties
are Blenheims, Grenadiers and
Howgates.*

3 large cooking apples
150ml (¼ pint) water
thinly pared rind and juice of ½ lemon
20g (¾oz) powdered gelatine
2 eggs
2 egg yolks
50g (2oz) caster sugar flavoured with bay
(see p. 33)
150ml (¼ pint) double cream, whipped

SAUCE
175g (6oz) caster sugar
thinly pared rind and juice of ½ lemon
300ml (½ pint) water
2 × 15ml spoons (2tbls) chopped apple mint

1   Peel, core and chop the apples and
put them into a pan with the water and
lemon rind. Bring to the boil, cover
and simmer for 10-15 minutes, until
the apples are soft. Set aside to cool.
2   Stir the gelatine into the lemon
juice and stir it over hot water to
soften.
3   Discard the lemon rind. Pour the
gelatine liquid and the apple mixture
into a blender or food processor and
work to a purée.
4   Whisk the eggs, egg yolks and
sugar over a pan of hot water or in the
top of a double boiler until thick.
5   Stir the egg mixture into the apple
purée. Fold in the cream.
6   Turn the mixture into a ring mould
rinsed in cold water. Cover and chill
for 2-3 hours, until set.
7   To make the sauce, put the sugar,
lemon rind, lemon juice and water into
a small pan. Stir over low heat until the
sugar has dissolved. Bring to the boil
and boil for 5-10 minutes, until the
mixture turns syrupy. Set aside to cool.
8   Discard the lemon rind. Stir in the
chopped mint.
9   Turn out the apple mould on to a
serving dish. Pour a little of the sauce
over it, to decorate. Serve the rest
separately.

SERVES 6

PEARS IN PLUM SAUCE

*Two fruits of the orchard combine in
this simple but tasty russet-coloured
dessert.*

4 large, ripe dessert pears
150ml (¼ pint) water
150ml (¼ pint) red wine
75g (3oz) demerara sugar
1 × 15ml spoon (1tbls) lemon juice
5cm (2in) piece of cinnamon stick
250g (9oz) plums or damsons

1   Peel the pears, leaving the stalks
intact. Scoop out the core with a sharp
knife.
2   Peel and stone the plums. Chop
finely.
3   Put the water, wine, sugar, lemon
juice and cinnamon in a pan. Stir over
low heat to dissolve the sugar. Bring to
the boil and simmer for 5 minutes.
4   Add the pears and poach them
until they are just tender. Lift out the
pears and stand them upright in a dish.
5   Strain the sauce, taste it and add a
little more sugar or lemon juice if
needed. Pour the sauce over the pears.
Leave to cool and serve cold.

SERVES 4

Variation Pears are equally delicious
poached in apricot sauce. Soak 175g
(6oz) dried apricots in 300ml (½ pint)
water or unsweetened orange juice,
then liquidize.

CHERRY FLAN

*Cherry and almond flavours go
especially well together in this party
flan.*

250g (9oz) flour
salt
100g (4oz) butter
1 × 15ml spoon (1tbls) icing sugar
about 3 × 15ml spoons (3tbls) water

FILLING
1kg (2¼lb) cherries, pitted
75g (3oz) sugar
2 eggs
100ml (3½fl oz) single cream
50g (2oz) ratafia biscuits, crumbled

1   Sift together the flour and salt. Rub
in the butter until the mixture is like
fine breadcrumbs. Stir in the icing
sugar and sprinkle on just enough
water to make a firm dough.
2   Form the dough into a ball. Cover
with cling film or foil and chill in the
refrigerator for at least 30 minutes.
3   Roll out the dough on a lightly
floured board and use it to line a
greased 25cm (10in) flat tin. Trim the
edges and prick the base with a fork.
4   Arrange the cherries in the flan
case.
5   Bake the flan in the oven, preheated to 200°C, 400°F, gas 6.
6   Beat the sugar, eggs and cream
and beat in the biscuit crumbs. Pour
the custard mixture over the cherries.
7   Continue baking for a further 20-25
minutes, until the filling is set.
8   Stand the flan on a wire rack and
leave to cool.

SERVES 6-8

Variation Once the cherry season is
over, you can use apples in a similar
way. Peel, core and quarter the apples.
Arrange them, round side up, in the
flan case. Sprinkle them with 2 × 15ml
spoons (2tbls) lemon juice before baking. Then follow the recipe times.

Cook's note

Crumble the ratafia biscuits lightly to
make coarse crumbs. The slightly coarse,
nutty texture is especially good with the
smooth, creamy custard filling.

STEAMED PUDDING WITH DAMSON SAUCE

100g (4oz) soft margarine
100g (4oz) caster sugar
2 eggs
100g (4oz) 81% wheatmeal self-raising flour
1 × 5ml spoon (1tsp) baking powder
a pinch of ground cinnamon
a pinch of grated nutmeg
1 × 5ml spoon (1tsp) grated lemon rind

SAUCE
350g (12oz) damsons
4 × 15ml spoons (4tbls) water
50g (2oz) sugar
2 × 15ml spoons (2tbls) sweet sherry

1   This is a 'one-step' pudding. Beat all the pudding ingredients together until the mixture is smooth and has a soft, dropping consistency.
2   Turn the mixture on to a 30cm (12in) square of greased cotton and shape it into a ball. Cover the pudding ball with foil, press it to the shape and overlap the joins to make them water-tight.
3   Place the pudding in the top of a steaming pan, or in a trivet in a pan with fast-boiling water. Cover the pan and steam the pudding for 1¾ hours.
4   To make the sauce, put the damsons, water and sugar into a pan and stir over low heat to dissolve the sugar. Simmer the damsons until they are tender. Rub the fruit through a sieve then stir the sherry into the purée.
5   Turn out the pudding on to a heated dish. Drizzle a little sauce over it and serve the rest separately.

SERVES 4-6

In olden days

This round shape is traditional for boiled and steamed puddings of all kinds. They were originally tied with string and suspended in the boiling broth over an open fire — a truly one-pot meal.

MIXED FRUIT OMELETTE

1 large cooking apple
1 large dessert pear
8 dessert plums
100g (4oz) butter
75g (3oz) sugar
4 × 15ml spoons (4tbls) double cream
2 × 15ml spoons (2tbls) rum
5 eggs

1   Peel, core and slice the apple and pear. Quarter the plums, removing the stones.
2   Melt half the butter and add the fruit. Cook over moderate heat, stirring frequently, until all the fruit is tender.
3   Remove from the heat and cool slightly. Stir in 2 × 15ml spoons (2tbls) of the sugar, the cream and rum.
4   Separate 2 of the eggs. Beat the yolks with the 3 remaining eggs. Beat in 1 × 15ml spoon (1tbls) sugar. Whisk the 2 egg whites until they are stiff. Fold the egg whites into the beaten eggs.
5   Melt the remaining butter in a frying pan. Pour in the omelette mixture and cook over moderate heat until it is firm and well browned on the underside.
6   Spread the fruit over the omelette. Slide it on to a heatproof serving dish and flip it so that it folds in half.
7   Sprinkle the remaining sugar over the omelette. Caramelize it under a hot grill for 3-4 minutes. Serve the omelette at once, sliced.

SERVES 4

GREENGAGE TART

300g (11oz) flour
200g (7oz) butter
75g (3oz) icing sugar, sifted
1 × 5ml spoon (1tsp) grated lemon rind
1 × 5ml spoon (1tsp) lemon juice
1 egg, beaten

FILLING
350g (12oz) full-fat soft cheese
2 eggs
1 × 15ml spoon (1tbls) cornflour
grated rind of ½ lemon
50g (2oz) caster sugar flavoured with rosemary (see p. 33)
50g (2oz) ground almonds
1kg (2¼lb) greengages, quartered and stoned
40g (1½oz) demerara sugar

1   Sift the flour into a bowl. Rub in the butter until the mixture is like fine breadcrumbs. Stir in the icing sugar and lemon rind. Sprinkle on the lemon juice and use just enough egg to make a firm dough.
2   Knead the pastry lightly in the bowl. Cover and chill in the refrigerator for about 1 hour.
3   To make the filling, beat the cheese until it is softened. Beat in the eggs one at a time. When they have been incorporated, beat in the cornflour, lemon rind, sugar and ground almonds.
4   Roll out the pastry on a lightly floured board. Line a greased 25cm (10in) flan ring on a greased baking sheet. Trim the edges and prick the base with a fork.
5   Spread the cheese filling into the pastry case and level the surface.
6   Arrange the greengage segments, cut side up, over the filling in neat rings. You will see that the fruit formation looks like a water lily. Sprinkle the demerara sugar over the fruit.
7   Bake in the oven, preheated to 200°C, 400°F, gas 6, for 30-35 minutes. Cover the top with foil towards the end of the cooking time if the top browns too quickly.
8   Stand the baking tray on a wire rack to cool slightly before releasing the flan. Serve it warm or cold.

Soured cream or thick and creamy yoghurt flavoured with lemon rind and lemon juice go well with this dessert.

SERVES 6-8

THE VEGETABLE GARDEN

For ten thousand years and more, people have been cultivating vegetables on any patch of ground that will take seed – rocky hillside, fertile valley and swampy marshland – and learning the incomparable satisfaction of 'growing your own'.

Incomparable it certainly is. No matter where you buy vegetables, they can never have that 'straight from garden to table' flavour of those that you gather just before you cook and eat them. And no matter what price you are prepared to pay for them, vegetables in the shops will never have been selected with a more discerning eye than those you have watched develop, day by day, from your kitchen window.

To the home gardener, nothing can match the pure pleasure of wandering round the garden, basket in hand, selecting tender young vegetables at the peak of perfection. A handful of broad bean pods, so tiny you can cook them whole; the first early peas, so crisp the pods pop like champagne corks; new potatoes not much larger than marbles and carrots scarcely the size of your little finger, to cook with a handful of mint; long slender roots of salsify, justifiably known as the 'vegetable oyster' and intriguing black-skinned scorzonera, so delicious yet virtually unobtainable in the shops: with produce like this in your basket, you're what an old East Anglian countryman friend of mine calls a 'garden millionaire'.

'How much space do I need?' and 'What crops can I grow?' are two questions that many would-be vegetable gardeners ask. The answers are ambiguous, but favourable – for happily, vegetable gardening can be all things to all people. You can plan your planting precisely to suit the size of your garden or allotment, the likes of your family, and the amount of time you have available. Skill doesn't really come into it. Plant seeds are perfect little packages, containing all the components you need to reproduce a replica of the parent plant in the following year. All you have to do is to provide favourable conditions in which to grow them!

Space is the main factor determining how many and what crops you can grow. Many people are heavily into self-sufficiency these days, and growing your own produce plays an enormous part in satisfying that desire. Not everyone can achieve the full never-buy-a-thing status of course. It is generally reckoned that you need a plot of about 335 square metres (400 square yards), with the crops rotated on a three-year cycle, to supply most of the fruit and vegetables a family of four would need throughout the year. That, and a fair commitment of time – a rough estimate puts it at 200 hours' work a year, with the work heavily concentrated into the spring (planting) and autumn (preparing the ground) seasons.

Every gardener's dream, a basket of crisp and colourful vegetables to take to the kitchen.

Even in a small garden, however, you can achieve a good balance and selection of year-round crops. A plot just 84 square metres (100 square yards) is ample to fill your garden trug with salad vegetables, green beans, broad beans, peas, courgettes, spinach and tiny carrots and turnips in summer; and leeks, cabbages, Brussels sprouts and a few root vegetables in winter.

You might decide instead to go for the luxury of an asparagus bed, which occupies the ground permanently, planting rows of, say, spinach, lettuce and cabbage in between; or to major on some of the more unusual vegetables – asparagus peas, kohlrabi, spaghetti marrow (its name describes it exactly) – and so on.

If your garden is already laid out with flower beds, there's still space for vegetables: herbs, decorative cabbages, carrots, beetroot, corn salad, and globe artichokes all have attractive foliage. And remember that runner beans, tomatoes and asparagus were grown for their appearance long before they were eaten.

Even a patio or balcony has space for vegetables. You can grow runner beans on a wigwam frame in a tub or trough, or train them to trail over a trellis against a wall. Grow dwarf beans and peas in troughs, courgettes, marrows even, and tomatoes in grow-bags, and herbs and salads in window boxes. Trailing herbs are pretty in hanging baskets. Vegetable gardening can indeed be all things to all plots.

PLANNING YOUR GARDEN

Planning your vegetable garden is rather like designing a dress or a house – it's best to draw it to scale on a piece of graph paper so that you can see exactly what the finished result will look like and whether it will be practical.

In the case of a garden, there are all kinds of considerations to be taken into account, and every family will have different priorities. The size and aspect of the plot are invariable – that is, until you get so hooked on growing your own vegetables and fruit that you keep encroaching on the flower beds, the lawn and the patio to give yourself more space, or do a deal with a neighbour, offering him a share of the produce in exchange for the use of his plot.

The soil – the product of millions of years of geological change and activity – will have the natural characteristics of the region. But if these are unfavourable to cropping, it doesn't mean that you are stuck with them. In fact, the perfect soil doesn't exist – at least that's the opinion you would get talking to any group of gardeners – without a fair amount of preparatory work and additives.

What you decide to grow depends on what you like to eat and the space you have available. In a small area you may have to limit your production of the space-hungry plants – such as Brussels sprouts, cabbages, cauliflowers, Jerusalem and globe artichokes and so on – to a precious few of each, forgoing any thoughts of neat, soldier-like rows. But where you do have space to go into a reasonable amount of production, neatness definitely equals efficiency. It is easier by far to plant, hoe, weed, fertilize and eventually harvest crops in well-defined areas – be they rows, blocks, circles or whatever.

Crop merry-go-round

Going back to your graph-paper plan, you need to plot it on a three-year cycle. Rotation of crops is a phrase more associated with the agriculture of years gone by than with gardening, but it has just as much relevance on the domestic scene. Plan your kitchen garden in four separate areas. One will be for the permanent or semi-permanent crops such as asparagus, perennial herbs and soft fruits. The other three plots should be occupied in turn by each of three groups of vegetables; first, peas and beans, the onion family, celery and some saladings; second, brassicas and spinach; and third, all the root crops. It's a game of musical plots, with each group of crops moving round each year. Disregard this at your peril! It's a time-honoured practice to get the best from the soil and to lessen the chance of plant diseases. If a row of brassicas is infested by cabbage root fly one year, the pest will not thrive on the root crops that follow.

The first group of vegetables are those that need a rich, well-fertilized soil, with plenty of farmyard manure or well-rotted compost dug in. The legumes, peas and beans leave the soil richer in nitrogen – just the element the brassicas, in group two, need in the following year. They'll need a supplementary dressing of a general fertilizer too, and lime if the garden shows a deficiency.

Then the following year, in that same plot comes the third group, the root crops – two years after the rich manure was dug in. They too, will need a dressing of general fertilizer.

If you have space and the inclination to grow main-crop potatoes, you need to plot an extra area because their requirements are different from those of the other roots. Potatoes do need manure and humus to produce a good yield, but hate lime.

Soil classification

Each category of soil has its advantages and drawbacks, its likely successes and failures among the various crops, and needs additives, dressings and downright first aid in varying degrees. Clay soil – the heaviest and sometimes the most depressing to work – is least favourable to root crops. It has poor draining ability, retains moisture to the point of squelchiness and is slow to warm up in the spring – bad news for seeds, which need warmth and a friable soil to germinate. It's a long-term project to dig in manure, sharp sand and peat to improve the texture and fertility of this soil.

At the opposite end of the scale, sandy soil drains too quickly, which means that not only the moisture but also the nutrients you add are soon drawn away. Strangely enough, the same remedial action is needed as for clay – a vigorous input of compost, or humus. Sandy soil warms up quickly in the spring so, as long as it is kept well watered, it makes a good nursery for seeds and seedlings. It also ensures a good start for soft fruits, tree fruits, legumes, cauliflowers and potatoes.

In the chalky regions of the country, there is the problem of an excess of lime in the soil. Again, this means barrow loads of organic matter, garden or mushroom compost, peat and farmyard manure to redress the balance and bring it to something like the acidity level that vegetables prefer. Even then it's best to accept defeat on main-crop potatoes and major on the crops that will tolerate such a level of lime – fruit, legumes and brassicas.

Every gardener's dream, but by no means every garden's inheritance, is a rich loamy soil, which has just the right balance of sand, clay and organic matter that food crops thrive on. If by happy chance or hard endeavour your garden has this soil, you can spend longer contemplating your crops from a deckchair than any of your fellow gardeners who are still battling with the rigours of other soil types.

Preparing the ground

People who find gardening therapeutic, who treat it as a form of exercise, or who just love it anyway can make it seem harder work than it actually needs to be. It's a bit like making bread: if you find it relaxing to push and pull the dough, you will naturally turn a blind eye to the appliances and the short cuts that others take for granted.

So digging, probably the hardest work in the garden, can be one of the best forms of exercise or the greatest chore; it depends on your point of view. It is generally recommended that the vegetable garden is dug thoroughly – to the depth of the spade, or 'spit' – once a year in the autumn or winter. This aerates the soil, exposes the maximum surface to the frost – a helpful means of breaking down large lumps of clay – and is your chance to add manure and compost.

But you can get away without doing it and still grow successful crops. Especially in a small area, you can take the lazy option and plant vegetables in a shallow layer of peat or compost, leaving the soil below un-dug and to its own devices.

By the time you come to planting seeds or seedlings, the soil – whatever its type – needs to be broken down into smaller particles and raked free of stones. This desirable state is what gardeners call a fine tilth.

Depending on the crop, dig trenches, make channels (called drills) with a draw hoe, or make individual holes with a dibber in rows. The best-laid garden plans have rows running roughly from north to south. This way each side of the row has an opportunity to bask in the sun.

Seed packets nowadays are obligingly full of detailed cultivation advice, and a general guide to sowing many crops is given in the 'seasonal harvest' sections following the recipes in this chapter. As a rough rule of thumb, the larger the seed the deeper it needs to be sown.

Thickness of sowing is another factor that can make or break your success rate. Generous sowing, crowding the seeds on top of each other, does not mean the chance of a higher germination rate: quite the reverse. They *all* fight a losing battle. You can either sow seed thinly along the row, and plan to thin out the seedlings still further, or in 'stations' – four larger seeds together and then a gap. Old gardeners used to reckon that this gave you about the right chance of a reasonable crop: 'one for the rook, one for the crow, one to rot and one to grow' was an old country saying with a degree of acceptance that the gardener does not always have the last word. If the rook and the crow don't take their allotted share, you have the job of thinning out the weakest seedlings. That leaves the healthiest plants to grow into a bumper harvest – your raw materials for the recipes that follow.

Spring

As the season advances, the vegetable garden holds all the promise and all the reward of a treasure hunt. The hardier vegetables make way for the first tender leaves of spinach, succulent stalks of asparagus and slender spring onions. At first there's just a taste, enough for a salad or garnish, then suddenly there's plenty – and the chance to try new recipes.

SPINACH & RICOTTA SQUARES

Pizza dough with a vegetable filling makes a ravioli look-alike.

15g (½oz) dried yeast
120ml (4fl oz) warm water
500g (1¼lb) flour
salt
3 × 15ml spoons (3tbls) olive oil

FILLING
50g (2oz) cooked spinach, well drained
50g (2oz) ricotta cheese
75g (3oz) Parmesan cheese, grated
freshly ground black pepper
1 egg white, lightly whisked
oil, for deep-frying

1 Dissolve the yeast in the water. Sift the flour and salt on to a working surface. Stir in the yeast liquid, then add the oil and just enough water to make a soft dough. Knead the dough lightly until it is smooth. Cover with oiled polythene and leave to rise in a warm place for 30 minutes.
2 Flatten the dough with a rolling pin and roll out to a thickness of 5mm (¼in). Using a tooth-edge rotary pastry wheel, cut the dough into 5cm (2in) squares.
3 Purée the spinach in an electric blender or food processor. Mix with the ricotta and Parmesan cheeses and season with pepper.
4 Place 1 × 5ml spoon (1tsp) of the spinach mixture in the centre of half the pizza squares. Brush the edges of these squares with the whisked egg white, then cover with the remaining dough squares. Press the edges together to seal them, and make little 'cushions'.
5 Heat the oil in a deep frying pan to 190°C, 375°F, or until a cube of day-old bread browns in 50 seconds. Deep-fry the squares a few at a time until they are golden brown. Lift them out with a draining spoon and dry them on absorbent kitchen paper. Keep each cooked batch hot while you cook the remainder.

Serve with a green salad and Tomato and thyme sauce (see following page).

SERVES 6

Capture the flavour of Italy! Make tiny Spinach and ricotta squares and deep-fry them to crisp, and irresistibly golden brown.

ASPARAGUS CROWN

This is a highly decorative dish for a salad buffet or special dinner.

500g (1¼lb) asparagus, trimmed
500g (1¼lb) new carrots, scraped and diced
salt
2 × 5ml spoons (2tsp) aspic jelly crystals
300ml (½ pint) water
15g (½oz) gelatine
40g (1½oz) sugar
1 × 15ml spoon (1tbls) mustard powder
3 eggs, lightly beaten
freshly ground black pepper
6 × 15ml spoons (6tbls) white wine vinegar
300ml (½ pint) single cream
2 × 15ml spoons (2tbls) chopped tarragon
250g (9oz) lean ham, cut into fingers

1   Cook the asparagus and carrots separately in boiling, salted water until they are tender. Drain the vegetables (reserving a little liquid for the gelatine). Finely dice the carrots.
2   Make up the aspic jelly with the crystals and the water. Pour it into a 900ml (1½ pint) decorative mould, rolling the mould round in your hands to coat evenly.
3   Arrange the asparagus around the mould, with the tips to the centre. Cut the asparagus stems to fit if necessary. Chop and reserve any trimmings.
4   Dissolve the gelatine in 3 × 15ml spoons (3tbls) of the vegetable liquid.
5   Mix the sugar and mustard together. Stir in the eggs, and season.
6   Boil the vinegar, then cool slightly and pour on to the egg mixture, beating constantly.
7   Pour the mixture into a bowl over a pan of simmering water or the top of a double boiler and stir over low heat until the sauce thickens – about 10 minutes. Do not allow the water to boil, or touch the container. Pour in the gelatine.
8   Remove from the heat and stand the bowl or upper pan in cold water. Leave to cool, then chill.
9   When the mixture is just beginning to set, stir in the cream and tarragon.
10   Stir the carrots, ham and any chopped asparagus into the sauce. Pour into the mould, then chill for 2 hours, or until the mould is set.
11   Run a knife around the mould to release it. Turn it out on to a plate.

SERVES 6

TOMATO & THYME SAUCE

All versions of tomato sauce freeze well, so it's a good idea to make larger quantities and store them for the gaps in the fruiting season.

25g (1oz) butter
1 × 15ml spoon (1tbls) olive oil
1 medium onion, peeled and chopped
2 garlic cloves, peeled and finely chopped
500g (1¼lb) tomatoes, skinned and sliced
2 × 15ml spoons (2tbls) tomato purée
2 × 15ml spoons (2tbls) chopped thyme
salt
freshly ground black pepper

1   Heat the butter and oil in a small pan and fry the onion over moderate heat for 3 minutes, stirring once or twice. Add the garlic, tomatoes and tomato purée and simmer for 20 minutes.
2   Stir in the thyme, season with salt and pepper and simmer for a further 3-5 minutes.

MAKES ABOUT 450ML (¾ PINT)

Variation Stir in 2 × 15ml spoons (2tbls) chopped capers – especially good with bland vegetables such as cauliflower, and with chicken.

The moment you have been waiting for! The first asparagus is ready to serve with Hollandaise sauce (recipe on page 60).

SORREL SOUP

250g (9oz) sorrel leaves
25g (1oz) butter
1 litre (1¾ pints) chicken stock
2 medium potatoes, peeled and chopped
1 × 5ml spoon (1tsp) lemon juice
150ml (¼ pint) single cream
1 egg yolk, lightly beaten
salt
freshly ground black pepper

CROÛTONS
2 thick slices white bread
50g (2oz) butter
3 × 15ml spoons (3tbls) chopped chervil

1   Wash the sorrel and strip off the stalks. Melt the butter and stir in the sorrel over moderate heat until it collapses. Add the stock, potatoes and lemon juice and bring to the boil. Simmer for 15 minutes.
2   Cut the crusts from the bread and cut it into 1cm (½in) squares. Melt the butter and when it is hot fry the bread over moderate heat, stirring frequently, until it is golden brown. Lift out the bread and toss it at once in the chopped chervil.
3   Stir the cream and egg yolk into the soup and season with salt and pepper. Heat gently.
4   Serve the soup hot with the herb croûtons separately.

SERVES 4

ASPARAGUS WITH HOLLANDAISE SAUCE

Choose perfect asparagus tips, all the same size, for this simply luxurious spring dish. Other thinner spears can be used for soups and casseroles.

1kg (2¼lb) asparagus
salt
2 × 15ml spoons (2tbls) chopped marjoram

SAUCE
3 egg yolks
1 × 15ml spoon (1tbls) warm water
175g (6oz) unsalted butter, softened
1 × 15ml spoon (1tbls) orange juice
freshly ground black pepper

1 Wash and trim the asparagus. Using a sharp knife and working downwards towards the base, scrape off any fibrous scales. Tie the asparagus into bundles of 10 or 12 spears.
2 Stand them upright in a deep pan with boiling, salted water to come halfway up the stems. Cover the pan with a lid, or make a dome of foil, pressing it around the rim of the pan. Take care not to damage the delicate tips. Cook for 10-20 minutes, depending on the thickness of the stems.
3 To make the sauce, whisk the egg yolks and water in a bowl over a pan of simmering water, or in the top of a double boiler. Do not let the water boil, or come into contact with the container.
4 When the egg yolks are thick and creamy, add the butter a little at a time, whisking constantly. Whisk in the orange juice and season with salt and pepper.
5 If it is not convenient to serve the sauce at once, closely cover the surface with a piece of wetted greaseproof paper and stand the bowl in a pan of warm (not hot) water. Whisk in 1 × 15ml spoon (1tbls) warm water just before serving.
6 Drain and dry the asparagus (reserve the liquid for soup). Arrange it on a heated serving dish and sprinkle with the marjoram. Serve the sauce separately.

SERVES 4

SPINACH ROULADE

This impressive-looking spinach roll makes a good main course or can be served as a first course for a dinner party when it would serve 6-8.

500g (1¼lb) spinach
salt
25g (1oz) butter
4 eggs, separated
freshly ground black pepper
a pinch of grated nutmeg
1 × 5ml spoon (1tsp) lemon juice
50g (2oz) Parmesan cheese, grated

FILLING
15g (½oz) butter
2 spring onions, peeled and chopped
175g (6oz) shelled prawns, chopped
15g (½oz) flour
200ml (7fl oz) milk
a pinch of cayenne
3 × 15ml spoons (3tbls) double cream
1 × 15ml spoon (1tbls) chopped parsley

1 Wash the spinach and strip off the stalks. Put it in a pan, add a little salt, cover and cook over moderately low heat for 5 minutes.
2 Drain the spinach in a colander and chop it finely.
3 Beat in the butter, cut into small pieces, add the egg yolks, one at a time. Season with salt, pepper, nutmeg and lemon juice.
4 Whisk the egg whites until stiff. Fold them into the spinach mixture.
5 Spread the mixture evenly over a Swiss roll tin lined with silicone paper. Bake it in the oven, preheated to 190°C, 375°F, gas 5, for 10-12 minutes, or until the roulade feels dry.
6 Melt the butter, fry the onions over moderate heat for 2-3 minutes, stir in the prawns and cook for 1 minute. Stir in the flour and gradually pour on the milk, stirring constantly. Bring to the boil and simmer for 2 minutes. Season with salt, pepper and cayenne and stir in the cream and parsley. Remove from the heat.
7 Spread the grated cheese over a piece of greaseproof paper. Turn out the roulade and remove the paper.
8 Spread the filling over the roulade. Lift up the greaseproof paper on one short end of the roulade and roll up. Serve warm or cold.

SERVES 4

STIR-FRIED CHICKEN WITH CASHEWS

2 boneless breasts of chicken, about 750g (1½lb)
8 spring onions, peeled
3 × 15ml spoons (3tbls) sesame oil
1 garlic clove, peeled and finely chopped
1 piece fresh ginger, peeled and chopped
250g (9oz) broccoli spears, sliced diagonally
75g (3oz) cashew nuts

SAUCE
1 × 5ml spoon (1tsp) cornflour
3 × 15ml spoons (3tbls) dry sherry
1 × 15ml spoon (1tbls) soy sauce
3 × 15ml spoons (3tbls) chicken stock
salt
freshly ground black pepper

1 Mix the sauce ingredients to a smooth paste.
2 Thinly slice the chicken into 10cm (4in) strips.
3 Thinly slice 4 of the onions. Trim most of the green tops from the remainder. Make a criss-cross slit in each one from the top almost to the base. Put them in ice-cold water for 20-30 minutes for the tops to frill out.
4 Heat the oil in a wok or heavy-based frying pan and stir-fry the garlic and ginger over moderately high heat for 1 minute.
5 Add the chicken and broccoli and stir-fry for 3 minutes. Add the rest of the spring onions, sliced, and cashews and stir-fry for 2 minutes.
6 Pour on the sauce, stir well and bring to the boil. Stir for 1 minute. Serve at once, with the onion garnish.

Stir-fried spring greens with ginger (see below) are a good accompaniment to this crunchy chicken dish.

SERVES 4

Spring greens with a difference

Stir-fry 1 piece of ginger and 2 cloves of garlic, peeled and finely chopped, for 30 seconds in a little peanut or sesame oil. Add 450g (1lb) of prepared greens and thinly sliced onions and stir-fry for 2 minutes. Add 3 × 15ml spoons (3tbls) each of soy sauce and sherry with a dash of ground ginger. Bring to the boil and serve at once.

SPRING HARVEST

How many crops you have to harvest during the spring depends to a great extent on how many you leave in the ground over the winter, and on whether you grow early or late varieties. If the cabbage, cauliflower, salsify and seakale were too tempting during the winter months, then you might be relying, from February to May, on a relatively small selection of vegetables.

Sprouting broccoli, one of the most versatile of brassicas, spring greens, one of the most hardy of vegetables, spinach, sorrel, salad (or spring) onions and, towards the end of the season, asparagus give you good culinary variety – as the recipes on the previous pages show.

You have to plan well ahead to have sprouting broccoli to enjoy in spring, to serve simply with hollandaise sauce, in an open flan, stir-fried or steamed with a crunchy walnut topping. Like most brassicas, **sprouting broccoli** likes a rich, deep soil – not something every garden is blessed with – and benefits from a good ration of general fertilizer early in the growing season, and a dressing of lime before winter.

Seeds are sown thinly in a prepared seedbed in 2.5cm (1in) drills, 30cm (12in) apart. As soon as seedlings are big enough to handle they should be transplanted 15cm (6in) apart. You can sow seed from April onwards until August and September, when you should allow 6 months for the plants to reach maturity. Cut the centre heads first to allow the side shoots to develop.

As for maintenance, keep down weeds by hoeing between rows, and keep the broccoli moist. You can grow a 'catch crop', such as lettuce or spinach, between the rows.

Spinach has a much shorter growing cycle, from 8 to 11 weeks. There are spring, summer and winter-harvesting varieties, and a perpetual type, known as spinach beet, which, as long as you keep cutting it and do not allow it to go to seed, will flourish continually for several months.

Spinach should be sown in 2.5cm (1in) drills, 30cm (12in) apart. Sow it at three-weekly intervals and you greatly extend the harvesting period. Protect over-wintering spinach under cloches and never pick every last leaf from a plant or you will weaken it – terminally. Ideally, spinach likes a good loamy soil with lime. It will tolerate heavy clay – good news for Londoners! – but will bolt and prematurely produce seed in a light, well-drained soil.

Other members of the spinach family are worth their space in gold. **Spinach beet**, sown in April and June, gives a year-round harvest. The leaves can be used just as spinach, in salads, quiches, sauces and so on, and the stalks finely chopped in salad or lightly braised, as a milder-tasting alternative to celery. **Good King Henry**, also known as wild spinach and Mercury, is sown from May onwards – it likes rich humus in the soil – to harvest from April the following year. It's a dual-purpose vegetable with the leaves being used as spinach and the shoots as a substitute (some say a poor man's one!) for asparagus.

Another close cousin of spinach is **seakale beet**, sown in April and July. The spring sown crops can be harvested from July onwards; the July sowing, protected under cloches

during the winter, provides another light and refreshing leaf crop in spring.

Sorrel, which is rather like a lemon-tasting spinach, has the great advantage of being a perennial. The seed is sown in April, or you can plant divided roots in spring and autumn. If you remove all flowering stems, you will encourage new leaf growth – especially in early spring.

Asparagus, that most luxurious of vegetables, is a long-term project. It is best to plant 'crowns' (roots) in well-drained loamy soil in a sunny position in March and April. Asparagus needs space, so plant the crowns 60cm (2ft) apart in 25cm (10in) deep trenches, 90cm (3ft) apart. In February and March dress the ground with a general fertilizer, and in summer enrich it with manure. Then sit back and wait: you cannot cut the stalks at all for the first two years, and even in the third year you must restrict your harvest to one or two stalks from each plant. Pick off all the berries from the female plants in autumn, and always keep the bed well weeded.

Salad or spring onions, another crop which spans the seasons, gives a 'lift' as a garnish, in stir-fries and omelettes early in the year. Sow under glass in February, August and September and in open ground from March to June in 1cm (½in) drills, 25cm (10in) apart. Harvest the onions when they are as thick as a pencil.

SUMMER

Harvesting the early-summer vegetables is one of gardening's incomparable joys. And eating those that you have grown yourself, watched over impatiently and gathered at the peak of perfection – young, small and tender – puts every meal in the gourmet class. Plan your meals around this feast of vegetables, and let them take their rightful place as the centre of attention.

PEA POD SOUP

In the old country tradition of 'waste not, want not', especially when it has tasty potential, this soup uses the pods which otherwise might be discarded.

50g (2oz) butter
1 large onion, peeled and sliced
500g (1¼lb) pea pods
1 litre (1¾ pints) chicken stock
1 bay leaf
2-3 sprays mint leaves
150ml (¼ pint) single cream
½ × 5ml spoon (½tsp) lemon juice
salt
freshly ground black pepper
2 × 15ml spoons (2tbls) chopped mint,
to garnish

1   Melt the butter in a large pan and fry the onion over moderate heat for 3-4 minutes, stirring once or twice. Add the pea pods, stock, bay leaf and mint sprays. Bring to the boil, cover and simmer for 1 hour, or until the pea pods are tender – this will largely depend on age and size.
2   Discard the bay leaf and mint. Liquidize the pea pods and stock in a blender or food processor, then rub the purée through a sieve or work it through a vegetable mill.
3   Return the purée to the pan, stir in the cream and lemon juice and season with salt and pepper. Reheat gently. Sprinkle the soup with the chopped mint to garnish.

SERVES 4

A pod of flavour

There's a wealth of flavour in pea pods. Country cooks always added two or three 'shucks' when cooking fresh peas – the perfect complement.

STIR-FRIED GARDEN VEGETABLES

2 small new carrots
250g (9oz) mangetout peas
250g (9oz) courgettes
salt
4 × 15ml spoons (4tbls) peanut oil
1 garlic clove, peeled and finely chopped
1 × 15ml spoon (1tbls) sesame seeds

SAUCE
1 × 15ml spoon (1tbls) soy sauce
2 × 15ml spoons (2tbls) dry sherry
2 × 5ml spoons (2tsp) honey
3 × 15ml spoons (3tbls) water

1   Trim the carrots and cut them into matchstick strips. Top and tail the mangetout peas. Thinly slice the courgettes. Blanch the carrots and peas in boiling, salted water for 2 minutes, then drain and dry them.
2   Mix together the soy sauce, sherry, honey and water.
3   Heat the oil in a wok or heavy-based frying pan and stir-fry the garlic over moderately high heat for 30 seconds. Add the carrots, mangetout peas and courgettes and stir-fry for 2 minutes. Pour on the sauce, bring to the boil, add salt and boil for 2 minutes, or until almost dry.
4   Stir in the sesame seeds and serve.

SERVES 4

Spring onion frills

These are frequently served as a decorative garnish to Chinese meals and are pretty with meat salads. You can make them in advance, drain and dry them and store them in the refrigerator overnight.

WHOLE-POD BROAD BEANS

Only when you grow your own, or have access to pick broad beans from a local grower, can you enjoy them in this 'mangetout' way. Pick them when they are very small – no more than 7.5-10cm (3-4in) long.

500g (1¼lb) whole broad bean pods
150ml (¼ pint) chicken stock
2 sprigs mint
15g (½oz) butter
100ml (3½fl oz) double cream
2 × 15ml spoons (2tbls) chopped savory
salt
freshly ground black pepper

1   Top and tail the bean pods if necessary, and wash them very thoroughly.
2   Cook the bean pods in the stock with the mint sprigs for 10 minutes, or until they are just tender. Drain the beans, return them to the pan and toss them in the butter.
3   Pour on the cream, stir in the savory and season the sauce with salt and pepper. Serve at once.

Broad beans cooked this way are specially good with boiled or baked ham and bacon, and with roasted or grilled pork.

SERVES 4

Variation Slightly older broad bean pods, once you have shelled them, can be made into a tasty soup. Follow the recipe for the pea pod soup on the left, substituting savory or chervil for the mint. Add a swirl or two of soured cream with the garnish.

BEANS IN EGG & LEMON SAUCE

500g (1¼lb) runner beans
200ml (7fl oz) chicken stock
2 sprigs savory
2 egg yolks, beaten
2 × 15ml spoons (2tbls) lemon juice
salt
freshly ground black pepper

1   Top and tail the runner beans and cut them diagonally into 7.5cm (3in) slices.
2   Bring the stock to the boil, add the beans and savory and return to the boil. Cover and cook for 10-12 minutes, or until the beans are tender. Drain the beans, reserving the stock and discard the savory.
3   Beat the egg yolks and lemon juice and beat in 3 × 15ml spoons (3tbls) hot stock. Season with salt and pepper.
4   Pour the sauce over the beans, stir well and heat very gently. On no account allow the sauce to boil.

SERVES 4

COURGETTE & BASIL SALAD

175g (6oz) mangetout peas
salt
500g (¼lb) courgettes, thinly sliced
1 small onion, thinly sliced into rings
3 × 15ml spoons (3tbls) basil leaves
4 thin slices orange, to garnish

DRESSING
4 × 15ml spoons (4tbls) olive oil
½ × 5ml spoon (½tsp) grated orange rind
1 × 15ml spoon (1tbls) orange juice
1 × 15ml spoon (1tbls) red wine vinegar
1 × 5ml spoon (1tsp) clear honey
freshly ground black pepper
1 garlic clove, peeled and crushed

1   Blanch the peas in boiling, salted water for 2 minutes. Drain and dry them.
2   Mix all the ingredients for the dressing.
3   Toss together the mangetout peas, courgettes and onion rings. Pour over the dressing and toss well. Cover and set aside for 1-2 hours.
4   Toss the basil leaves with the salad. Garnish it with the orange slices.

SERVES 4

Two of summer's luxuries, Beans in egg and lemon sauce left, and Courgette and basil salad with tiny mangetout peas.

PEAS BRAISED WITH LETTUCE

1kg (2¼lb) peas, shelled
12 button onions, peeled
salt
50g (2oz) butter
1 small lettuce heart, shredded
4 × 15ml spoons (4tbls) chicken stock
freshly ground black pepper
2 × 5ml spoons (2tsp) sugar
sprigs of mint, to garnish

1   Blanch peas and the whole onions in boiling, salted water for 3 minutes. Drain them.
2   Melt the butter, add the onions, peas, lettuce and stock and season with salt and pepper. Cover and simmer for 5 minutes. Add the sugar and simmer for a further 3-5 minutes, until the peas are just tender. Garnish the vegetables with the mint.

SERVES 4

GLOBE ARTICHOKES WITH TUNA

4 large globe artichokes
salt
lemon juice
200g (7oz) can tuna fish
4 hard-boiled eggs, chopped
2 × 15ml spoons (2tbls) olive oil
2 × 15ml spoons (2tbls) double cream
3 × 15ml spoons (3tbls) herb mayonnaise
1 × 15ml spoon (1tbls) chopped fines herbes
freshly ground black pepper
a pinch of cayenne
vinaigrette dressing, to serve

1   Cut off the stalks and the dark outside leaves of the artichokes and cut off the tips of the leaves, so that the top is level.
2   Cook the artichokes in boiling, salted water with 2 × 5ml spoons (2tsp) lemon juice for 25-30 minutes or until the base of the vegetables is tender. Pierce with a fine skewer to test. Drain the artichokes and leave them upside down on a draining board.
3   When they are cool enough to handle, open out the centres. Scoop out the thistle-like 'choke' with a spoon and pull out the thin, light-coloured leaves in the centre. Trim a little more from the base, so that the artichokes will stand level and brush all the exposed surfaces with lemon juice. Set aside to cool.
4   Drain, flake and mash the tuna fish, discarding any bones. Mix it with the chopped egg, oil and ½ × 5ml spoon (½tsp) lemon juice. Gradually beat in the cream and mayonnaise, then stir in the herbs. Season well with salt, pepper and cayenne.
5   Pack the filling into the artichoke centres. Cover, and chill for 1-2 hours.

SERVES 4

Variation As a less substantial first course, one of the delights of summer, you can serve the artichokes without the filling. Prepare and cook them as described, and serve them with vinaigrette dressing or mayonnaise. And finger-bowls!

BROAD BEANS WITH HAM

1kg (2¼lb) broad beans, shelled
100ml (3½fl oz) chicken stock
15g (½oz) butter
3 egg yolks, lightly beaten
150ml (¼ pint) double cream
salt
freshly ground black pepper
½ × 5ml spoon (½tsp) lemon juice
100g (4oz) lean ham, chopped
2 × 15ml spoons (2tbls) chopped savory
or chervil

1   Put the beans, chicken stock and butter in a pan, bring to the boil, cover and simmer for 5-10 minutes until the beans are barely tender. If any liquid remains, uncover the pan and fast-boil to evaporate it.
2   Beat the egg yolks and cream, season with salt and pepper and stir in the lemon juice. Pour the sauce over the beans and stir over very low heat for 3-4 minutes until it thickens. Stir in the ham. Serve at once, garnished with the chopped herb.

SERVES 4

Tough skins

When the beans are large, towards the end of the season, their skin may be tough and should be removed before cooking. It's a job children love — press each bean between thumb and forefinger and pop the seed out of the skin.

GREEN BEANS À LA GRECQUE

Use runner beans or French beans for this recipe, sometimes called 'snap' beans because when they are very fresh and crisp you can easily break them in half.

500g (1¼lb) small green beans
300ml (½ pint) water
4 × 15ml spoons (4tbls) tomato purée
4 × 15ml spoons (4tbls) olive oil
2 garlic cloves, peeled and finely chopped
1 medium onion, peeled and finely chopped
2 stalks celery, thinly sliced
2 × 15ml spoons (2tbls) chopped savory
or parsley

1   Top and tail the beans removing any strings. Cut in half if they are large.

2   Put all the remaining ingredients except the herbs into a pan, stir over low heat to blend in the purée, then bring to the boil. Boil for 10 minutes.
3   Add the beans, return to the boil. Cover the pan and simmer for 20 minutes, or until the beans are tender and the sauce is reduced by half. Garnish with the savory or parsley and serve hot or as a first course, cold.

This garlicky tomato dish, which has its own sauce, is especially good with roast or grilled meats.

SERVES 4

LEG OF LAMB BOULANGERE

4 garlic cloves, peeled
25g (1oz) butter
750g (1½lb) new potatoes, scrubbed
salt
250g (9oz) button onions, peeled
1.5kg (3¼lb) leg of lamb
freshly ground black pepper
200ml (7fl oz) chicken stock
2 × 15ml spoons (2tbls) chopped parsley

1   Halve one of the garlic cloves and rub it over the inside of a baking dish. Rub the dish with the butter.
2   Partly cook the potatoes in boiling, salted water for 3 minutes, then add the onions and cook for 2 minutes. Drain them.
3   Place the lamb in the dish. Arrange the potatoes and onions round it. Chop the remaining garlic and sprinkle it over the potatoes. Season with salt and pepper and pour on the stock.
4   Roast the meat in the oven, pre-heated to 180°C, 350°F, gas 4, for 1¼-1½ hours, turning the meat over once. Sprinkle the parsley over the potatoes to serve.

Serve the meat with whole baked courgettes and tomatoes, cooked in the oven at the same time, or with Peas braised with lettuce (see p. 63).

SERVES 4-6

SUMMER HARVEST

When it comes to summer vegetable crops, the size of your plot and the time you have to spare are the only limits. Peas, beans of all kinds, courgettes, calabrese – the less hardy cousin of sprouting broccoli – globe artichokes, new potatoes, not to mention tiny carrots and golfball turnips – the choice is delicious enough to make vegetarians of us all.

There's always an air of impatience for the first taste of these delightful crops, and friendly rivalry among local gardeners. If you want to be among the first with your harvest – and who doesn't? – the maxim is to sow early. And in our temperate climate this means starting off trays or pots of seeds in a glasshouse, under cloches or, for sure-fire quick germination, in an electrically heated **propagator** – the modern version of a covered seed box on a shelf in the airing cupboard. Start off peas, French beans, runner beans, courgettes and calabrese in this way and you can plant out the seedlings weeks ahead of the 'grown-where-sown' crops.

For **planting out of doors**, the order – depending on which varieties you choose and where you live (plant three weeks later in the north of England) – is first, broad beans (February to April – though some people sow them in the late autumn, hoping to advance the shoots enough to beat the spring onslaught of blackfly); then peas (March to May, or even June); French and dwarf beans (April to June); and then runner beans (not earlier than May to mid June).

Planting depth for **peas, French beans** and **dwarf beans** is about 4cm (1½in) with 7.5cm (3in) and 15cm (6in) respectively between each seed and 60cm (2ft) between rows. **Broad beans** and **runner beans** need at least 1m (3ft) between rows and 15cm (6in) between each seed, which are planted 5cm (2in) deep.

All legumes (peas and beans) like a rich, well-manured soil: use farm manure, well-rotted garden compost or a good general fertilizer to improve yield. All except the dwarf types need sticks, wires or string to support the climbing tendrils.

Courgettes need a rich soil. Some people go to the length of building a mound of compost and manure so that the roots never touch ordinary *terra firma*. To advance the fruiting season, sow seed in soil blocks in heat in April and May, or outdoors from mid May onwards. Ready-grown plants can go in the ground from early June onwards. Transplant seedlings with a good block of soil round them – the roots hate being disturbed.

Plant the courgettes 50cm (20in) apart in a trench filled with manure and water well around the roots. Give the plants a weekly feed of liquid manure when the first fruits form. And that's not all: scatter slug bait around them. Slugs are partial to both the leaves and the fruit.

If any courgette or marrow flowers do not germinate, all is not lost. Dip them in a light batter and deep-fry them. The Greeks serve them as a delicious first course with egg and lemon sauce.

Calabrese seed is planted in April in good, firm soil and transplanted (or bought plants set out) in late May. The plants need to be 50cm (20in) apart in rows spaced 60cm (2ft) apart, and well watered if they are to form good 'heads'. Cut the centre heads first, from July to September, and then spread general fertilizer around the plants to encourage the side shoots to develop.

Globe artichokes are so decorative they can be mistaken for one of the thistle-type flowers, and do not look out of place among the hollyhocks at the back of the flower bed. They do like the sun, and plenty of room. Plant roots of this perennial from March to May, allowing 75cm (30in) between them. The heads will be ready to cut from June into October and should be harvested before the scales open.

What garden would be complete without at least a few **new potatoes**. To beat the calendar, try growing some in pots in an unheated greenhouse, in used grow-bags or large plastic bags filled with moist compost. For crops in open ground, sow seed potatoes from late March to mid April. The well-sprouted tubers should be sown 30cm (12in) apart in rows 60cm (2ft) apart, and 10cm (4in) below soil level. A dressing of two parts superphosphate of lime to one part sulphate of potash at planting time will increase the yield and reduce the chance of plant disease.

Not so much a vegetable, more a flavouring, plant single cloves of **garlic** 15cm (6in) apart from November to March in a sunny position. Then in July and August, when the stems collapse, harvest the bulbs – they bring out the flavour of many other vegetables.

AUTUMN

The season of misty mornings and warm golden sunlight is a generous one in the vegetable garden. Willow trugs come into the kitchen laden with long pale stalks of celery, leeks and fennel; chubby roots of celeriac, beetroot and kohlrabi, colourful as can be; bunches of plump onions, prize-winning marrows and fragrant tomatoes. This is a harvest to celebrate!

FISH & SWEETCORN CHOWDER

A typical New English dish, combining the harvests of both sea and land.

750g (1½lb) cod or haddock fillets
100g (4oz) salt pork
2 corn cobs
15g (½oz) butter
1 large onion, peeled and sliced
25g (1oz) flour
900ml (1½ pints) milk
2 bay leaves
350g (12oz) potatoes, peeled and diced
salt
freshly ground black pepper
4 × 15ml spoons (4tbls) double cream
2 × 15ml spoons (2tbls) chopped parsley, to garnish

1 Skin the fish and cut it into 5cm (2in) slices. Cut the rind from the pork and cut the meat into 1cm (½in) cubes. Using a sharp knife, strip the kernels from the corn cobs.
2 Heat the butter and fry the pork in a flameproof casserole over moderate heat until the fat runs. Lift it out with a draining spoon and set aside.
3 Fry the onion for 3-4 minutes, stirring once or twice. Stir in the flour and, when it has thickened, gradually pour on the milk, stirring constantly. Bring the milk to simmering point.
4 Add the fish, pork, corn kernels, bay leaves and potatoes and season with salt and pepper.
5 Cover and simmer for 20 minutes, or until the potatoes and corn are tender. Discard the bay leaves.
6 Stir in the cream and sprinkle the dish with parsley. Serve in deep soup bowls, with plenty of hot, crusty bread.

SERVES 4

LEEK & POTATO CAKE

This is a distant cousin of Spanish omelette, a medley of vegetables fried in an egg custard and then finished under the grill.

3 medium leeks
2 medium potatoes, peeled
1 small onion, peeled and chopped
1 × 15ml spoon (1tbls) snipped chives
5 eggs, beaten
3 × 15ml spoons (3tbls) single cream
salt
freshly ground black pepper
75g (3oz) Gruyère cheese, grated
2 × 15ml spoons (2tbls) sunflower oil
parsley sprigs, to garnish

1 Trim the leeks, strip off the outer leaves and cut off the green tops. (Use these in soup; you need only the white part for this dish.) Wash the leeks well and dry them thoroughly. Thinly slice them into rings.
2 Grate the potatoes. You can use a food processor, but take care not to reduce them to a pulp.
3 Mix together the leeks, potatoes, onion and chives. Beat in the eggs and cream and season well.
4 Heat the oil in a pan. Pour in the omelette mixture, cover and cook over low heat for 10-15 minutes, or until the omelette is set. Sprinkle on the grated cheese. Preheat the grill to moderate and grill the omelette for 2-3 minutes, to brown the top. Slide it on to a heated plate and serve garnished with the parsley.
  Cut into wedges like a moist, savoury cake and serve warm, with ham, bacon or cold meats, or cold with salad. It's especially good as a picnic snack or as part of a packed lunch.

SERVES 4

PORK & LEEK MEATBALLS

1kg (2¼lb) leeks
salt
500g (1¼lb) lean pork, minced
50g (2oz) white breadcrumbs
2 × 15ml spoons (2tbls) chopped marjoram
2 eggs, beaten
freshly ground black pepper
200ml (7fl oz) chicken stock
3 × 15ml spoons (3tbls) lemon juice
15g (½oz) butter

1 Trim the leeks, strip off the tough outer leaves and the tough green tops. Wash them very thoroughly to remove all traces of sand and grit. Cook the leeks in boiling, salted water for 8-10 minutes, until they are just tender. Drain them and dry them on absorbent kitchen paper. Mince the leeks or chop them finely.
2 Beat and mash the meat with a wooden spoon until it makes a smooth, moist paste. Add the leeks, breadcrumbs and marjoram and beat well. Beat in the eggs and season the mixture with salt and pepper.
3 Wet your hands and shape the mixture into rounds about the size of golf balls.
4 Put the stock, lemon juice and butter into a pan and bring to the boil. Add the meatballs, cover and simmer slowly for 20-25 minutes, shaking the pan frequently. By then most of the sauce should have been absorbed.
  You can serve the meatballs with rice and crisp, green salad, or just with salad and crusty bread.

SERVES 4-6

ROAST FENNEL CHICKEN

1.25kg (2¾lb) oven-ready chicken
40g (1½oz) butter, softened
2 medium bulbs fennel
½ small marrow, or 4 courgettes
4 large tomatoes
2 × 15ml spoons (2tbls) chopped parsley
2 × 5ml spoons (2tsp) flour
120ml (4fl oz) dry cider

STUFFING
1 small bulb fennel
40g (1½oz) wholewheat breadcrumbs
2 × 15ml spoons (2tbls) chopped
fennel leaves
½ × 5ml spoon (½tsp) grated lemon rind
1 × 5ml spoon (1tsp) lemon juice
½ × 5ml spoon (½tsp) caraway seeds
salt
freshly ground black pepper
40g (1½oz) butter, melted

1   Wipe the chicken inside and out with damp kitchen paper and dry it. Lift up the skin and, using your fingers, rub the butter over the flesh.
2   To make the stuffing, trim the fennel, tear off any stringy or discoloured outer leaves and chop the bulb finely. Mix the chopped fennel with the breadcrumbs, fennel leaves, lemon rind, lemon juice and caraway seeds and season with salt and pepper. Pour on the melted butter and mix through.
3   Pack the stuffing into the cavity and close the cavity with a skewer. Season the skin with salt and pepper.
4   Place the chicken in a roasting pan. Roast it in the oven, preheated to 220°C, 425°F, gas 7, for 20 minutes.
5   Trim the fennel bulbs, discard the outer leaves and halve bulbs lengthways. Blanch in boiling, salted water for 10 minutes, drain and dry. Roughly chop the courgettes or peel the marrow, halve it, remove seeds and cut it into thick slices. Prick the tomatoes.
6   Arrange the fennel and marrow slices around the chicken and baste the vegetables and the bird with the pan juices. Reduce the oven heat to 200°C, 400°F, gas 6 and continue cooking for 30 minutes. Add the tomatoes, baste all the vegetables again and cook for 10 minutes more.
7   Test that the chicken is cooked by piercing the thick part of the thigh with a fine skewer. The juices should run clear, and not be red.

8   Transfer the chicken to a heated serving dish and arrange the vegetables around it. Sprinkle them with parsley to garnish.
9   Pour off most of the fat from the pan. Stir in the flour and pour on the cider. Bring to the boil and season with salt and pepper.
Serve the sauce separately.

SERVES 4

There's a hint of Greece, where wild fennel is one of the most prolific herbs, in this unusual chicken dish. The bird is cooked with fennel, courgettes and tomatoes – all from the garden – and served with a cider sauce.

BEETROOT AU GRATIN

500g (1¼lb) small beetroots
salt
1 × 15ml spoon (1tbls) caraway seeds

SAUCE
40g (1½oz) butter
25g (1oz) flour
300ml (½ pint) milk
freshly ground black pepper
5 × 15ml spoons (5tbls) double cream
50g (2oz) Cheddar cheese, grated
50g (2oz) Parmesan cheese, grated

1   Wash the beetroots and cook them in boiling, salted water for 45 minutes – 1 hour, or until they are tender. Drain them and, when they are cool enough to handle, skin and slice them.
2   To make the sauce, melt the butter in a small pan, stir in the flour and gradually pour on the milk, stirring constantly. Bring to the boil and simmer for 3 minutes. Season with salt and pepper and stir in the cream and grated Cheddar cheese.
3   Arrange the beetroot in a greased baking dish and sprinkle with the caraway seeds. Pour on the cheese sauce and sprinkle the Parmesan cheese on top.
4   Bake the dish in the oven, preheated to 190°C, 375°F, gas 5, for 15-20 minutes, until the topping is well browned. Serve at once.

SERVES 4

CELERIAC REMOULADE

2 celeriac roots
salt
2 × 15ml spoons (2tbls) lemon juice
2 hard-boiled eggs, chopped
2 × 15ml spoons (2tbls) chopped chervil

SAUCE
150ml (¼ pint) mayonnaise
4 × 15ml spoons (4tbls) double cream
1 garlic clove, peeled and crushed
½ × 5ml spoon (½tsp) mustard powder
2 × 5ml spoons (2tsp) capers
1 × 15ml spoon (1tbls) chopped chervil
1 × 15ml spoon (1tbls) chopped tarragon
freshly ground black pepper

1   Scrub the celeriac roots. Cook them in boiling, salted water with half the lemon juice for 30-40 minutes,

until just tender, then drain them.
2   Peel the celeriac and slice into matchstick strips. Toss them in the remaining lemon juice.
3   Mix all the sauce ingredients together, seasoning well with salt and pepper.
4   Toss the celeriac in the sauce.
5   Pile the celeriac salad on to a serving dish. Arrange lines of chopped egg white, egg yolk and chervil over it, to garnish.

SERVES 4-6

Variation Other unusual vegetables can be turned into a delicious salad in the same way. Ring the changes with kohlrabi, salsify, scorzonera – and even parsnips and potatoes.

CORN ON THE COB KEBABS

2 large corn cobs
8 button onions, peeled
100g (4oz) smoked bacon
8 small tomatoes
8 button mushrooms, trimmed
4 bay leaves
1 × 15ml spoon (1tbls) snipped chives

DRESSING
4 × 15ml spoons (4tbls) sunflower oil
1 × 5ml spoon (1tsp) red wine vinegar
freshly ground black pepper
1 × 5ml spoon (1tsp) paprika
1 garlic clove, peeled and crushed

1   Mix the dressing and set aside.
2   Remove the husks and silky threads from the corn cobs. Cook them in boiling water for 7 minutes. Add the whole onions and cook for 2-3 minutes. Drain the vegetables.
3   Cut the corn cobs into 2.5cm (1in) slices, cut the rind from the bacon and cut it into cubes.
4   Thread the corn slices, onions, bacon, tomatoes, mushrooms and bay leaves on to 4 skewers. Lay them in a flat dish, pour over the dressing and turn to coat them evenly.
5   Heat the grill to high. Grill the kebabs for about 10 minutes, turning them frequently and brushing them with the dressing. Serve them at once, sprinkled with the chives.

These colourful kebabs go well with risotto or jacket-baked potatoes.

SERVES 4

COTTAGERS' CHOICE

This is a typical country recipe combining pork from the pig kept in almost every cottage garden, and tender young root vegetables.

750g (1½lb) lean boneless pork
50g (2oz) butter
250g (9oz) button onions, peeled
2 garlic cloves, peeled and finely chopped
350g (12oz) kohlrabi
150ml (¼ pint) dry cider
5 × 15ml spoons (5tbls) chicken stock
2 bay leaves
2 × 5ml spoons (2tsp) fennel seeds
salt
freshly ground black pepper
150ml (¼ pint) cream
2 × 15ml spoons (2tbls) chopped chervil

1   Trim excess fat from the meat and cut it into 4cm (1½in) cubes.
2   Melt half the butter in a pan and sauté the meat over moderate heat, stirring frequently, to brown it evenly on all sides. Lift out the meat.
3   Add the remaining butter, and fry the onions and garlic for 2 minutes.
4   Peel the kohlrabi and cut it into 2cm (¾in) cubes. Add them to the pan, stir well, and pour on the cider and stock. Bring to the boil.
5   Return the pork to the pan, add the bay leaves and fennel seeds and season with salt and pepper. Cover and simmer for 45 minutes, until the pork is cooked and the kohlrabi is tender. Discard the bay leaves.
6   Stir in the cream, adjust the seasoning if needed and garnish with the chopped chervil. Serve with new potatoes boiled in their skins.

SERVES 4

Cooking kohlrabi

Harvest kohlrabi when the bulbs are very small — about 7.5cm (3in) is ideal. Trim off the roots, stems and leaves. Just before you are ready to cook the vegetable, peel off the thin outer skin.

AUTUMN HARVEST

A utumn, the season of mellow fruitfulness, provides a feast of vegetables ripened by the summer sun and ready for the kitchen.

Sweetcorn needs a good summer and plenty of sun, and even then it may not grow 'as high as an elephant's eye' to fulfil the words of the song. But it does seem the very essence of a golden harvest. For early crops, plant the pea-sized seeds under glass in April or early May, preferably in fibre-pot trays so that they can be transplanted without disturbing the roots. For later maturing, seeds can be sown where they are to grow in late May. In both cases, sow the seeds 2.5cm (1in) deep and in open ground, space them 45cm (18in) apart with 60cm (2ft) between rows. The female cobs are pollinated more successfully if the plants are grown in blocks of, say, four short rows rather than one long one.

Some of the more unusual root vegetables provide a bumper harvest in the autumn. **Celeriac**, for example, which looks like a large brown turnip but has the flavour of celery, needs heat to germinate the seed. Transplant young seedlings in a cold frame or tunnel cloche to harden off, finally planting them 30cm (12in) apart in open ground in May or early June. The brown, bulbous swelling is formed just above soil level. You can leave some in the garden through to November.

Another 'above ground' root is **kohlrabi**, a member of the cabbage family which also looks like a turnip, though it can be purple or green. The seed can be sown directly in the ground 2.5cm (1in) deep in rows 30cm (12in) or so apart. Apply a dressing or two of lime, and thin the seedlings to give them space to mature. Don't let them grow bigger than the size of a large golf ball, however, or they'll get stringy.

Florence fennel, another vegetable which forms above the ground, has an aniseed flavour and the texture of celery. Sow the seeds *in situ* in April and thin the seedlings to 20cm (8in) apart. When the bulbs are nearly golf ball size, pile up soil around them to exclude light and blanch the roots. Keep the soil moist with a liquid manure solution and leave the bulbs to develop to about 13cm (5in) across.

For main crop **beetroot**, sow seed in late May or early June, to harvest in October and store through winter.

Celery, a near cousin of celeriac, can be tricky to grow, it has to be said, and it is a proud gardener who can produce the size and quality of the best commercial varieties. If you like a challenge, plant the minute seed in a heated greenhouse between February and April, transfer the seedlings to a cold frame to harden off, and transplant at the beginning of June. Or buy plants and set 30cm (12in) apart in trenches of the same depth, and 90 to 120cm (3 to 4ft) apart. Use plenty of manure in the trenches, water the plants well, and give them dressings of liquid manure and a general fertilizer. Pile up the earth around the stalks to blanch them, and remove side shoots to encourage growth. Cross your fingers and harvest from early November onwards. Alternatively you can buy a self-blanching type, which avoids the earthing-up process. Seed is sown in a greenhouse at the end of March and planted out in June 23cm (9in) apart. The stalks will never be snow-white but will be crisp and tasty.

If you have been busy cutting the small, delicately flavoured courgettes during the summer, you should be able to grow prize-winning **marrows**, and all their near relations in the squash family. Sow the seeds three to a pot in seed compost in the greenhouse in May, or out of doors (they favour a warm compost heap) a month later. Transplant seedlings when they have their second pair of leaves. As for courgettes, the soil should be well dug with manure and well watered. Try some yellow marrows for a change and, while you're at it, pumpkins too.

No vegetable garden should be without a row or two of **onions** and **leeks**. The advantage with onions is that they can be ripened, lifted and stored by mid-August and a catch crop of, say, **spinach** or late **Brussels sprouts** seedlings planted in their place. Plant onion 'sets' – small, commercially raised bulbs – in rich soil in March or April, 25cm (10in) apart with 45cm (18in) in between rows. Mild-flavoured pickling or button onions are harvested before they are fully developed.

Close relations to the onion family, **leeks** are best sown in seed trays in the greenhouse (for greenhouse you can read garden room or even kitchen!) in early April, with the sturdiest seedlings planted out in June. Make a 10cm (4in) hole with a dibber, fill it with water, then pop in the leek. Keep filling the hole with water, odd though it seems.

WINTER

There's no shortage of vegetables to give colour and flavour to hearty soups, stews and casseroles throughout the winter, or to serve as side dishes in guises as varied as fritters and purées. Brassicas and root vegetables will crop plentifully throughout the chilliest days, and you can add even more variety with dried beans and peas from the store-cupboard, the preserve of summer's bounty.

ARTICHOKE & ORANGE SOUP

500g (1¼lb) Jerusalem artichokes
1 × 15ml spoon (1tbls) lemon juice
25g (1oz) butter
2 medium onions, peeled and sliced
900ml (1½ pints) chicken stock
2 strips thinly pared orange rind
2 bay leaves
salt
freshly ground black pepper
juice of ½ orange
150ml (¼ pint) single cream
2 × 15ml spoons (2tbls) chopped parsley
4 thin slices of orange, to garnish

1   Peel and chop the artichokes and drop them straight into water acidulated with lemon juice.
2   Melt the butter and fry the artichokes and onions over low heat for 10 minutes, stirring once or twice. Pour on the stock, add the orange rind and bay leaves and bring to the boil. Cover and simmer for 20 minutes. Discard the orange rind and bay leaves.
3   Purée the vegetables and stock in a blender or food processor. Return the purée to the pan, season with salt and pepper, stir in the orange juice and cream and heat gently.
4   Sprinkle the parsley over the soup and garnish each serving with a slice of orange.

SERVES 4

Variation For a more sophisticated garnish, thinly pare the rind of half an orange, cut it into matchstick strips and poach in boiling water for 15 minutes. Drain the orange strips and pat them dry.

GREEK BEAN SALAD

This makes a substantial first course, or can be served as a high-protein dish in a salad meal, with rice salad and leeks vinaigrette, for example.

250g (9oz) dried haricot beans, soaked and drained
a few stalks of parsley
2 bay leaves
1 small onion, peeled and halved
salad leaves, to serve
4 tomatoes, sliced into rings
2 large onions, peeled and sliced into rings
100g (4oz) feta cheese, crumbled

DRESSING
2 garlic cloves, peeled and crushed
6 × 15ml spoons (6tbls) olive oil
4 × 5ml spoons (4tsp) red wine vinegar
1 × 5ml spoon (1tsp) lemon juice
1 × 5ml spoon (1tsp) chopped marjoram
a pinch of sugar
salt
freshly ground black pepper

1   Put the beans, parsley, bay leaves and halved onion into a pan, cover with boiling water and bring to the boil. Cover the pan and fast-boil for 15 minutes, then simmer for 1 hour or until the beans are tender.
2   Drain the beans and discard the flavourings.
3   Mix all the dressing ingredients.
4   Pour the dressing over the beans while they are still warm. Set aside to marinate and cool.
5   Line a serving dish with salad leaves, such as lettuce, spinach, endive. Arrange the tomato and onion rings around the outside. Pile the bean salad in the centre and scatter the crumbled cheese over it.

SERVES 4

POT ROAST OF BEEF

1.25kg (2¾lb) topside of beef
3 × 15ml spoons (3tbls) flour
salt
freshly ground black pepper
40g (1½oz) butter
100g (4oz) streaky bacon, rinded
300ml (½ pint) light ale
1 bouquet garni
1 large carrot, peeled and sliced
1 large onion, peeled and sliced
2 stalks celery, thinly sliced
1 small swede, peeled and diced

1   Wipe the beef with damp kitchen paper and dry it. Rub it on all sides with the flour seasoned with salt and pepper.
2   Melt the butter in a flameproof casserole. Cut the bacon into squares and fry it over moderate heat for 3 minutes, stirring once or twice. Add the meat and brown it on all sides. Pour on the ale, add the bouquet garni and vegetables, and bring to the boil.
3   Cover the dish and cook in the oven, preheated to 160°C, 325°F, gas 3, for 2 hours, or until the meat is tender. Discard the bouquet garni.
4   Transfer the meat to a heated serving dish and arrange the vegetables around it. Skim the fat from the stock, adjust the seasoning and serve separately. Serve with boiled or mashed potatoes.

SERVES 4-6

A real winter warmer – Artichoke and orange soup followed by Pot roast of beef cooked with winter vegetables taken straight from the garden.

CASSEROLE OF VEAL

750g (1½lb) pie veal
350g (12oz) celeriac
1 × 15ml spoon (1tbls) lemon juice
25g (1oz) butter
1 large onion, peeled and sliced
750ml (1¼ pints) chicken stock, hot
a strip of thinly pared lemon rind
100g (4oz) flageolets, cooked
2 × 15ml spoons (2tbls) chopped parsley

SAUCE
25g (1oz) butter
2 × 15ml spoons (2tbls) flour
2 egg yolks, beaten
1 × 15ml spoon (1tbls) lemon juice
salt
freshly ground black pepper

1   Cut any excess fat from the veal. Cut the meat into 2.5cm (1in) cubes. Peel and dice the celeriac, dropping it at once into water acidulated with lemon juice.

2   Melt the butter and fry the meat over moderate heat, stirring it often, until it is evenly brown. Lift it out with a draining spoon and set aside.

3   Fry the onion and celeriac for 3-4 minutes, stirring once or twice. Pour on the stock, add the lemon rind and return the meat to the pan.

4   Bring slowly to the boil, cover and simmer for 45 minutes.

5   Add the flageolets and simmer for 15 minutes.

6   Discard the lemon rind. Pour off the stock and reserve.

7   To make the sauce, melt the butter in a small pan, stir in the flour and gradually pour on most of the stock, stirring constantly. Bring to the boil and simmer for 3 minutes, until the sauce thickens. Pour the remaining hot stock on to the egg yolks, beat in the lemon juice and pour into the sauce. Stir over very low heat for 1-2 minutes. Season with salt and pepper.

8   Stir the sauce into the meat and vegetables and sprinkle with the parsley. Serve this dish with boiled potatoes, or with brown rice.

SERVES 4

BRUSSELS SPROUT SALAD

350g (12oz) small Brussels sprouts
175g (6oz) lean bacon
15g (½oz) butter
4 stalks celery, thinly sliced
1 small onion, sliced into rings
2 tomatoes, quartered

DRESSING
6 × 15ml spoons (6tbls) olive oil
1 × 15ml spoon (1tbls) cider vinegar
2 × 5ml spoons (2tsp) lemon juice
a pinch of sugar
50g (2oz) Roquefort cheese, crumbled
freshly ground black pepper

1   Trim the Brussels sprouts and discard any damaged outer leaves. Slice them thinly.
2   Cut the rind from the bacon and snip it into squares. Melt the butter and fry the bacon, stirring it often, until it is dry. Set aside to cool.
3   Mix the dressing ingredients.
4   Toss together the Brussels sprouts, bacon, celery and onion rings, pour the sauce over and toss well.
5   Serve the salad garnished with tomato wedges. It is good with cold ham, pork and poultry.

SERVES 4

POTATO & PARSNIP LAYER

3 large potatoes, peeled and thinly sliced
2 large parsnips, peeled and thinly sliced
1 large onion, peeled and sliced into rings
salt
freshly ground black pepper
2 × 15ml spoons (2tbls) chopped parsley
50g (2oz) butter
150ml (¼ pint) milk or single cream

1   Grease a shallow baking dish. Arrange layers of potato, parsnip and onion, seasoning each with salt, pepper and parsley, and beginning and ending with potato.
2   Cut the butter into small pieces. Dot it over the potatoes and pour on the milk or cream.
3   Bake the dish in the oven, preheated to 190°C, 375°F, gas 5, for 1-1¼ hours, until the potatoes are tender and the top is crisp and well browned. Cover the top with foil if necessary.

SERVES 4-6

CABBAGE LEAF PARCELS

12 Savoy cabbage leaves
salt
40g (1½oz) butter
1 medium onion, peeled and chopped
1 garlic clove, peeled and finely chopped
250g (9oz) minced lamb
50g (2oz) wholewheat breadcrumbs
50g (2oz) sultanas
50g (2oz) blanched almonds, chopped
1 × 15ml spoon (1tbls) chopped mint
freshly ground black pepper
1 egg, beaten
300ml (½ pint) beef stock

SAUCE
25g (1oz) butter
1 × 15ml spoon (1tbls) flour
2 × 15ml spoons (2tbls) red wine
1 × 5ml spoon (1tsp) tomato purée

1   Cut away the tough stalks from the cabbage leaves and blanch them in boiling, salted water for 1 minute. Drain them, drop at once into cold water, then drain and dry them.
2   Melt the butter and fry the onion and garlic over moderate heat for 3 minutes, stirring once or twice. Add the meat and stir-fry to brown it evenly on all sides.
3   Remove from the heat and stir in the breadcrumbs, sultanas, almonds and mint and season with salt and pepper. Beat in the egg.
4   Divide the filling between the cabbage leaves, placing it in the centre. Fold up the bottom of the leaf, fold over the 2 sides then fold down the top to enclose the filling.
5   Place the parcels, join side down, in a shallow pan. Pour on the stock, cover, bring to the boil and simmer for 20 minutes. Transfer the parcels to a heated serving dish and keep warm, reserving the stock.
6   Melt the butter in a small pan, stir in the flour and pour on the reserved stock and wine, stirring occasionally. Stir in the tomato purée, bring to the boil and simmer for 3 minutes. Season with salt and pepper. Pour the sauce over the cabbage parcels to serve.

SERVES 4

MIXED VEGETABLE FRITTERS

A dish of puffed up and crispy golden vegetables is a delicious accompaniment to grilled steak, chops or fish. A sauce of soured cream or Greek-style yoghurt stirred with chopped onion and mint makes a good accompaniment.

1 large onion, peeled
½ small cauliflower
2 small parsnips
salt
oil, for deep frying
8 small button mushrooms, trimmed
lemon wedges to serve

BATTER
125g (5oz) flour
salt
2 × 15ml spoons (2tbls) sunflower oil
4 × 15ml spoons (4tbls) milk
150ml (¼ pint) warm water
2 egg whites

1   Slice the onion into 5mm (¼in) rings. Break the cauliflower into florets, discarding the stalk. Peel the parsnips and cut them into 1cm (½in) slices.
2   Blanch the cauliflower and parsnip slices in separate pans of boiling, salted water for 3 minutes. Drain the vegetables, plunge them at once into cold water, then drain and dry them.
3   To make the batter, sift the flour and salt, stir in the oil and beat in the milk and water. Just before using the batter, stiffly whisk the egg whites and fold them in.
4   Heat the oil in a deep pan to 190°C, 375°F, or until a cube of bread browns in 50 seconds.
5   Dip the vegetables in the batter and drain off any excess. Fry the vegetables, each type separately, in the hot oil for 2 minutes, or until they are golden brown. Lift them out with a draining spoon, toss them on crumpled kitchen paper to dry them and keep the cooked vegetables warm while you cook the remainder. Serve the fried vegetables with lemon wedges.

SERVES 4

WINTER HARVEST

No matter whether you dig your main crops of root vegetables towards the end of summer, through the autumn or even later, they form an important part of winter's menu because they can be so successfully stored. Add Brussels sprouts, cabbages and winter cauliflowers, not to mention onions and dried beans and peas from the store-cupboard, and you can see that winter offers a bumper harvest for the table.

Among the main root crops, in order of sowing, **turnips** are sown from February to July and can be harvested from 10 weeks onwards; early sowing, of course, gives you the small, sweet summer **snowball turnip**. And in spring and summer the leaves, or 'tops', make a delicious green vegetable.

Parsnips, sown from February to April, have a long growing cycle, from seven and a half months. Old hands reckon that they are never sweet enough until they've had a touch of frost. But once the foliage has died down it can be a job to locate them on a cold winter's morn.

Carrot seed goes in from March to July; sow in succession and harvest continually, starting two and a half months later. Thin out the seedlings, pencil thin, for small sweet summer

vegetables leaving the main crop to develop.

Salsify, the 'vegetable oyster', and its black-skinned cousin **scorzonera**, both considered luxury crops and hard to come by in the shops, are sown in April. Being very hardy, they can be left in the ground into the winter. The problem is, however, that when the ground is frozen, they're impossible to lift because the long, slender stems snap. A bonus with scorzonera is that if roots are left in the ground and earthed up, the young shoots can be used in salads or cooked like (very early) spinach.

Jerusalem artichokes, like **potatoes**, are grown not from seed but from small tubers set in early spring. This is a vegetable that grows to a great height, like a wall. It acts as an effective windbreak for other crops, but needs staking and wiring in an exposed position. You can lift the knobbly crop as late as March, though you have to bait the slugs to beat them to it.

Swedes sown from seed in May and June can be lifted from five months later. This is another hardy, dig-as-you-please crop; choose between lifting early and storing in clamps (see pages 74 and 75) or harvesting to the demands of the kitchen.

To give an idea of what mountainous crops grow from minuscule seed, 15g (½oz) of carrot seed will sow the equivalent of a 15m (50ft) row, and yield 18kg (40lb) of large, main-crop vegetables, or 6.75kg (15lb) of summer harvest. One beginner's mistake to avoid: never plant root crops in ground recently fertilized with manure. Such a rich diet confuses them and the roots split and spread in all directions.

Brussels sprouts, cabbages and cauliflowers are among the best brassicas – hardy green crops – to look winter squarely in the eye. Sow **Brussels sprout** seed on prepared seed beds in March and April, according to variety, and plant out seedlings in firm ground in May and June not less than 60cm (2ft) apart each way. Choose F_1 hybrid varieties, specially selected for healthier, disease-resistant plants. In exposed ground, the plants may need staking; in pigeon territory they need netting too.

Cabbages come in so many varieties, you can enjoy a succession of them all year round. Sow the seed for winter varieties, like the crinkly-leaved Savoy, in prepared drills by mid-May, and transplant seedlings in July and August into ground that has had a good sprinkling of lime worked in. This is to prevent the dreaded club-root.

Winter **cauliflowers** with their firm, snow-white heads are one of the delights of the culinary year. Like other brassicas they are greedy for space. Plant seed in April, transplanting when the seedlings are at least 15cm (6in) tall, or buy a bundle of plants going for a song at most markets. Cauliflowers need a rich soil and one or two applications of fertilizer. What they don't like is frost. Snap off the upper leaves and fold them over the heads to protect them – they grow with their own built-in frost shield and umbrella! Keep a close watch on the heads once they are fully mature and cut them when they are still tight: once they open out, they are over the top and will taste bitter.

DRYING AND STORING

Willow trays of broad bean seeds drying in the sun and wind; whole haricot bean plants and bunches of onions, shallots and garlic hanging under the eaves; sliced runner and French beans layered in crocks of salt; root vegetables nestling under a 'clamp' of sand or peat; strings of red and green peppers like bead curtains in a doorway; rows of glistening chutneys and sun-gold pickles packing the larder shelves: this was the scene not so many years ago, when every season's harvest turned every cottage into a mini industry.

Modern commercial and home preserving techniques haven't captured our hearts. Tradition dies hard, and old country ways of preserving home-grown products by means of natural resources – the sun and wind – have an emotional appeal, even today.

Drying vegetables
If you have a plentiful bean crop, turn back the clock and dry some to use in the winter in pulse dishes as varied as soups and salads, pâté and casseroles.

Haricot beans and marrow fat peas are left practically to their own devices. Leave the plants until the pods turn brown, then pull them up, including the roots, tie them in bunches and hang them upside-down. Choose a dry, covered place with a good circulation of air, such as a car-port. When the pods are dry enough to rattle, shell the seeds, spread them on trays and finish drying them in the sun or the airing cupboard. Cool them thoroughly before storing in a covered jar.

Broad beans are left to mature in the pod, then shelled and blanched for 2-3 minutes in boiling water to stop the growth of harmful enzymes. Drain, cool and dry them – a whizz in a salad spinner does this in moments. And then comes the evocative bit, when you spread them on trays to dry.

More evocative still, you can dry whole runner beans, French beans, mangetout peas or very young pea pods (gathered while they are still flat and before the seeds develop). Top and tail the pods, then blanch them for 2-3 minutes. Plunge them at once into

cold water, to avoid further cooking, then drain and dry them. Thread the pods necklace fashion and hang them out each day to dry in the sun and wind. Bring them in each evening – or the dew would undo all the good work.

To salt beans, top, tail and slice them, then layer them in a crock or jar (never a metal container) with half their weight in coarse salt. Cover the jar and leave it in a cool, dry place. To cook salted beans, soak them overnight in fresh water.

Red and green peppers bring a touch of the Mediterranean as they hang on strings to dry. Peppers don't need blanching. Simply thread them whole or halved on strings, or spread them on trays, turning them frequently. They will take up to 3-4 days to dry in the sun, or somewhat longer in the airing cupboard.

All dried vegetables benefit from a final flourish of heat, either in hot sun or, failing that, in the oven. Spread them on racks and process them for 10 minutes at 80°C, 175°F, gas ¼. Then cool them thoroughly before storing.

Most dried vegetables need soaking to restore the moisture content before cooking. Dried pea and bean seeds need the longest soaking. The slow way is to soak them overnight in cold water; a quicker way is to bring them to the boil from cold, and leave them in the water until it becomes cold. Drain and wash them, then cook them in boiling unsalted water for 45 minutes to 1 hour. All dried pulses must be fast-boiled for the first 15 minutes to destroy the harmful toxins.

Whole dried bean pods should be soaked for several hours, peppers soaked in warm water for 1 hour, or added in their dried state to high-liquid dishes such as soups and stews.

Drying fruits
Tree fruits dry very rewardingly. How satisfying to build up a store of creamy apple rings; pale green pear halves; golden apricots and peaches; russety figs and glinting black plums.

Peel, core and halve pears; halve and stone apricots, peaches and plums; and halve large figs. Drop the

prepared fruit at once into water, acidulated with lemon juice. Drain the fruit, pat it thoroughly dry, then thread it on strings or spread on trays.

Choose between drying in the sun or in the oven, at 50°C, 120°F (gas ¼ with the door open), turning the fruit often. It will take 4-5 days to dry, but the process need not be continuous. You can put the fruit in the oven each time you have finished cooking. Keep it covered with a cloth meanwhile.

Give dried fruit a final flourish in hot sun or in the oven for 15 minutes at 80°C, 175°F, gas ¼. Cool before storing.

Storing vegetables and fruit
The onion family and all root vegetables, will keep satisfactorily for several months with no form of processing. Harvest onions, shallots and garlic once the leaves have withered and turned yellow. Tie them in bunches and hang them in a cool, airy place. Protect them from frost.

Store root vegetables in the old-fashioned way, in a 'clamp' of dry sand or peat to protect them from frost.

Select only perfect tree fruits for storing – blemished ones can be cut and used in preserves. Do not wash the fruit – the 'bloom' on the skins forms a protective cover. Wrap each fruit separately in waxed paper or newspaper and store in racks or on cardboard trays in a cool – but frost-free – airy place. Check the fruits periodically and remove any bruised or damaged ones. That old saying, that it only takes one rotten apple to damage the entire crop, is sad but true.

Making pickles, chutneys and other preserves has a time-honoured social history, too, as a delicious way of storing a bumper vegetable harvest. The different sections throughout the book have recipes that illustrate the variety of preserves – sweet and sour, hot and spicy – that you can make with produce from the kitchen garden.

Onions and herbs hanging to dry, carrots covered with dry, fine sand, apples carefully wrapped in paper, jars of dried beans and preserves – there's a deep satisfaction in 'salting' away your produce.

SPICED BEETROOT

This hot-spiced pickle is especially good with a ploughman's lunch of bread and cheese, and with cold meats and smoked mackerel.

500g (1¼lb) small beetroots
salt
100g (4oz) horseradish
125g (5oz) seedless raisins, chopped
150ml (¼ pint) red wine vinegar
1 × 5ml spoon (1tsp) mustard seeds
1 × 5ml spoon (1tsp) sea salt

1   Wash the beetroots and cook them in boiling, salted water for 45 minutes – 1 hour, until they are tender. Cool them, then peel and grate them.
2   Peel the horseradish and grate it finely. Or chop it and grate it in a blender or food processor.
3   Mix together the beetroot, horseradish and raisins and pack into warm, sterilized jars.
4   Bring the vinegar and mustard seed to the boil. Add the sea salt and pour into the warm jars. Cover with vinegar-proof lids and seal. Cool, label and store in a cool, dry place for up to 3 months.

MAKES ABOUT 750G (1½LB)

COURGETTE CHUTNEY

1kg (2¼lb) courgettes, trimmed
500g (1¼lb) tomatoes, skinned and chopped
250g (9oz) onions, peeled and sliced
4 garlic cloves, peeled and chopped
750g (1½lb) light Muscovado sugar
75g (3oz) sultanas
1 × 15ml spoon (1tbls) salt
1 × 15ml spoon (1tbls) pickling spice
1 × 5ml spoon (1tsp) ground ginger
500ml (18fl oz) white vinegar

1   Cut the courgettes into 2.5cm (1in) slices.
2   Put the ingredients into a pan and bring slowly to the boil, stirring until the sugar has dissolved.
3   Simmer for 1½ hours, stirring frequently, until it is thick.
4   Pour the chutney into warm, sterilized jars. Cover the surface with waxed paper discs. Cover the jars with vinegar-proof lids. Cool, label and store in a cool, dry place for up to 6 months.

MAKES ABOUT 2KG (4½LB)

GREEN TOMATO & DATE CHUTNEY

500g (1¼lb) green tomatoes, chopped
250g (9oz) onions, peeled and chopped
250g (9oz) cooking apples, peeled, cored and chopped
250g (9oz) stoned dates, chopped
1 × 5ml spoon (1tsp) mixed spice
350g (12oz) light Muscovado sugar
1 × 15ml spoon (1tbls) salt
750ml (1¼ pints) malt vinegar

1   Put the tomatoes, onions, apples and dates into a pan and stir over low heat for 10 minutes. Add the remaining ingredients and stir until the sugar has dissolved.
2   Bring to the boil and simmer for 1-1¼ hours until the chutney is thick.
3   Pour into warm, sterilized jars. Cover the surface with waxed paper discs and cover the jars with vinegar-proof lids.
4   Cool, label and store in a cool, dry place for up to 1 year.

MAKES ABOUT 1.5KG (3¼LB)

PRESERVING PANS

Use a good quality stainless steel, aluminium or (as long as it's not chipped) enamel pan for vinegar-based preserves or, for small quantities, use a non-stick saucepan. Not suitable are copper and brass pans – keep them for jams and jellies and for the pure pleasure of looking at their gleaming surfaces.

PICCALILLI PICKLE

The magic of this popular pickle is that each vegetable retains its characteristic shape and texture, all blended together in a golden mustard sauce.

1.5kg (3¼lb) mixed vegetables (see below)
150g (5oz) coarse salt
1.5 litres (2½ pints) water
2 × 5ml spoons (2tsp) mustard powder
½ × 5ml spoon (½tsp) ground ginger
1 × 15ml spoon (1tbls) ground turmeric
600ml (1 pint) white vinegar
1 × 15ml spoon (1tbls) cornflour
100g (4oz) sugar

1   Pickles are intended to preserve the glut of the harvest, but try to select vegetables which contrast well, such as cauliflower, marrow, onion and runner or French beans. Cut the cauliflower into florets. Peel, seed and dice the marrow. Peel and slice the onions. Top and tail the beans and slice them diagonally into 4cm (1½in) slices.
2   Put the prepared vegetables into a glass or china bowl (not a metal pan). Mix in the salt and water, cover and set aside overnight or for several hours.
3   Tip the vegetables into a colander and run cold water through them to rinse off the brine. Put the vegetables into a stainless steel or aluminium pan.
4   Mix together the mustard, ginger and turmeric, and gradually pour on the vinegar, reserving 3 × 15ml spoons (3 tbls), stirring constantly.
5   Pour the spiced vinegar over the vegetables, stir well and bring slowly to the boil. Simmer for 45 minutes or until the vegetables are just tender.
6   Stir the remaining vinegar into the cornflour, stir in the sugar and add to the pan. Bring to the boil and simmer, stirring, for 3 minutes.
7   Pack the pickle into warm, sterilized jars. Cover with vinegar-proof covers.
8   Cool, label and store in a cool, dry place.

MAKES ABOUT 1.25KG (2¾LB)

PEPPER & CUCUMBER RELISH

This colourful, moist relish is especially good with cold meats and with bread and cheese.

500g (1¼lb) cucumber, peeled and seeded
salt
2 large red peppers, cored and seeded
2 large green peppers, cored and seeded
1 large onion, peeled and chopped
250ml (8fl oz) red wine vinegar
1 × 15ml spoon (1tbls) pickling spice
1 × 15ml spoon (1tbls) lemon juice

1　Grate the cucumber. Put it into a colander and sprinkle with salt. Leave it to drain for about 45 minutes. Run cold water through the colander and drain it well. Wring out the cucumber in a clean tea towel to squeeze out as much moisture as possible.
2　Thinly slice the peppers. Mix together the cucumber, peppers and onion in a stainless steel or aluminium pan.
3　Boil the vinegar with the pickling spice for 5 minutes.
4　Pour the spiced vinegar and the lemon juice over the vegetables, bring to the boil and simmer for 15 minutes.
5　Pour the pickled vegetables into warm sterilized jars. Cover with vinegar-proof lids.
6　Cool, label and store in a cool, dry place for up to 6 months.

MAKES ABOUT 1KG (2¼LB)

Variation You can use courgettes or marrow in place of the cucumber.

COVERING PICKLES

The keeping quality of pickles depends to a large extent on the way you cover them. Paper jam-pot covers are not enough – the preserve shrinks visibly in the jar. Use screw-on lids with non-corrosive linings – vinegar in contact with corrosive metals spells rust.

The ideal solution is to use clean, sterilized coffee or similar jars for the preserve; their plastic-lined lids seem purpose-made for pickles.

TOMATO SAUCE

1.5kg (3¼lb) ripe tomatoes
250g (9oz) onions, peeled and chopped
1 × 5ml spoon (1tsp) salt
8 black peppercorns, lightly crushed
2 dried red chillies, split
½ × 5ml spoon (½tsp) mustard seeds
300ml (½ pint) red wine vinegar
75g (3oz) sugar
2 × 5ml spoons (2tsp) paprika

1　Put the tomatoes, onions, salt, peppercorns, chillies, mustard seeds and vinegar into a stainless steel or aluminium pan. Bring to the boil and simmer for 1 hour, stirring frequently.
2　Press the tomato purée through a sieve and return it to the pan.
3　Add the sugar and paprika and stir over low heat until the sugar has dissolved. Boil for 3-5 minutes, until the sauce is smooth and thick.
4　Pour the sauce into warm, sterilized bottles and cover with sterilized corks wired or tied in place (do not press in), or with screw tops.
5　Stand the bottles on a trivet, folded cloth or wad of newspapers in a deep pan with boiling water to come up to the tops. Simmer for 20 minutes – the temperature should be 88°C, 190°F.
6　Press corks firmly into the bottles. Leave them to cool, then brush the tops with melted paraffin wax to seal them completely. Tighten screw caps. Leave to cool.
7　Label and store in a cool, dry place for up to 6 months.

MAKES 600ML (1 PINT)

PENNSYLVANIA CHOW CHOW

1 small cauliflower, cut in florets
2 red peppers, seeded and sliced
2 green peppers, seeded and sliced
1 large onion, peeled and sliced
2 courgettes, diced
2 corn cobs
75g (3oz) coarse salt
100g (4oz) dried haricot beans, soaked and drained

SPICED VINEGAR

1 litre (1¾ pints) cider vinegar
2 × 15ml spoons (2tbls) pickling spice
1 × 15ml spoon (1tbls) mustard powder
1 × 5ml spoon (1tsp) ground turmeric
1 × 5ml spoon (1tsp) ground ginger
175g (6oz) light Muscovado sugar

1　Put the cauliflower, peppers, onions and courgettes into a glass or earthenware bowl. Strip the kernels from the corn cobs and add them to the other vegetables. Add the salt and cover the vegetables with water. Stir well, cover and set aside for at least 24 hours.
2　Drain the vegetables, rinse them under cold running water and drain again.
3　Cook the dried haricot beans in boiling, unsalted water. Fast-boil them for at least 15 minutes, then simmer for 45 minutes, or until they are tender. Drain the beans. Cool them and then stir them into the other vegetables.
4　In a stainless steel or aluminium pan, bring the vinegar to the boil with all the spices. Boil for 5 minutes. Add the sugar and stir over low heat until it has dissolved. Bring to the boil.
5　Pack the vegetables into warm, sterilized jars. Pour over the spiced vinegar to cover the vegetables. Put on vinegar-proof lids and leave to cool.
6　Label the jars and store them in a cool, dry place. Leave for at least 2 months before using.

MAKES 1.75KG (4LB)

SOFT FRUITS

Growing soft fruits is a joy not to be missed – a kaleidoscope of experiences, colours and flavours: garden baskets lined with strawberry leaves and filled to overflowing with glistening fruit; sitting under the beating sun stringing trusses of shiny blackcurrants and red and white currants into a colander; the bitter-sweet taste of lesser-known fruits, such as blueberries, huckleberries and tayberries; dodging the thorns to gather the innermost yellow-green gooseberries; and stretching to your limit for the furthermost loganberry and blackberry.

There are the strawberry teas after school, the golden scones toppling with fluffy cream; the tang of berries in rich-tasting sauces to complement poultry and game; light-as-air mousses and moulded creams to end a meal with memorable flourish; tempting jars and bottles of jam, jelly, syrup and liqueur to preserve the fruit from now until next year; and, perhaps best of all, the fruits that never quite made it to the basket and are eaten, sun-warm, in the garden. Who would expect such luxuries without a little honest endeavour, with fair shares of hoeing, weeding and pruning?

An early advertisement by W. Atlee Burpee and Co. of Philadelphia, drawing attention to their Parker Earle, Dayton and Timbrell varieties of strawberry, proudly claims that 'God never made a better berry.' Which serves to remind us Britons, who tend to think of the strawberry as our own invention, that the first berries crossed the Atlantic from the eastern states of America in the 17th century.

One of the problems with strawberries has always been disease – and, of course, the weather. Breeders have concentrated their efforts on developing strains with greater resistance to grey mould (botrytis) which strikes in damp, humid conditions and when over-ripe fruit is left on the plants. Mildew will attack the leaves in dry weather, and virus diseases are ever a possibility. Always buy runners which are certified free from disease, and renew plants every three years. Three rows, each one replaced in turn, gives you a continually bumper crop.

Strawberries don't have to creep along at ground level but can make a spectacular garden decoration trained up a trellis, shinning up a pole in a tub, trailing over the rim of a container or peeping out of the holes in a strawberry pot. Mount Everest – appropriately – is a good climbing variety. At the end of harvest, sad moment that it is, cut back strawberry plants, removing all withering foliage to give the new growth a chance to form.

Gooseberry, red and white currant bushes should be pruned in June, cutting all side shoots back to five leaves. This opens up the bushes and neatens cordon-grown plants,

Facing page: The soft deep blue of the tiny round blueberry 'Ivanhoe' and the showy splendour of strawberry Chiloensis (left) show the attractive variety of our soft fruit harvest.

allowing a free circulation of air, without which you're just asking for an attack of mildew. Winter pruning is a somewhat lengthier operation. To build up strong branches you have to cut back the leaders by one-third to a half, and always to a bud that faces upwards. This way you train the growth the way you want it to grow. Cut out all weak, dead or interweaving stems level with the main stem, and cut lateral shoots to 7.5cm (3in). And all this, needless to say, should be done with the sharpest of secateurs or, in the old-fashioned way, with a razor-sharp pruning knife.

You may think that all currants need the same pruning treatment – but they don't. Blackcurrants, for example, carry the best crops on the previous year's new growth, so in the winter it's the old wood you cut back, plus any damaged or crossing shoots.

Raspberry canes cry out for attention and you will find that they are starting to die back even as you are gathering in the last of summer's harvest. Once they have fruited, cut back the old canes to just above ground level. Cut out any new canes which are weak or damaged and, in any case, leave only five or six to a plant, tying them in to the vertical wires. In winter cut back the tips of the canes by 7.5-10cm (3-4in) to a strong bud. Loganberries and blackberries need similar treatment. Autumn-fruiting raspberries get their down-to-ground-level pruning in chilly February and the fruit will develop on new canes in the same year.

Wear good protective gloves for pruning and burn all discarded wood and canes. Hoe only lightly around roots, water plants well, especially once they start fruiting, and protect all fruit diligently from birds. Growing on a largish scale almost certainly means erecting a netting cage. Then you can sit back and reap the rewards of your labours.

FRUIT ROUND-UP

Alpine strawberry A perennial strawberry which you can grow from seed. Plant it under heat (for example, in a propagator) in February and March, harden off the seedlings and plant out, after the last frosts, in a moist, shady position. Without heat plant seeds in April, but be prepared to wait until the following year for a sizeable crop.

You can harvest the small, cone-shaped fruits all through summer and autumn, but for late cropping it is best to sacrifice the first fruits and pick off the early blossom. Varieties include Délices, Ruegen and – a bird-cheater – Alpine Yellow, with sun-gold fruits.

Bilberry Smaller and less juicy than blueberries, bilberries grow wild in northern Europe and Asia and ripen in midsummer. The bushes can occasionally be found in specialist nurseries.

Blackberry Cultivated blackberries like a reasonably well-drained but heavy soil. The canes can extend to 4m (13ft) and need to be woven in and out of wire supports or tied to a wall or fence. You can increase your stock by rooting cuttings taken from the tips of canes in July and August, to plant out, once they have rooted, in the autumn.

There's a variety which grows upright, Wilson's Early, and a thornless variety, Oregon Giant, which ripens in September and October and avoids the battling-with-barbed-wire element of gathering wild berries.

Blueberry In May the bush is a mass of white, bell-shaped flowers, from July to September it is heavy with round blue-black fruits (which, incidentally, don't stain the fingers), and in the autumn the leaves turn variegated red. It likes full sun or partial shade, dislikes lime or chalky soil, and grows to a height of 1.75m (5ft). Gold Traube is a 'giant'-fruiting variety.

Boysenberry A hybrid of US origin with a strong resemblance to the loganberry, it does well on light soils, survives drought but is not hardy to the fiercest of winters. The deep crimson fruits, harvested from early July, are sharp-tasting but good in compotes and preserves.

Cranberry With their bitter-sweetness, even cultivated cranberries *taste* wild, and few varieties can be eaten raw. One low-growing variety, which makes an evergreen ground cover, is Pilgrim, with extra-large, brilliant red fruits that are harvested in the autumn. You can store cranberries simply – they will keep in the refrigerator in a covered jar of water for up to eight months – or make them into traditional preserves and desserts.

Currants Blackcurrants and redcurrants were first cultivated in Europe in the 16th century. White currants, actually a very pale green, are an albino strain of the red fruits, and have a sweeter, less strident flavour. The small round fruits are carried in large trusses, rather like bunches of grapes.

Currants are greedy for space. Plant the bushes soon after the end of October 1.75m (5ft) apart with 2m (6ft) between rows. Red and white currants can also be grown as single and double cordons, 40cm (16in) and 60cm (2ft) apart respectively. They like a good, rich and slightly acid soil and full sun, though they will tolerate partial shade. It is recommended to treat currant bushes with a lime sulphur spray when the first flowers open, and then three weeks later to protect them against mites.

Blackcurrant varieties begin with Boskoop Giant, the first to crop, then Wellington XXX, Seabrook's Black, Malling Jet and Amos Black. Redcurrants include Laxton's No. 1, Red Lake, Jonkheer van Tets and the late-cropping Wilson's Long Bunch. White Grape, Weisse Perle and the extra-sweet white Versailles are all mid-season white currants.

Gooseberry Normally grown as tightly compact and painfully prickly bushes, the gooseberry is the most adaptable of soft fruits. You can grow them as cordons trained along a wall or supporting frame and even as a fruitful hedge.

They are not over-fussy about soil conditions and will thrive in practically any type, from clay to sandy loam. For the highest yield, the soil should be well drained, enriched with well-rotted manure or compost and given a light dressing of potash. Avoid high-nitrogen fertilizers, which invite an attack of mildew.

Buy two- or three-year-old bushes and plant them from autumn through to early spring. Give each bush 1.2m (4ft) space all round, and plant single, double or triple cordons from 40-80cm (16-32in) apart. Once you have established plants, you can propagate them by taking cuttings from first-year wood in late September or early October.

Given the right conditions, the bushes will crop heavily and it is advisable – and delightful! – to pick the small early fruits of both dessert and cooking varieties from early May to encourage continuous cropping. Use these unripe (and rather sour) fruits in desserts and preserves.

Dessert gooseberries, when left to ripen on the bush until July and August, are one of the most delicious summer fruits, with a firm texture and fresh flavour and can, of course, also be used for cooking. Whinham's Industry has large, oval fruits which become deep purplish pink, while the fruits of Leveller, by contrast, are bright yellow-green and heavily veined. Careless carries heavy crops of firm, small green berries for cooking and preserving.

Your bushes will not bear fruit at all unless you remember to cover them as early as November, when the bullfinches start swooping at the first appearance of the buds. It doesn't matter what you use – old netting, soft curtaining, cheesecloth, bird-scaring fibre – but protect the bushes right through the winter and spring.

Huckleberry This is a semi-tropical plant with small black berries too bitter to eat raw but delicious in pies, puddings and preserves. Sow the seeds under glass in spring, prick out into boxes or pots and transplant into the garden once there is no danger of frost. Allow 30cm (12in) between each plant and 1m (3ft) between rows. One word of warning: the plant and berries look remarkably like deadly nightshade and have been known to be discarded in their prime!

Loganberry A fan-trained or horizontally woven loganberry cane is an ideal way to use – and conceal – a fence, wall or partition. The canes like a good, medium loam or light soil, well dug with organic matter.

Flowering begins in late May and continues after cropping starts in July, so even in frost pockets some harvest is guaranteed. Like other hybrid berries, the long oval, deep red fruits are self-fertile. The Thornless variety makes harvesting more pleasant.

Raspberry Here's a fruit that works so hard to fill your baskets with the very essence of summer only 18 months after planting that it pays to give it near-perfect conditions. The canes like a well-drained but not too dry, loamy soil, rich in organic matter, and will fall far short of expectations in undernourished or soggy ground.

Get them off to a good start by digging a trench 30cm (12in) deep and 75cm (30in) wide, and layering it with compost. Once the canes have taken up residence, you will never be able to feed the roots this thoroughly again. Rows should run from north to south and, in an open site, have good protection from wind.

Plant canes from late October, 45cm (18in) apart in rows 1.75m (5ft) apart, supporting them and tying them to horizontal wires. Two weeks after planting, take courage, cut the canes to 25cm (10in) from the ground, and anticipate a harvest the year after next.

Most varieties fruit from late June to August, some in September and October. Malling Jewel, Promise, Delight and Leo all bear the name of Malling Research Station, in Kent. Other early varieties include Glen Cora and Haida, which has short sturdy canes and needs no staking. Zeva is an autumn cropper.

Strawberry The plants like well-manured loamy and slightly acid soil, and will tolerate chalk. Give them the sunniest possible position and diligent maintenance. A neglected strawberry bed equals a disappointing crop. Set plants in the ground in August and September for fruiting the following year or in late autumn or spring for harvest the year after; in this case nip off the blossom in the intervening season – the plants won't be strong enough to bring it to fruition.

Set plants 38-45cm (15-18in) apart with 75cm (2½ft) between rows. Dig two holes for each plant, dividing the roots between them; the crown sits on the soil surface. Alternatively, make a shallow tunnel of black polythene and set plants in rows along it; this protects them from excessive damp and consequent mould.

Remove runners as they appear, though by August they are your propagation material; you simply peg them

down in pots or in the ground. Keep the beds meticulously weeded and tuck straw around the plants, under the leaves, once they start fruiting. Use cloches to encourage both early and late fruiting. Net and bait the plants against birds and slugs, and spray them with derris dust against aphids.

Cambridge Rival is an early variety; Royal Sovereign wins points for flavour but is prone to diseases; Cambridge Favourite, Grandee and Tamella are all good mid-season choices; Templar and Cambridge Late Pine crop well into the autumn; and Gento and Bordurella are 'perpetual' fruiting varieties, or remontants.

Tayberry A hybrid similar to loganberry, it has purplish red fruits up to 5cm (2in) long, which are good for desserts and preserves, and freeze well. The bush grows to 2m (6ft) high and crops from early July to mid August.

Wineberry Also known as the Japanese wineberry, the canes have numerous thin red spines and small bright red pippy fruits. They are good for flavouring spirits; make wineberry gin as you do sloe gin.

Worcester berry The small black gooseberry-like fruits reveal the parentage. The bush is a cross between the Whinham's Industry variety of gooseberry (from which it takes its cultivation requirements) and a blackcurrant.

Youngberry Hybrid cane fruit, very similar to the boysenberry.

NEW ENGLAND FAVOURITES

*The Pilgrims who landed in New England found a rich
and colourful wild harvest of native North American berries –
cranberries, of course, blueberries, huckleberries,
dewberries and others. With characteristic ingenuity, they adapted
their own recipes to use these fruits, cousins
of those back home, and these dishes have become firm favourites.*

CHICKEN & CRANBERRY PIE

*This pie, with the spectacular layer of
cranberries through the centre, is an
attractive centrepiece for a buffet, and
ideal to take on a special picnic.*

275g (10oz) flour
salt
65g (2½oz) butter
65g (2½oz) lard
3-4 × 15ml spoons (3-4tbls) water
1 egg, beaten, to glaze

FILLING
1.5kg (3¼lb) oven-ready or boiling chicken
1 bay leaf
a few parsley stalks
25g (1oz) butter
1 medium onion, peeled and chopped
1 garlic clove, peeled and crushed
175g (6oz) button mushrooms, chopped
1 × 15ml spoon (1tbls) chopped parsley
freshly ground black pepper
120ml (4fl oz) water
250g (9oz) sugar
500g (1¼lb) cranberries
1 × 5ml (1tsp) powdered gelatine

1   Put the chicken into a pan with the
bay leaf and parsley. Cover with water,
bring to the boil, cover the pan and
simmer for about 1 hour, or until the
chicken is cooked.
2   Lift out the chicken. Skim the fat
from the stock and discard the herbs.
Reserve the stock. Cut the meat from
the bones and chop it roughly.
3   Melt the butter and fry the onion
and garlic over moderate heat for 3
minutes, stirring once or twice. Add
the mushrooms and cook for 2 minutes more. Stir in the parsley and
season the mixture with salt and pepper. Set aside to cool.
4   Put the water and sugar into a pan,

stir over low heat to dissolve the
sugar, then increase the heat and bring
to the boil. Boil for 5 minutes. Add the
cranberries and simmer for 10 minutes, stirring occasionally, or until the
sauce thickens. Set aside to cool.
5   To make the pastry, sift together
the flour and salt. Rub in the butter
and lard until the mixture is like fine
crumbs. Sprinkle on the water and mix
to a firm dough. Knead the dough on a
lightly floured board until it is smooth.
6   Divide the dough into 3 pieces.
Roll two pieces to circles 18cm (7in) in
diameter. Place one circle in the base
of a greased cake tin of that size and
dampen the edge. Roll out the third
piece to make a long strip 13cm (5in)
thick. Place the strip around the side of
the tin and press it to seal the join.
7   Place half the chicken mixture in
the pastry case. Cover with the cranberries and then with the remaining
chicken. Dampen the top of the pastry
strip and press the lid in place.
8   Re-roll the pastry trimmings and
cut leaf shapes.
9   Brush the pastry top with the egg,
press a hole in the centre, arrange the
decoration and brush the leaves with
the glaze.
10   Bake the pie in the oven preheated to 200°C, 400°F, gas 6 for 30
minutes. Reduce the heat to 180°C,
350°F, gas 4 and continue cooking the
pie for 40-45 minutes.
11   Stand the tin on a wire rack and
leave to cool.
12   Dissolve the gelatine in 100ml
(3½fl oz) of heated chicken stock.
Leave it to cool slightly, then pour it
into the pie through the hole in the lid.
Leave the pie for about 2 hours before
serving, for the jelly to set. Garnish
with a little fresh parsley.

SERVES 6-8

BLUEBERRY MUFFINS

250g (9oz) self-raising flour
2 × 5ml spoons (2tsp) baking powder
½ × 5ml spoon (½tsp) salt
100g (4oz) caster sugar
1 egg, beaten
250ml (8fl oz) buttermilk
50g (2oz) butter, melted
150g (5oz) blueberries

1   Sift together the flour, baking
powder and salt and stir in the sugar.
Beat in the egg, buttermilk and melted
butter and beat the batter until it is
smooth. Stir in the blueberries.
2   Pour the batter into 12 greased
muffin tins.
3   Bake the muffins in the oven,
preheated to 220°C, 425°F, gas 7, for
20-25 minutes, until they are well risen
and firm but springy to the touch.
4   Cool the muffins in the tins for 2-3
minutes, then turn them out. Serve
them warm with clotted cream.

MAKES 12 MUFFINS

Variation Other firm, soft fruits can be
substituted for blueberries – blackcurrants and redcurrants both give
lovely results.

For the next morning

*Tender, melt-in-the-mouth muffins speckled
with blueberries are a favourite breakfast
dish. You can make the batter the night
before, then beat it well and stir in the
fruit just before cooking.*

BLUEBERRY GRUNT

This pudding was first made by the Pilgrims from the wild berries they found in the New England countryside. Without quite their pioneer spirit or home-grown produce you could use frozen berries.

500g (1¼lb) blueberries, bilberries or blackberries
100g (4oz) caster sugar
225g (8oz) flour
2 × 5ml spoons (2tsp) baking powder
large pinch of ground cinnamon
salt
25g (1oz) butter
100ml (3½fl oz) milk

1   Toss the fruit in half of the sugar and put it in the base of a greased 1 litre (1¾ pint) pudding bowl.
2   Sift together the flour, baking powder, cinnamon and salt. Rub in the butter until the mixture is like fine crumbs. Stir in the remaining sugar. Pour in just enough milk to make a soft dough.
3   Spoon the dough into the bowl and level the top.
4   Cover the bowl with a piece of foil, pleated along the centre to allow for expansion. Tie the foil under the rim.
5   Place the bowl on a trivet or a folded cloth in a large pan with boiling water to come half-way up the side, or in the top of a steaming pan.
6   Cover the pan and boil for 1¼ hours, topping up with more boiling water as needed.
7   Run a knife around the inside of the bowl and turn out the pudding on to a heated serving plate. Serve the pudding hot, cut into wedges.

Clotted cream makes a lovely accompaniment, in keeping with the farmhouse origins of this pudding. Soured cream stirred with a little orange rind and 1 × 5ml spoon (1tsp) of orange juice is just as good.

SERVES 4

Native North American fruits add their sharp, tangy flavour to a variety of dishes, to Chicken and cranberry pie *(below, right)* and *steamed Blueberry grunt (below, left).*

STRAWBERRY JELLO CHEESECAKE

50g (2oz) butter
25g (1oz) caster sugar flavoured with rosemary (see p. 33)
120g (4½oz) chocolate-covered digestive biscuits

FILLING
150g (5oz) packet strawberry jelly
150ml (¼ pint) boiling water
250g (9oz) full-fat soft cheese
2 eggs, separated
100g (4oz) caster sugar flavoured with rosemary
300ml (½ pint) double cream, whipped
250g (9oz) strawberries, hulled
scented geranium leaves, to decorate

1   Melt the butter and sugar and stir over low heat until the sugar has dissolved. Crush the biscuits and stir the crumbs into the melted butter.
2   Press the mixture into a greased 20cm (8in) flan case. Chill in the refrigerator.
3   To make the filling, break the jelly into squares, stir in the boiling water and stir until it has dissolved. Set aside to cool.
4   Beat the cheese until it is smooth and beat in the egg yolks, one at a time. Beat in half of the sugar and slowly pour on the cooled jelly, stirring. Fold in half of the cream. Chill for about 20 minutes, until the mixture is syrupy and beginning to set.
5   Whisk the egg whites until they are stiff and fold in the remaining sugar. Fold this meringue into the jelly mixture.
6   Pour the filling into the biscuit case and level the top. Chill in the refrigerator for at least 2 hours.
7   Pipe the remaining cream around the top and base of the cheesecake. Decorate with the strawberries and small scented leaves.

SERVES 6-8

Set the style

Americans claim the uncooked 'set' cheesecake as their own. Try other popular variations of matching fruit and jelly such as raspberries and blackcurrants, or strawberry jelly with cranberries.

RASPBERRY CREAM PIE

For 'pie' in American cookery, read 'flan' in Britain! This one uses an old country recipe for vinegar pastry, which is especially good for a pie with a rich creamy filling.

200g (7oz) flour
salt
75g (3oz) butter
1 × 5ml spoon (1tsp) sugar
1 egg
4 × 5ml spoons (4tsp) water
1 × 5ml spoon (1tsp) distilled vinegar

FILLING
50g (2oz) flour
120g (4½oz) light Muscovado sugar
salt
2 eggs
300ml (½ pint) double cream
juice of 2 oranges
1 × 5ml spoon (1tsp) grated orange rind
350g (12oz) raspberries

1   To make the pastry, sift together the flour and salt. Rub in the butter until the mixture is like fine crumbs, then stir in the sugar. Beat the egg with the water and vinegar. Pour this into the dry ingredients and mix to form a firm dough.
2   Roll out the dough on a lightly floured board. Line a greased 25cm (10in) flan ring with the dough. Trim the edges, and prick the base all over with a fork.
3   Line the flan case with foil and fill it with 'baking beans'. Bake the case 'blind' in the oven, preheated to 190°C, 375°F, gas 5, for 25 minutes. Remove the beans and foil and dry the case in the oven for a further 5 minutes.
4   To make the filling, put the flour, sugar and salt in a bowl, fitted over a pan of simmering water, or into the top of a double boiler. Beat in the eggs and cream. Stir over simmering water until the custard thickens. Do not allow the water to boil, or to touch the upper container.
5   Stir in the orange juice and rind and cook for a further 5 minutes. Set the custard aside to cool slightly.
6   Pour the custard into the pie shell. When it has cooled, arrange the raspberries on top and serve with cream.

SERVES 6

HUCKLEBERRY DUMPLINGS

225g (8oz) self-raising flour
1 × 15ml spoon (1tbls) baking powder
salt
25g (1oz) butter
1 × 15ml spoon (1tbls) caster sugar
about 250ml (8fl oz) milk
500g (1¼lb) huckleberries
2 bay leaves
4-5 × 15ml spoons (4-5tbls) demerara sugar

SAUCE
120ml (4fl oz) water
100g (4oz) sugar
strip of thinly pared orange rind
juice of 1 orange

1   Sift the flour, baking powder and salt. Rub in the butter until the mixture is like coarse meal, then stir in the sugar. Stir in just enough of the milk to make a stiff dough. Fold in 100g (4oz) of the huckleberries.
2   To make the sauce, put the water, sugar, orange rind and juice into a pan and stir over low heat until the sugar has dissolved. Increase the heat, bring to the boil and boil for 5 minutes. Add the remaining huckleberries and simmer for about 12 minutes, until the fruit is just tender. Discard the strip of orange rind. Keep the sauce warm.
3   Form the dough into small balls about the size of a golf ball. Drop them into a large pan of boiling salted water with the bay leaves. Keep the water at a brisk boil. Cook the dumplings for 10-12 minutes, until they are light and fluffy and rise to the surface.
4   Lift out the dumplings with a draining spoon. Dry them with kitchen paper and toss them at once in the demerara sugar.

Serve the dumplings hot, with the sauce separately.

SERVES 4

Variation Cranberries, blackcurrants, redcurrants and white currants (though these lack the colour contrast) can all be used instead of huckleberries.

HUCKLEBERRY WAFFLES

150g (5oz) self-raising flour
½ × 5ml spoon (½tsp) salt
½ × 5ml spoon (½tsp) baking powder
2 eggs
50g (2oz) butter, melted
300ml (½ pint) buttermilk
300ml (½ pint) soured cream, to serve

FILLING
75g (3oz) sugar
100ml (3½fl oz) water
350g (12oz) huckleberries
(or other soft fruit)
2 scented geranium leaves

1   To make the filling, stir the sugar
and water over low heat until the sugar
has dissolved. Increase the heat, bring
to the boil and boil for 10 minutes. Add
the berries and geranium leaves and
simmer for 5-6 minutes, until tender.
Do not allow to break up. Set aside.
2   To make the waffles, sift together
the flour, salt and baking powder. Beat
in the eggs, one at a time, and the
melted butter. Gradually pour on the
buttermilk, beating constantly. Beat
until the batter is smooth.
3   Heat a waffle iron and grease it if
necessary. Pour in just enough of the
batter to cover. Close the iron and
cook the waffles until they are crisp
and golden brown. Keep each batch
warm while you cook the remainder.
4   Gently reheat the huckleberry filling. Sandwich pairs of waffles together
with the fruit between them. Serve hot,
with soured cream.

SERVES 4

BERRY BOWL WITH BUTTERSCOTCH SAUCE

150g (5oz) strawberries, hulled
150g (5oz) raspberries
150g (5oz) loganberries

SAUCE
50g (2oz) butter
75g (3oz) light Muscovado sugar
25g (1oz) caster sugar flavoured with bay
(see p.33)
100g (4oz) golden syrup
150ml (¼ pint) double cream

1   To make the sauce, heat the butter, sugars and golden syrup over low
heat, stirring to dissolve the sugar.
Increase the heat, bring to the boil and
simmer for 5 minutes.
2   Gradually stir in the cream and
beat over low heat until the sauce is
smooth and glossy.
3   Toss all the fruits together in a
bowl. Drizzle a little of the sauce over
to decorate. Serve the rest of the sauce
separately, either hot or cold.

SERVES 4

Variation For a more authentic version of the melt-in-the-mouth sauce,
replace the everyday golden syrup
with corn syrup or much more expensive maple syrup.

CRANBERRY SAUCE

*This sauce, made from wild
cranberries, was served with turkey at
the first Thanksgiving Dinner. No
celebration dinner would be complete
without it!*

250g (9oz) sugar
250ml (8fl oz) water
juice and grated rind of 1 orange
350g (12oz) fresh or frozen cranberries

1   Put the sugar and water into a pan
and stir over low heat to dissolve the
sugar. Bring to the boil and boil for 5
minutes.
2   Add the orange juice, orange rind
and cranberries and stir with a
wooden spoon, taking care not to
crush the fruit. Simmer for 5 minutes
until the sauce is translucent and
berry-bright.
3   Cool the sauce, then pour it into a
lidded container. Store it in the refrigerator for up to 2 weeks, or freeze.

MAKES ABOUT 450ML (¾ PINT)

RICE & CRANBERRY STUFFING

*This quantity is enough to stuff a 5kg
(11lb) turkey; halve the ingredients, or
divide as appropriate, for a smaller
bird.*

350g (12oz) long-grain rice
salt
75g (3oz) butter
1 large onion, peeled and finely chopped
2 × 15ml spoons (2tbls) chopped parsley
1 × 5ml spoon (1tsp) chopped thyme
a pinch of ground cloves
a pinch of grated nutmeg
300ml (½ pint) cranberry sauce (see above)
freshly ground black pepper

1   Cook the rice in a large pan of
boiling, salted water for 10-12 minutes,
until it is just tender. Drain the rice
into a colander, run cold water
through it and drain it again.
2   Melt the butter and fry the onion
over moderate heat for 3-4 minutes,
stirring once or twice. Remove from
the heat.
3   Stir in the rice, herbs, spices and
cranberry sauce. Season with salt and
pepper and set aside to cool before
packing into the turkey.

HIGHLAND DINING

*Living off the fat of the land in the Highlands
means enjoying a varied menu, based on wild and cultivated
berries such as cranberries, blueberries and bilberries; hardy root
crops, like turnips and swedes; oatmeal and, of course, game shot
on the moors. Our recipes show how imaginatively – and
temptingly – these local ingredients are brought together.*

GAME & RASPBERRY SOUP

75g (3oz) butter
2 pheasant carcasses, chopped
4 rashers bacon, halved
100g (4oz) calves' liver, sliced
1.75 litres (3 pints) chicken stock
salt
freshly ground black pepper
2 juniper berries, crushed
a few parsley stalks
2 bay leaves
1 carrot, trimmed and halved
2 stalks celery, sliced
1 medium onion, peeled and sliced
250g (9oz) raspberries
4 × 15ml spoons (4tbls) sherry
2 × 5ml spoons (2tsp) flour

1   Melt 50g (2oz) of the butter in a pan and cook the pheasant bones, bacon and liver over moderate heat, stirring frequently, until they are evenly brown. Add the stock, salt, pepper, juniper berries, parsley, bay leaves, carrot, celery and onion.
2   Bring to the boil, skim off any foam that rises to the top and cover the pan. Simmer, stirring often, for 2 hours.
3   Strain the stock. Scrape off the flesh from the pheasant bones. Cut the rind from the bacon. Mince the pheasant, bacon and liver, or work it in a food processor.
4   Reserve a few raspberries to garnish. Sieve the remainder.
5   Return the stock to the pan. Stir in the minced meat, raspberry purée and sherry. Heat gently.
6   Make a paste with the remaining butter and the flour and stir it into the soup. Stir the soup until it thickens slightly. Garnish it with the reserved raspberries.

SERVES 6

CRANBERRIED TURNIPS

These clear, bright red berries turn an everyday root crop into a dish fit for a dinner party – and a perfect accompaniment to roast game.

4 small turnips, peeled and diced
salt
100g (4oz) cranberries
3 × 15ml spoons (3tbls) clear honey
25g (1oz) butter
freshly ground black pepper

1   Steam the turnips over a pan of boiling, salted water for 3-4 minutes, until they are barely tender.
2   Put the cranberries, honey and butter in a pan over low heat, until the honey and butter are blended.
3   Put the turnips in a baking dish, stir the cranberry mixture and pour it over them.
4   Cover the dish and bake in the oven, preheated to 190°C, 375°F, gas 5, for 20 minutes.

SERVES 4

Right. All set for a Highland feast of Pigeon breasts with loganberries, a perfect partnership of rich meat with tangy fruit, and Bilberry kissel with junket.

No good cook misses the opportunity, with pheasant carcasses to spare, of making one of Scotland's classic dishes, Game soup.

PIGEON BREASTS WITH LOGANBERRIES

The meat is first marinated in red wine and oil, to moisten and tenderize it, so start this dish the day before you wish to serve it.

4 pigeons
1 medium onion, peeled and sliced
40g (1½oz) butter
2 × 5ml spoons (2tsp) flour
250g (9oz) loganberries
2 × 15ml spoons (2tbls) raspberry jelly
freshly ground black pepper

MARINADE
3 × 15ml spoons (3tbls) olive oil
1 medium onion, peeled and chopped
1 stalk celery, sliced
a few parsley stalks
2 garlic cloves, peeled and chopped
6-8 green peppercorns, lightly crushed
4 juniper berries, lightly crushed
salt
150ml (¼ pint) red wine

1 Heat the oil for the marinade and fry the onion and celery over moderate heat for 3 minutes, stirring once or twice. Add the remaining marinade ingredients and bring slowly to the boil. Boil for 5 minutes, then set aside to cool.

2 Cut the breasts from the pigeons and dry them. Place them in a shallow dish and set aside.

3 Chop the pigeon carcasses and cook them in a non-stick pan over moderate heat, turning them frequently to brown them on all sides. Just cover them with water, add the onion, cover the pan and bring to the boil. Simmer for 30-45 minutes, until the stock is well reduced. Skim any foam from the stock and strain it. Discard the carcasses.

4 Pour the cooled marinade over the pigeon breasts, cover and set aside in a cool place for several hours, or overnight.

5 Lift out the pigeon breasts and dry them. Strain and reserve the marinade to make the sauce.

6 Melt the butter in a pan and fry the pigeon breasts over moderate heat for 5-8 minutes on each side, until they are just cooked. Do not overcook them, or they will become tough.

7 Lift out the pigeon breasts and keep them warm. Stir in the flour, then gradually pour on the marinade and 150ml (¼ pint) of the reserved pigeon stock. Bring to the boil and boil for 2-3 minutes. Add the loganberries and raspberry jelly, season the sauce with salt and pepper and simmer for 5 minutes, or until the fruit is tender.

8 Pour the sauce over the pigeon breasts and, if liked, garnish with a spray of leaves.

Serve with potatoes boiled in their skins and a green vegetable such as curly kale.

SERVES 4

Variation You can use redcurrant jelly instead or raspberry jelly if you wish. The loganberry flavour will dominate.

PHEASANT & BILBERRY CASSEROLE

You can use the pheasant carcasses left after making this dish to make Game soup (see page 86)

2 pheasants, dressed
65g (2½oz) butter
2 × 15ml spoons (2tbls) vegetable oil
1 small onion, peeled and chopped
225g (8oz) bacon, minced
1 garlic clove, peeled and crushed
salt
freshly ground black pepper
1 bay leaf
6 × 15ml spoons (6tbls) chicken stock
250g (9oz) bilberries
150ml (¼ pint) single cream
2 × 15ml spoons (2tbls) brandy
100g (4oz) button mushrooms, sliced
watercress, to garnish

1   Fry the pheasants in 25g (1oz) of the butter and the oil in a flameproof casserole until they are well browned on all sides. Remove them from the dish and set aside.
2   Melt 15g (½oz) of the remaining butter and fry the onion, bacon and garlic over moderate heat for about 5 minutes.
3   Return the pheasants to the casserole, breast sides down, season with salt and pepper, add the bay leaves and stock, and bring to the boil.
4   Cover the dish and cook in the oven, preheated to 170°C, 325°F, gas 3, for 1 hour.
5   Stir in the bilberries, cream and brandy, cover and cook for a further 4-5 minutes. Lift out the birds.
6   Melt the remaining butter in a small pan. Fry the mushrooms for 3-4 minutes, then stir them into the sauce. Taste and adjust seasoning.
7   Slice the pheasants and arrange the meat on a heated serving dish. Pour over a little of the sauce to garnish the dish, and serve the rest separately. Arrange the watercress.
   Game chips are the traditional accompaniment. They are made with potatoes sliced paper-thin on a mandoline, washed, dried and deep fried.

SERVES 4

ROAST GROUSE WITH CRANBERRIES

2 grouse, dressed
salt
freshly ground black pepper
100g (4oz) butter
1 × 5ml spoon (1tsp) grated orange rind
175g (6oz) cranberries
4 × 15ml spoons (4tbls) rolled oats
4 sprays rosemary
4 rashers bacon, rind removed
2 × 5ml spoons (2tsp) flour
8 × 15ml spoon (8tbls) chicken stock
1 × 15ml spoon (1tbls) whisky (optional)

SAUCE
1 small onion, peeled and halved
2 sprays rosemary
200ml (7fl oz) milk
25g (1oz) butter
50g (2oz) white breadcrumbs
pinch of grated nutmeg
30ml (2tbls) double cream

1   Season the grouse inside and out with salt and pepper. Melt half the butter. Stir together the orange rind, cranberries, rolled oats and pour on the butter. Mix well. Pack the grouse with the cranberry mixture.
2   Place the birds in a roasting pan with the remaining butter. Place a spray of rosemary on the breasts and cover with a rasher of bacon.
3   Roast the birds in the oven, preheated to 190°C, 375°F, gas 5, for 40 minutes. Remove the bacon, baste the birds with the pan juices and continue cooking for 10 minutes.
4   To make the sauce, put the onion, rosemary, milk and butter into a pan and bring slowly to the boil. Add the breadcrumbs and nutmeg and simmer for 15 minutes. Remove the onion and rosemary and beat the sauce until it is smooth. Cover the top closely with a piece of wetted greaseproof paper to stop a skin forming, and set aside.
5   Transfer the grouse to a heated serving dish. Pour off most of the fat from the pan. Stir in the flour, then pour on the stock and whisky (if you like it). Bring to the boil, season with salt and pepper and simmer for 2-3 minutes.
6   Stir the cream into the bread sauce and reheat gently. Serve the bread sauce and the gravy separately.

SERVES 4

BILBERRY KISSEL WITH JUNKET

500g (1¼lb) bilberries
4 × 15ml spoons (4tbls) heather honey
150ml (¼ pint) water
3 × 15ml spoons (3tbls) fine oatmeal
scented geranium leaves, to decorate

JUNKET
600ml (1 pint) milk
1 × 15ml spoon (1tbls) liquid rennet
3 × 15ml spoons (3tbls) whisky
grated nutmeg

1   Put the bilberries, honey and water in a pan over low heat. Simmer for about 10 minutes, until the fruit is just tender.
2   Stir a little of the juice into the oatmeal and mix to a smooth paste. Mix it into the fruit and stir over low heat until the mixture thickens. Turn it into a serving dish and set aside to cool.
3   To make the junket, heat the milk without boiling. Remove from the heat, stir in the rennet and whisky and pour into heatproof serving dishes. Leave undisturbed at room temperature to cool.
4   Sprinkle a little grated nutmeg over the junket before serving. Decorate the edge of the fruit dish with a spray of scented leaves; the combination of the purple-coloured fruit and the fresh green is most attractive.

SERVES 4

Variation You can substitute blackcurrants for the bilberries or make a lovely berry-bright kissel with redcurrants, in just the same way.
   If you prefer, you can liquidize the fruit and juice in a blender before thickening the purée with the oatmeal. This makes a half-liquid, half-solid consistency and is sometimes called 'swaying fruit'.

What's in a name?

Bilberries, small, round, blueblack and somewhat smaller than blueberries, have a number of romantic-sounding names. They are known variously as blaeberries, whortleberries and hurtleberries and, in France, as myrtilles.

RASPBERRY CREAMS

6 × 15ml spoons (6tbls) medium oatmeal
450ml (¾ pint) double cream
4 × 15ml spoons (4tbls) caster sugar
8 × 15ml spoons (8tbls) whisky
350g (12oz) raspberries

1   Heat the grill to low. Spread the oatmeal on a baking tray and toast it for 3-4 minutes, stirring frequently, until it is light brown. Set aside to cool.
2   Whip the cream until it is stiff. Stir the sugar into the whisky and stir it, little by little, into the cream. Do not add too much at once or the cream will curdle.
3   Reserve 12 of the best raspberries and 2 × 5ml spoons (2tsp) of the toasted oatmeal for decoration. Fold the remaining raspberries and oatmeal into the cream.
4   Divide the dessert between 4 individual serving glasses. Decorate them with the reserved raspberries and oatmeal. Serve chilled.

SERVES 4

Variation As an alternative, use lightly toasted porridge oats in place of the oatmeal. They give a pleasantly nutty texture.

GROSET FOOL

500g (1¼lb) gooseberries
5 × 15ml spoons (5tbls) water
100g (4oz) sugar
2 heads of elderflowers
300ml (½ pint) double cream
herb leaves, to decorate

1   Put the gooseberries in a pan with the water, sugar and elderflowers and stir over low heat until the sugar has dissolved.
2   Remove the flowers and press the fruit through a sieve or a vegetable mill.
3   Whip the cream until it just holds its shape. Gradually fold the fruit purée into it.
4   Divide the dessert between 4 individual serving glasses and decorate each one with herb leaves. The pale green and cream variegated pineapple mint is especially pretty.
Serve with sponge finger biscuits or Almond butter biscuits (see page 93).

SERVES 4

DOUBLE-CRUST FRUIT PIE

175g (6oz) flour
salt
1 × 15ml spoon (1tbls) icing sugar
40g (1½oz) butter
40g (1½oz) lard
1 small egg, separated
1 × 15ml spoon (1tbls) water
3 × 15ml spoons (3tbls) caster sugar

FILLING
250g (9oz) redcurrants
350g (12oz) raspberries
100g (4oz) caster sugar
2 × 15ml spoons (2tbls) fine oatmeal

1   Sift together the flour, salt and icing sugar. Rub in the butter and lard until the mixture is like fine crumbs. Beat the egg yolk and water, add to the dry ingredients and mix to a firm dough.
2   Divide the dough into 2 pieces. Roll it out on a lightly floured board. Line a greased 17.5cm (7in) pie plate with one piece.
3   Mix together the filling ingredients and fill the pie case.
4   Dampen the edge of the pie and cover with the second piece of dough. Trim and flute the edges. Re-roll the trimmings and cut them into decorative shapes.
5   Lightly beat the egg white. Brush it over the pastry top. Arrange the decoration and brush the shapes with egg white. Sprinkle the caster sugar over the top.

6   Bake the pie in the oven, preheated to 190°C, 375°F, gas 5, for 30 minutes. Cover the top with foil if it browns too quickly and the sugar starts to burn. Serve warm or cold with cream.

SERVES 4

BILBERRIES IN WHISKY

After dinner in the Highlands, what could be more pleasant, or appropriate, than a small glass of bilberry liqueur?

250g (9oz) bilberries
120g (4½oz) sugar
450ml (¾ pint) whisky

1   Prick the bilberries with a sterilized darning needle and put them into a screw-topped jar.
2   Add the sugar and whisky, cover the jar and shake well.
3   Leave the jar in a cool, dark place for at least 3 months, shaking it occasionally.
4   Strain off the bilberries, pressing them against the side of the sieve to extract the maximum flavour.
5   Pour the liqueur into a bottle and cover it. Label the bottle and store for at least 3 months away from the light, before drinking.

MAKES 450ML (¾ PINT)

SUMMER TREATS

*It's all too short, the season when you can line baskets
and punnets with strawberry leaves and pile them high with the
glistening berries and currants of summer. The question is
whether to serve them now, in desserts and tea-time treats,
or to preserve them for the months to come.
There's nothing for it – you'll simply have to do both!*

RODGROD

250g (9oz) strawberries, hulled
250g (9oz) redcurrants
100g (4oz) caster sugar
300ml (½ pint) water
25g (1oz) cornflour
2 bay leaves
150ml (¼ pint) whipping cream, whipped
1 chocolate flake bar, crushed

1   Reserve 4 strawberries to decorate
the dessert. Put the remaining strawberries, the redcurrants, sugar and
water into a blender or food processor
(you may have to do this in 2 batches)
and blend to a purée.
2   Sieve the purée to remove the
pips.
3   Stir a little of the purée into the
cornflour to make a smooth paste.
4   Put the remaining purée into a pan
with the bay leaves and bring slowly to
the boil. Blend the purée with the
cornflour paste and stir over moderate
heat until the purée thickens and
clears. Remove from the heat and
discard the bay leaves.
5   Pour the purée into 4 individual
bowls – cool the dessert first if they
are not heatproof – and leave to
become cold.
6   Pipe cream to decorate the dessert
and place the reserved strawberries on
top and sprinkle with a little chocolate
flake. Serve chilled.
Serve with Almond butter biscuits
(see page 93).

SERVES 4

*Rodgrod, a soft fruit purée as bright as the
berries themselves, is shown with Almond
butter biscuits (recipe on page 93).*

RASPBERRY JELLY

*This jelly is good with roast game,
poultry and pork, and as a tea-time
spread. It can also be used to glaze fruit
flans and tarts.*

1kg (2¼lb) raspberries
4 blackcurrant leaves, washed
about 500g (1¼lb) sugar

1   Put the raspberries and 2 of the
blackcurrant leaves into a pan and stir
them over low heat until the juice
runs. Increase the heat and simmer the
fruit for 30-45 minutes, until it is soft.
Stir and mash it with a wooden spoon
from time to time.
2   Turn the fruit into a scalded jelly
bag and leave it to drain into a bowl
overnight. Do not squeeze the bag, as
this makes the jelly cloudy.

3   Measure the fruit juice and allow
250g (9oz) of sugar to each 300ml (½
pint) of fruit juice.
4   Put the fruit juice and sugar into a
pan with the 2 remaining blackcurrant
leaves and heat over low heat, stirring
occasionally until the sugar has dissolved. Increase the heat, bring to the
boil and fast-boil for 10 minutes, or
until setting point is reached (see page
34). Discard the leaves.
5   Pour the jelly into warmed sterilized jars. Cover the surface with waxed
paper discs and the jars with jam-pot
covers. Cool.
6   Label the jars and store them in a
cool, dry place.

MAKES ABOUT 750G (1½LB)

Variation If you prefer, you can mix
raspberries and redcurrants in equal
proportions.

SCONES WITH STRAWBERRY CREAM

225g (8oz) self-raising flour
1 × 5ml spoon (1tsp) baking powder
¼ × 5ml spoon (¼tsp) salt
a pinch of ground ginger
40g (1½oz) butter
40g (1½oz) caster sugar
1 egg yolk
about 120ml (4fl oz) buttermilk, plus
extra for brushing

FILLING
200ml (7fl oz) double cream
1 egg white
250g (9oz) strawberries, hulled

1   Sift together the flour, baking powder, salt and ginger. Rub in the butter until the mixture is like fine crumbs. Stir in the sugar. Beat the egg yolk and buttermilk and add just enough to make a light dough.
2   Knead the dough lightly. Roll it out on a lightly floured board to a thickness of 2.5cm (1in). Cut the dough into rounds with a 5cm (2in) cutter. Re-roll the trimmings and cut more rounds.
3   Place the scones on a baking sheet and brush the tops with buttermilk.
4   Bake the scones in the oven, preheated to 230°C, 450°F, gas 8, for 10 minutes, until they are well risen and golden brown. Cool the scones on a wire rack.
5   To make the filling, whip the cream. Whisk the egg white until it is stiff, then fold it into the cream. Slice the strawberries, reserving a few whole ones to decorate the bowl. Fold the strawberries into the cream.
6   Serve the scones filled with strawberry cream.

MAKES 10 SCONES

Variation Buttermilk, readily available in health food shops and supermarkets, has just the right acidity to make light, fluffy scones. But if you can't find it, stir 1 × 5ml spoon (1tsp) lemon juice or 2 × 5ml spoons (2tsp) plain yoghurt into milk.

Crisp and snowy Blackcurrant coconut meringues (recipe on page 92) and split Scones with strawberry cream filling are two of the tastiest joys of summer cooking.

UNCOOKED RASPBERRY JAM

1kg (2¼lb) raspberries
1kg (2¼lb) sugar

1   Put the raspberries and sugar into 2 separate heatproof bowls.
2   Heat the fruit and sugar in the oven, preheated to 180°C, 350°F, gas 4, for 25-30 minutes, until very hot.
3   Mix the fruit and sugar together and beat with a wooden spoon until the sugar has dissolved.
4   Pour the jam into warmed sterilized jars. Cover the surface with waxed paper discs and cover the jars with jam-pot covers or screw-on lids. Cool.
5   Label the jars and store in a cool place – the refrigerator is ideal.

MAKES ABOUT 1.5KG (3¼LB)

GOOSEBERRY CURD

1kg (2¼lb) gooseberries
3 × 15ml spoons (3tbls) water
3 scented geranium leaves
75g (3oz) butter
3 eggs, lightly beaten
500g (1¼lb) sugar

1   Simmer the gooseberries with the water and geranium leaves for about 20 minutes, until they are soft.
2   Sieve the fruit, pressing it against the sides to extract the maximum moisture.
3   Put the gooseberry purée, butter, eggs and sugar into a bowl fitted over a pan of simmering water or the top of a double boiler. Cook, stirring frequently, for 25-30 minutes until the curd thickens.
4   Pour the curd into warmed, sterilized jars. Cover the surface with waxed paper discs and cover the jars with jam-pot covers. Cool.
5   Label the jars and store in a cool, dry, dark place. The preserve will keep for 3-4 months.

MAKES ABOUT 1KG (2¼LB)

STRAWBERRY & REDCURRANT JAM

1.5kg (3¼lb) strawberries, hulled
500g (1¼lb) redcurrants
1.75kg (4½lb) sugar

1   Put the strawberries and redcurrants into a pan and stir over low heat until the juice begins to run. Bring to the boil and simmer for about 20 minutes, or until the fruit is tender.
2   Meanwhile, spread the sugar on baking trays and warm it in the oven at 110°C, 225°F, gas ¼.
3   Add the warm sugar to the fruit and stir over low heat until the sugar has dissolved. Increase the heat, bring to the boil and fast-boil for about 15 minutes, or until setting point is reached (see page 34).
4   Pour the jam into warmed, sterilized jars. Cover the surface with waxed paper discs and the jars with jam-pot covers. Cool.
5   Label the jars and store them in a cool, dry place.

MAKES ABOUT 2.75KG (6LB)

BLACKCURRANT COCONUT MERINGUES

2 egg whites
50g (2oz) caster sugar
50g (2oz) demerara sugar
40g (1½oz) desiccated coconut

FILLING
250g (9oz) cooking apples, peeled, cored and sliced
40g (1½oz) sugar
2 × 15ml spoons (2tbls) water
250g (9oz) blackcurrants
150ml (¼ pint) double cream, whipped
scented geranium leaves, to decorate

1   Stiffly whisk the egg whites. Fold in the caster sugar and whisk again. Fold in the demerara sugar and coconut.
2   Line a baking sheet with non-stick silicone paper. Using a large star nozzle, pipe the meringue into 4 circles 11.25cm (4½in) in diameter. Pipe a rim around the outside to make a 'wall'.
3   Bake the meringues in the oven, preheated to 130°C, 250°F, gas ½, for 2 hours, until they are dry.
4   Peel off the silicone paper and cool the meringues on a wire rack.
5   To make the filling, cook the apples with the sugar and water until tender. Purée and return to the pan.
6   Add the blackcurrants and simmer until they are just tender. Cool.
7   Fold the cold fruit mixture into the cream. Fill the meringues just before serving. Decorate with the leaves.

SERVES 4

LINZER TORTE

This is a delicious way of using raspberry jam, in a tart which originated in Linz, in Austria (hence the name). The unblanched almonds, ground complete with their brown skins, give the pastry an unusual depth of colour.

175g (6oz) flour
salt
1 × 5ml spoon (1tsp) ground cinnamon
pinch of ground cloves
150g (5oz) caster sugar
150g (5oz) unblanched almonds, ground
¼ × 5ml spoon (¼tsp) grated lemon rind
175g (6oz) butter, grated
2 × 5ml spoons (2tsp) lemon juice
2 eggs, beaten
250g (9oz) raspberry jam
1 × 15ml spoon (1tbls) icing sugar

1   Sift together the flour, salt and spices. Stir in the caster sugar, ground almonds and lemon rind, and rub in the butter lightly. Sprinkle on the lemon juice and stir in the eggs. Mix to a firm dough, using a palette knife.
2   Knead the dough lightly. Wrap it in cling film or foil and chill it for at least 30 minutes.
3   Cut off one-third of the dough. Press the remainder into a greased and floured 23cm (9in) flan case, pressing it well into the corners and up the sides. Trim the edges and prick the base all over with a fork.
4   Spread the jam over the flan base.
5   Roll out the dough on a lightly floured board and cut it into narrow strips. Dampen the edge of the pastry case and arrange the strips over the top to make an open lattice pattern. Trim the edges and dampen them. Arrange one long strip around the rim to cover the lattice edges.
6   Bake the flan in the oven, preheated to 180°C, 350°F, gas 4, for 40 minutes, until the pastry is dark golden brown.
7   Sift icing sugar over the top. Stand the flan on a wire rack and leave to cool.

SERVES 6

ALMOND BUTTER BISCUITS

175g (6oz) butter
75g (3oz) caster sugar
175g (6oz) flour
25g (1oz) ground almonds
25g (1oz) flaked almonds

1   Beat the butter and sugar until light and fluffy. Add the flour and ground almonds. Mix to a firm dough.
2   Break the dough into walnut-sized pieces and flatten them between your hands.
3   Place the dough rounds well apart on 2 greased baking sheets. Press flaked almonds into the top of each biscuit.
4   Bake in the oven, preheated to 160°C, 325°F, gas 3, for 20 minutes, until the biscuits are golden brown.
5   Allow the biscuits to cool on the baking sheets for 1-2 minutes, then transfer them to a wire rack. Once they are completely cold, store the biscuits in an airtight container, where they will keep fresh for up to 10 days.

MAKES 24 BISCUITS

BLACKCURRANT SYRUP

This is a lovely sauce to serve with ice cream and to stir into plain yoghurt.

1kg (2¼lb) blackcurrants
2 blackcurrant leaves
150ml (¼ pint) water
about 250g (9oz) sugar

1   Put the blackcurrants and leaves into a pan with the water. Cover the pan and simmer for 20 minutes, or until the fruit is soft. Mash it with a wooden spoon.
2   Sieve the fruit, pressing it to extract as much juice as possible.
3   Measure the fruit juice and measure 200g (7oz) sugar to each 500ml (18fl oz) juice.
4   Put the fruit juice and sugar in the pan and stir over low heat until the sugar has dissolved. Increase the heat and fast-boil for 10 minutes.
5   Pour the syrup into warm, sterilized bottles and cover them with corks or non-corrosive lids. Cool.
6   Label the bottles and store them in a cool, dark place.

MAKES ABOUT 750ML (1½ PINTS)

RASPBERRY TRIFLE

500g (1¼lb) raspberries
75g (3oz) caster sugar
2 × 15ml spoons (2tbls) kirsch (optional)
1 layer sponge cake (see p. 30)

CUSTARD
3 egg yolks
25g (1oz) caster sugar
1 × 5ml spoon (1tsp) cornflour
300ml (½ pint) single cream
1 bay leaf
2 × 15ml spoons (2tbls) blanched almonds
25g (1oz) ratafia biscuits

1   Put the raspberries and sugar in a pan and stir over low heat until the sugar has dissolved. Simmer for 5 minutes, stir in the kirsch if you use it, then set aside to cool.
2   Cut the sponge cake to fit the base of a glass dish. Pour on the fruit.
3   To make the custard, beat the egg yolks, sugar and cornflour. Heat the cream with the bay leaf and when it reaches simmering point, pour it on to the egg yolks, beating constantly.
4   Strain the mixture through a sieve into a bowl fitted over a pan of simmering water, or the top of a double boiler. Stir until the custard thickens. Do not allow the water to boil or touch the upper container, or the eggs will scramble.
5   Cool the custard slightly. Pour it over the fruit and set aside to cool.
6   Decorate the top of the trifle with the almonds and ratafia biscuits.

SERVES 4-6

STRAWBERRIES IN TEQUILA

This is a luxury dessert, served with a little of the spirit-flavoured syrup. Any left-over syrup makes a lovely addition to fruit salad, or can be poured over ice cream and other creamy desserts.

500g (1¼lb) sugar
1 bay leaf
750ml (1¼ pints) water
600ml (1 pint) tequila
1.25kg (2¾lb) strawberries, hulled

1   Put the sugar, bay leaf and water in a pan and stir over low heat to dissolve the sugar. Bring to the boil and fast-boil for 5 minutes. Set aside to cool.
2   Stir the tequila into the syrup.
3   Pack the strawberries into sterilized jars and tap the jars to pack them tightly. Take care not to crush the fruit.
4   Pour on the spirit to cover the fruit completely. Cover the jars and leave to cool.
5   Label the jars and store in a cool, dry place – the refrigerator is ideal. Don't worry if the fruit floats to the top of the jars: this is inevitable as the juice is drawn out into the syrup.

FILLS 3 × 750G (1½LB) JARS

BLACKCURRANT GIN

The blackcurrants used to make this gin, steeped in spirit for all those weeks, are far too good to throw away. Serve them, stirred with a little of the liqueur, with ice cream, or as a base for a creamy dessert or kissel.

350g (12oz) blackcurrants
175g (6oz) sugar
450ml (¾ pint) gin

1   Put the blackcurrants in a bowl and crush them to release the juice. Add the sugar and stir until it dissolves. Stir in the gin.
2   Pour the mixture into a jar and put on the lid.
3   Leave the jar in a cool, dark place for 3 months, shaking it frequently.
4   Strain the fruit, pressing it to extract the maximum moisture.
5   Pour the liqueur into a sterilized bottle and store away from the light.

MAKES 450ML (¾ PINT) LIQUEUR

THE GLASSHOUSE

A touch of glass does marvellous things for your plant-raising potential. For a start, it makes spring, or at least spring temperatures, come a little earlier. This means that you can raise seed of half-hardy plants a month earlier, harden off the seedlings and plant them out well ahead of those you could grow outdoors. This is a godsend for anyone who is impatient for their first taste of tender young vegetables – lettuce or courgettes, for example.

To raise seed from more exotic plants, you need to maintain a temperature of at least 10°C (50°F) and a heated propagator can be the answer. Then at the other end of the calendar, even an unheated glasshouse or frame wards off the evil moment when you have to give in, admit the onset of winter and settle for only the hardiest of crops.

Fruit and 'vegetable fruit' crops that can be grown with reasonable success in the garden, such as apricots, peaches, figs, tomatoes, green peppers and aubergines, ripen earlier and more certainly behind glass, while others – more exotic ones which would be out of the question in a northern hemisphere garden – become exciting possibilities.

Imagine sitting snugly in a motor car, the sun beating on the windscreen, and watching people being blown along in the icy wind outside, and you will get an idea of what a glasshouse can do for your plants. The principle is simple: the short-wave rays from both direct sunlight and diffused light pass through the glass panels and heat the concrete base, soil or whatever. This then sends back the heat as long-wave rays, which cannot pass out through the glass. The heat is therefore trapped and, having nowhere to go, builds up behind the glass where it keeps your seedlings nice and cosy.

You can protect plants, according to their size, with clear glass or plastic of any form, shape or size. The simplest form of propagation for seeds is an upturned jam jar or its plastic equivalent over a pot, or a clear plastic lid fitted over a seed tray. Cloches – rounded, angled or 'barn' shape – of glass or lightweight plastic, create in-house conditions in the soil. Put them in place two weeks before sowing seed to warm up the soil, and choose a type with covered ends, or close them with a board or glass panel, to protect crops from those not-always popular visitors from the wild – birds and rabbits.

A garden frame, more spacious than a cloche but lacking the walk-in facility (and gardener comfort) of a greenhouse, provides a useful half-way house for seedlings grown under heat before they have to face up to the harsh reality of the world outside. This is where they stand, the sloping lid partly open and protecting them from rain and wind, to harden off, and where half-hardy seeds can be sown.

Facing page: *The white grape Muller and Thurgau is one of the most prolific, and melons* (left) *are one of the most satisfying of glasshouse crops.*

If your sights are set on branches hanging heavy with sun-warmed fruits, and troughs of vegetables to provide a feast of Mediterranean cuisine, then a lean-to glasshouse against a house wall or boundary fence, or a free-standing aluminium or wooden construction, is what you're after.

Raising seeds and plants out of their natural environment and in controlled conditions does mean that it's up to you to control those conditions in their favour. Unless you have the time and inclination to water plants in a glasshouse diligently and open fanlights every time the temperature builds up – and in the heat of summer even hothouse plants can have too much of a good thing – you will need some form of automatic watering, such as capillary matting or trays, and a temperature controlled ventilation system.

As for heating, it's a question of balancing the cost of paraffin, gas or electricity against your desire to create a tropical paradise in your own garden of Eden. If the spirit is willing but the finances aren't, there are still plenty of exciting crops you can grow, cheating both the climate and the calendar. A heavy crop of melons, and grapes hanging thickly on the vine; stone fruits that are sure to ripen, golden citrus fruits, exotic newcomers like Cape gooseberries and kiwi fruits, and versatile vegetables, they will all flourish behind a touch of glass.

GLASSHOUSE GLOSSARY

Apricot The fruit may ripen out of doors, especially on trees that are fan-trained against a south-facing wall, but frosts in March and April when the flowers form and, later, birds are problems. A glasshouse solves both. The flowers are self-fertile but, unless your glasshouse is a-hum with insects, you may have to give them a helping hand – a camel-hair brush flitted from one flower to the other does the trick.

Prune the trees in early spring to shape them. Fruits form on both old wood and last season's young shoots. Mulch the soil around the trees with well-rotted organic matter. Aphids which cause leaf-curl can menace apricots, so spray with dimethotate immediately after flowering.

Varieties with good flavour include New Large Early, Moorpark, Hemskerke and Luizet.

Aubergine The seeds of this semi-tropical plant need heat to germinate. The plants will bear fruit outdoors in a good summer against a sunny wall, but much more reliably so in a glasshouse or under cloches. Taller varieties, up to 75cm (2½ft) high, need staking and dwarf varieties, about 30cm (1ft), can be grown in windowboxes. Red spider mite can be a big problem, so spray with derris.

One variety, Easter Egg, which has large white fruit, illustrates why this normally purple-skinned 'vegetable' is also called eggplant.

Banana You'll never pose a threat to the greengrocer, but in a heated greenhouse you can produce mini-sized bananas. Soak the seed in warm water for 72 hours; they take 2-8 weeks to germinate at 21-27°C (70-80°F). The plants have huge, decorative leaves, and, according to variety, grow to 1.75m (5ft) – that's *Musa ensete* – and 1-1.2m (3-4ft) – that's *Musa coccinea*, the red mini-banana.

Cape gooseberry and **Golden berry** These fruits are related to Chinese lanterns, bearing small, firm, round golden fruits inside decorative husks. Sow seed in March in a temperature of 21°C (70°F) and transplant under glass in mid April or (risking restricted crops) in the open at the end of May in poor, light soil. Pinch out the growing shoots when plants reach 30cm (12in) and support on canes. Under glass you can harvest from mid July until late December, outdoors from late August until the first frost. The fruits can be stored, still in their husks, for several months.

Citrus fruits If you have visions of a conservatory lined with fragrant citrus trees, now is your chance! You can buy small orange, kumquat, lemon and grapefruit trees in pots. Keep them warm and well watered, especially sprinkled from above, and they will bear – albeit tiny – fruits.

Or grow your own from pips planted 1cm (½in) deep in a pot of damp potting compost. Cover them with plastic or glass and keep them in the dark until shoots appear. Transplant seedlings when they have 2 pairs of leaves. Don't get out the marmalade recipe yet – the trees will take 2-3 years to fruit!

Cucumber You can grow very tasty ridge cucumbers, with tough skins and large seeds, outdoors, but for prize-winning long and slender specimens you need a glasshouse. Plant seed in pots at 20-27°C (70-80°F) – the higher the temperature the better the results – then transplant to a well-manured bed in the glasshouse, or a grow-bag. Train the stems on canes or strings and nip off all side shoots after two leaves.

Remove male flowers as pollination causes a bitter flavour. Some F_1 hybrids produce only female flowers – Amslic, Athene, Fembaby, Monique, Pepinex and Petita are examples.

Fig A warm south-facing wall provides good ripening conditions, but a glasshouse is even better. Plant in well-drained soil with the roots restricted in a sunken bin or stone pit, otherwise there will be all growth and no fruit. Train the shoots against a wall and after several years and once the trees have matured, snip off side shoots, at the fifth leaf, in June: these will bear fruit the following summer.

Prune the trees to allow a free circulation of air and maximum light to the fruits, apply a good layer of mulch and keep it well watered. You can reckon to harvest the black-skinned fruits, such as Brown Turkey, or the green-skinned ones, such as White Marseille, from August to October.

Grape It's a wonderful sight, a well-established vine trained along a wire frame in a glasshouse, hanging with heavy bunches of black and green fruit. Yes, as long as you grow the most suitable varieties you can grow vines outdoors too – at least, it's possible but more chancy.

Vines like a light soil, three parts loam to one of sand, and need a top dressing of well-rotted organic matter. Plant the roots outside the glasshouse if they have to share it with other crops, and create an opening for the stem. This may mean removing a brick temporarily from the base, or cutting a hole in one of the side panels. Push through the stem, plant the roots, then make good the opening.

In the first year remove the flowers, and in the autumn prune one-third of the growth of the main stem. Once fruits form, spray the plants and water them well. Cut lateral shoots back to two buds beyond fruit trusses and snip out the smallest fruits at the centre. In autumn, when the leaves fall, prune the vine heavily – you have to be cruel to be kind.

Varieties to consider include Black Hamburgh (suitable for outdoors), Boskoop's Glory and, in a heated glasshouse, Muscat of Alexandria. Of the 'whites', Madeleine Sylvaner and Witte van der Laan are both wine-makers.

Kiwi fruit On their way from China (their other popular name is Chinese gooseberry), the fruits stopped at New Zealand, now the heart of the export trade. You can grow your own sturdy, climbing vines under glass, and you need at least one male plant, which can pollinate several female plants. The long oval fruits have greeny-brown hairy skins and a highly decorative black seed pattern.

They are ready to harvest in October and November. If picked slightly under-ripe they can be kept in a cool place for several months. Hayward is a good, vigorous variety.

Melon Glasshouses and melons were made for each other! Sow seed (on its side) in pots filled with compost in March (with heat) or May (without). Plant out seedlings in well-rotted manure under glass, and train the main stem up wires or canes. Pinch out the tip when it reaches 2m (6ft) and train laterals along wires. Remove those tips once the side shoots are 45cm (18in) long.

When at least 4 female flowers (they have tiny fruit already formed) are open, pollinate them for three or four days with the stamens of male flowers. Pick off the shoots beyond the fruits once they start to develop and feed the plants with liquid fertilizer. Support fist-sized fruits with nets. Keep up humidity by sprinkling with water.

With care you can grow such well-known varieties as Ogen, Cantaloup, Honeydew, Charentais and even water-melons.

Nectarine Now that nectarines, which look like smooth-skinned peaches, are more widely available in the shops, there is more interest in growing them. They have similar cultivation requirements to peaches and bear the fruit on the young shoots of the previous year's growth.

Pruning is planned to build up healthy laterals. Leave only one strong shoot every 10-15cm (4-6in) and one bud at the base of each fruit-bearing lateral. This is tied in alongside the fruiting lateral which it replaces in the autumn. Spray against pest attack as for peaches.

Lord Napier, Pineapple, Humbolt and El Rouge are reliable varieties.

Peach Peaches vie with apricots and nectarines for fan-training wall space in the garden or glasshouse and need well-drained soil with an organic mulching. All peaches are self-fertile, but be ready to do the job if there are no insects about. It is counter-productive to overload the tree; pick off some of the pea-sized fruits, then before the crop ripens remove surplus fruits so that the eventual crop is spaced 25cm (10in) apart.

Peach trees do need cosseting. Spray with tar oil in January and malathion after flowering, against greenfly; with 3 per cent lime sulphur in February, March and the autumn against peach leaf curl, destroying any affected leaves; and with sequestrene iron if the leaves turn silver green because of chlorosis.

Some varieties, in order of ripening, are Hales Early, Peregrine, Rochester and Diamond.

Pineapple Don't install a glasshouse specially to grow pineapples – you might be disappointed. But the way to do it is to cut off the leafy top with about 2.5cm (1in) of fruit and cut away the skin. Set aside to dry, cut off the shrivelled lower leaves and plant the 'crown' in a pot of damp sandy soil. Keep it at 18°C (68°F) and water it lightly. It takes 3-5 years to shoot up a flower head from the centre, which – with a bit of luck – will turn into a fruit.

Sweet pepper or Capsicum. It's a great feeling, gathering your own green, red or yellow peppers for salads and ratatouille. And it's not difficult to achieve.

Sow F$_1$ hybrid seed from late February to early April at 24°C (75°F). Transplanted seedlings should be grown between 13-24°C (55-75°F), and can then be planted outdoors or under glass. Support plants (except dwarf types) with stakes. Harvest the fruits from late July onwards.

Settle for green peppers and more will form, or wait 2-3 weeks for them to turn red or yellow, according to variety. Canape and Merit are among red-ripening varieties, Gold star a deep yellow.

Tomato You pay your money and you take your choice of tomato varieties. You can then grow them both outdoors and under glass.

Sow the seed in a good compost in January and February for early glasshouse crops, and in March for summer and autumn crops and for outdoor planting. The required temperature is 15°C (60°F). Prick out seedlings into pots and syringe flower trusses to help the fruit to set.

Some vines are described as 'determinate', which means that the terminal bud sets fruit after several trusses – encourage upward growth by selecting a side shoot; others, indeterminate, can go on almost indefinitely. There are also bush varieties. It is said that growing either basil or African marigolds near tomatoes repels whitefly.

Among popular varieties are Ailsa Craig, Gardener's Delight, Moneymaker, Alicante and Yellow Perfection, a lovely golden colour. Pixie and Minibel are good for window boxes.

MEDITERRANEAN/PROVENCE

Plants which thrive in the heat of the Mediterranean sun, and have given rise to popular regional dishes such as Ratatouille and Salade niçoise, will flourish in your garden. Red, green and yellow peppers, aubergines, cucumbers and tomatoes, exotic kiwi fruits, melons, figs, Cape gooseberries, grapes and delicate tree fruits such as apricots and peaches – grow them all in a glasshouse.

AUBERGINE DIP WITH CRUDITES

2 medium aubergines
1 small onion, peeled and grated
2 × 15ml spoons (2tbls) lemon juice
2 garlic cloves, peeled and crushed
120ml (4fl oz) olive oil
4 × 15ml spoons (4tbls) flat-leafed parsley

1   Preheat the grill to medium. Grill the aubergines, turning them frequently, until the skins are black and blistered. Hold the aubergines under cold, running water. Peel off the skins, using a small, sharp knife.
2   Halve the aubergines and scoop out the flesh. Mash the aubergine and beat in the onion, lemon juice and garlic. Add the olive oil little by little, beating constantly. Beat in half the parsley.
3   Turn the aubergine mixture into a bowl and sprinkle with the remaining parsley.

Serve the dip with warm pitta bread and sticks of crisp, raw vegetables: red, yellow and green peppers, cucumber, carrots, celery and cauliflower florets all make tasty 'dip-sticks'. Black olives are a good accompaniment.

SERVES 4-6

A Mediterranean flavour

Aubergine dip, well-flavoured with garlic and olive oil, evokes both Mediterranean and Middle-Eastern cuisines. Serve it as a filling for salad vegetables such as cucumber and celery boats and tomato cases.

HAM & FRUIT PLATE

Exotic fruits from the glasshouse make the most of the delicious but expensive Continental hams, such as Parma ham.

100-150g (4-5oz) very thinly cut ham
1 small melon
4 fresh black figs

1   Roll the ham.
2   Peel the melon, scoop out and discard the seeds, and cut the flesh into thin slices. Cut the figs almost through into quarters.
3   Arrange the ham, melon and figs on each of four individual serving plates. Serve chilled.

SERVES 4

RATATOUILLE WITH HERB CHEESE

2 medium aubergines, trimmed
coarse salt
5 × 15ml spoons (5tbls) olive oil
1 Spanish onion, peeled and chopped
1 green pepper, trimmed and chopped
1 red pepper, trimmed and chopped
250g (9oz) courgettes, sliced
250g (9oz) tomatoes, skinned and chopped
2 garlic cloves, peeled and crushed
freshly ground black pepper
3 × 15ml spoons (3tbls) chopped basil

DRESSING
175g (6oz) full-fat soft cheese
salt
1 × 15ml spoon (1tbls) chopped basil
1 × 5ml spoon (1tsp) chopped marjoram
2 garlic cloves, peeled and crushed
2 × 15ml spoons (2tbls) double cream

1   Thinly slice the aubergines. Put the slices into a colander and sprinkle with coarse salt. Leave to drain for about 1 hour. Rinse under cold running water and pat the slices dry with kitchen paper.
2   Heat the oil in a large pan. Cook the onion over moderate heat for 3-4 minutes. Add the aubergine and peppers and cook for 10 minutes. Add the courgettes and cook for a further 5 minutes. Add the tomatoes and garlic, season with salt and pepper and cook for 5 minutes more. Stir in the basil, taste and adjust the seasoning if needed. Leave to cool.
3   To make the dressing, beat the cheese and beat in all the remaining ingredients.

Serve the vegetables cold as a first course, with the herb cheese separate, as a dressing.

SERVES 4

FISH SOUP WITH PEPPER

750g (1½lb) white fish fillets
3 × 15ml (3tbls) olive oil
1 medium onion, peeled and chopped
2 garlic cloves, peeled and crushed
900ml (1½ pints) water
2 large tomatoes, skinned and chopped
1 bouquet garni
salt
freshly ground black pepper
50g (2oz) butter
8 slices French bread
2 × 5ml spoons (2tsp) chopped thyme

SAUCE
2 red peppers, seeded and trimmed
2 garlic cloves, peeled and crushed
3 × 15ml spoons (3tbls) white breadcrumbs
6 × 15ml spoons (6tbls) olive oil
½ × 5ml spoon (½tsp) paprika
pinch of cayenne pepper
2 × 5ml spoons (2tsp) lemon juice
1 egg yolk

1   Skin the fish, remove any bones and cut it into thick chunks.
2   Heat the oil and fry the onion and garlic over moderate heat for 3-4 minutes, stirring once or twice. Pour on the water, add the fish, tomatoes and bouquet garni. Season with salt and pepper. Bring slowly to the boil and simmer for 10 minutes until the fish is just tender.
3   While the soup is cooking, make the sauce. Use a blender or food processor to blend all the ingredients together, or chop the peppers finely and pound the ingredients to a paste in a mortar.
4   Heat the butter in a frying pan and fry the bread slices over moderate heat until they are golden brown on both sides.
5   Strain the soup and put the fish and vegetables into a heated serving dish. Discard the bouquet garni. Whisk all but 2 × 15ml spoons (2tbls) of the

sauce into the fish stock. Reheat the stock gently without letting it boil. Taste and adjust the seasoning if needed. Pour the stock over the fish and stir in the thyme.
6   Just before serving, float the bread slices on top of the soup and spoon a little of the remaining sauce on to each one.

Rust ~ coloured

The sauce is called 'rouille' which means rust in French and describes the beautifully deep red colour. It is also good to accompany grilled or poached white fish.

Mediterranean colours and flavour: Ham and fruit plate, with quartered black figs and slices of ham: Ratatouille with herb cheese dressing (back) and Grilled pepper salad (right).

AUBERGINE SALAD

2 medium aubergines
coarse salt
about 5 × 15ml spoons (5tbls) olive oil
1 medium onion, peeled and chopped
4 tomatoes, peeled and sliced
50g (2oz) feta cheese, crumbled
1 × 15ml spoon (1tbls) basil or
oregano leaves

DRESSING
4 × 15ml spoons (4tbls) olive oil
1 × 15ml spoon (1tbls) red wine vinegar
2 garlic cloves, peeled and crushed
salt
freshly ground black pepper
2 × 15ml spoons (2tbls) chopped flat-leafed
parsley

1   Trim the aubergines and cut them into 1cm (½in) dice. Put the cubes into a colander and sprinkle them with the coarse salt. Set aside to drain for about 1 hour. Rinse under cold water, drain and pat dry with kitchen paper.
2   Heat the oil in a frying pan and fry the aubergine over moderate heat for about 10 minutes, stirring frequently, until it is evenly brown. Remove the aubergine from the pan and leave to cool. Fry the onion for 3 minutes.
3   Mix the dressing ingredients.
4   Toss the aubergine and onion in half the dressing and pile it into a bowl. Arrange the tomato slices around the outside and pour the remaining dressing over. Sprinkle the feta and herb leaves over the salad. Serve chilled.
Serve this rich-tasting salad with grilled or spit-roasted meat or fish.

SERVES 4

STUFFED AUBERGINES

2 medium aubergines
coarse salt
4 × 15ml spoons (4tbls) olive oil
1 small onion, peeled and chopped
2 garlic cloves, peeled and crushed
1 stalk celery, finely chopped
75g (3oz) chicken livers, chopped
2 tomatoes, skinned and chopped
75g (3oz) lean ham, chopped
8 × 15ml spoons (8tbls) white breadcrumbs
2 × 15ml spoons (2tbls) chopped parsley
freshly ground black pepper
4 × 15ml spoons (4tbls) grated
Wensleydale cheese

1   Halve the aubergines. Scoop out the flesh, leaving firm 'walls'. Chop the flesh and put it into a colander. Sprinkle the aubergine shells and the chopped flesh with salt. Set aside for about 1 hour to drain. Rinse the aubergine under cold, running water and dry thoroughly.
2   Heat half the oil and fry the onion, garlic, celery and chopped aubergine over moderate heat for 3-4 minutes, stirring once or twice. Stir in the chicken livers and tomatoes, fry for 3 minutes then remove from the heat. Stir in the ham, breadcrumbs, and parsley. Season with salt and pepper.
3   Place the aubergine shells in a baking dish and pack them with the filling. Sprinkle the cheese on top and pour the remaining oil round them.
4   Bake in the oven, preheated to 190°C, 375°F, gas 5, for 25-30 minutes.
Serve with Tomato and thyme sauce (see page 59) and a green salad.

SERVES 4

PIPERADE

1 green pepper
1 red pepper
salt
25g (1oz) butter
3 × 15ml spoons (3tbls) olive oil
1 Spanish onion, peeled and chopped
2 garlic cloves, peeled and chopped
4 tomatoes, skinned and chopped
freshly ground black pepper
8 eggs, lightly beaten
2 × 15ml spoons (2tbls) chopped parsley

CROUTONS
25g (1oz) butter
2 × 15ml spoons (2tbls) olive oil
3 slices white bread
2 garlic cloves, peeled and crushed

1   Blanch the green and red peppers in boiling, salted water for 2-3 minutes. Drain and halve the peppers, removing the seeds and stem, and chop them.
2   Heat the butter and oil in a frying pan and fry the onion over moderate heat for 3-4 minutes, stirring once or twice. Add the garlic and peppers and cook for 10 minutes, stirring frequently. Stir in the tomatoes, season with salt and pepper and cook for a further 5 minutes.
3   To make the croûtons, heat the butter and oil. Cut the crusts from the bread and cut it into 2cm (¾in) cubes. Fry the garlic and bread cubes over moderate heat, stirring frequently, until the bread is golden brown and dry.
4   Pour the eggs over the pepper mixture, stir in the parsley and cook until the eggs are just set. Scatter the croûtons over the omelette and serve it cut into wedges.

SERVES 4

STUFFED PEPPERS

4 large green or red peppers
salt
5 × 15ml spoons (5tbls) olive oil
1 small onion, peeled and chopped
1 garlic clove, peeled and chopped
150g (5oz) cooked long-grain rice
12 black olives, stoned and chopped
2 × 15ml spoons (2tbls) chopped basil
1 × 5ml spoon (1tsp) chopped thyme
2 × 15ml spoons (2tbls) pine kernels
freshly ground black pepper
4 × 15ml spoons (4tbls) white breadcrumbs
6 × 15ml spoons (6tbls) grated
Parmesan cheese
¼ × 5ml spoon (¼tsp) paprika

1   Blanch the peppers in boiling, salted water for 2-3 minutes. Drain the peppers, cut a thin slice from the tops and discard the seeds and cores.
2   Heat 3 × 15ml spoons (3tbls) of the oil and fry the onion and garlic over moderate heat for 3-4 minutes, stirring once or twice.
3   Remove from the heat. Stir in the rice, olives, herbs and pine kernels and season with salt and pepper.
4   Stand the peppers in a baking dish. Fill them with the rice mixture.
5   Mix together the breadcrumbs, cheese and paprika. Pat the topping over the peppers.
6   Sprinkle the remaining oil over the peppers. Bake in the oven, preheated to 190°C, 375°F, gas 5, for 35-40 minutes, until the topping is crisp and golden brown.
Serve with 300ml (½ pint) Tomato and thyme sauce (see page 59).

SERVES 4

SALADE NICOISE

Served with crispy French bread, this makes a substantial lunch dish.

350g (12oz) tomatoes, skinned
½ cucumber
1 green pepper, seeded and trimmed
1 red pepper, seeded and trimmed
1 medium onion, peeled and sliced into rings
1 × 15ml spoon (1tbls) chopped parsley
2 hard-boiled eggs, shelled and quartered
50g (2oz) black olives
45g (1¾oz) can anchovies, drained

DRESSING
4 × 15ml spoons (4tbls) olive oil
1 × 15ml spoon (1tbls) lemon juice
1 garlic clove, peeled and crushed
salt
freshly ground black pepper
¼ × 5ml spoon (¼tsp) sugar

1   Cut the tomatoes into quarters. Draw the tines of a fork down the length of the cucumber skin to remove 'channels' of skin all around. Thinly slice the cucumber. Slice the green and red peppers into narrow strips.
2   Toss together the tomatoes, cucumber, peppers, onion rings and parsley and put them in a serving bowl.
3   Mix together the dressing ingredients, pour over the salad and toss well to coat it thoroughly.
4   Arrange the egg slices and olives on top. Split the anchovies lengthways. Arrange them over the salad in a criss-cross pattern. Serve chilled.

SERVES 4

Variation Some versions of this salad, which originated in Nice, include tuna fish. Drain and flake a 225g (8oz) can of tuna and toss it with the salad.

For a change

To make a variation of this mixed salad earlier in the season, before your peppers are ripe, substitute 225g (8oz) topped and tailed green beans cooked until they are just tender. It's just as authentic!

GRILLED PEPPER SALAD

1 green pepper
1 red pepper
1 yellow pepper
4 × 15ml spoons (4tbls) olive oil
1 × 15ml spoon (1tbls) red wine vinegar
salt
freshly ground black pepper
2 × 15ml spoons (2tbls) chopped marjoram
½ × 5ml spoon (½tsp) marjoram flowers
50g (2oz) stuffed green olives
50g (2oz) black olives

1   If you don't have a yellow pepper, substitute another green one or a red one. Preheat the grill to medium. Grill the peppers, turning them frequently, until the skins turn black and blister. Hold the peppers under cold, running water and peel off the skins.
2   Cut the peppers into quarters, removing the seeds and stems, and dry them.
3   Mix together the oil and vinegar and season with salt and pepper. Stir in the marjoram and marjoram flowers (if you have them). Toss the peppers in the dressing.
4   Arrange the peppers around the outside of a dish, grouped together for colour, and arrange the olives in the centre.
   Serve with wholewheat bread as a first course, or to accompany cold meat or poultry.

SERVES 4

CHICKEN BREASTS WITH GRAPES

4 boneless breasts of chicken, 100-150g
(4-5oz) each
1 × 15ml spoon (1tbls) lemon juice
50g (2oz) butter
2 × 15ml spoons (2tbls) flour
250ml (8fl oz) chicken stock
1 × 15ml spoon (1tbls) chopped chervil
120ml (4fl oz) double cream
salt
freshly ground black pepper
175g (6oz) green grapes, seeded
3 × 15ml spoons (3tbls) white wine

1   Sprinkle the chicken breasts with lemon juice and rub it in well.
2   Heat 40g (1½oz) of the butter in a frying pan and fry the chicken over moderate heat for 3 minutes on each side. Lift out the chicken.
3   Stir in the flour, gradually pour on the stock and bring to the boil, stirring constantly. Simmer for 3 minutes. Stir in the chervil and return the chicken to the pan. Cover and simmer for 20 minutes, until the chicken is cooked.
4   Stir in the cream, season with salt and pepper and heat gently without boiling.
5   Simmer the grapes in the wine over moderate heat until it has evaporated. Stir in the remaining butter and toss the pan to glaze the grapes.
6   Transfer the chicken to a heated serving dish and scatter the grapes over the top.
   Serve with a green vegetable such as mangetout or asparagus peas.

SERVES 4

EXOTIC DESSERTS

Fruits you have grown in the glasshouse – stone fruits like apricots and peaches and less familiar ones such as kiwi fruits, kumquats and Cape gooseberries – deserve to be served with a flourish. Creamy desserts decorated with candied angelica, exotic fruit salad and luxurious glacé fruits are all extra special when the fruit is home grown.

APRICOT SORBET

500g (1¼lb) fresh apricots, stoned
450ml (¾ pint) water
juice of ½ lime or lemon
175g (6oz) sugar
2 × 15ml spoons (2tbls) kirsch or
apricot brandy
1 egg white, stiffly whisked

1   Place the apricots in a pan with 150ml (¼ pint) of the water. Cover and simmer for 15 minutes, until the fruit is tender. Cool slightly.
2   Put the fruit, liquid and lime or lemon juice into a blender or food processor and blend to a purée.
3   Heat the remaining water and sugar in a pan over low heat, stirring frequently until the sugar has dissolved. Increase the heat, bring to the boil and fast-boil for 5 minutes.
4   Stir the syrup into the apricot purée and leave to become cold.
5   Stir in the liqueur and pour the mixture into a container. Cover and freeze for 2-3 hours, until it is half frozen. At the same time, chill a bowl.
6   Turn the partly-frozen sorbet into the chilled bowl and whisk to break down the ice crystals. Whisk in the egg white. Return the mixture to the container, cover and freeze for 2-3 hours, until set.
7   Transfer the sorbet to the refrigerator for 10 minutes before serving. Serve it in chilled glasses.

SERVES 6-8

Variation Once the apricot season is over you can make this sorbet with dried apricots. Soak 175g (6oz) dried fruit in 150ml (¼ pint) unsweetened orange juice. Make the syrup with 300ml (½ pint) water and 150g (5oz) sugar.

CARAMEL PEACHES

4-8 ripe peaches
225g (8oz) light Muscovado sugar
2 × 15ml spoons (2tbls) milk
15g (½oz) butter
150ml (¼ pint) double cream, whipped
4 × 15ml spoons (4tbls) toasted almonds

1   Put the peaches into boiling water for 2 minutes. Rub off the skins. Halve and stone the peaches and cool them.
2   Put the sugar, milk and butter into a pan and stir over low heat until the sugar has dissolved. Bring to the boil and boil for exactly 7 minutes.
3   Sandwich the peach halves together with the cream and arrange them in a bowl.
4   Remove the sauce from the heat and beat until the sauce thickens.
5   Pour the sauce over the peaches. Pipe or spoon over any remaining cream and scatter with the nuts.

SERVES 4

Variation Allow 2 peaches per person if they are not a really generous size. Nectarines are just as delicious with this sugary, buttery sauce.

BLACK FIG SORBET

8 ripe black figs, halved
300ml (½ pint) water
120g (4½oz) caster sugar
1 × 5ml spoon (1tsp) lemon juice
1 egg white, stiffly whisked

1   Liquidize the figs in a blender or food processor to make a smooth purée. Rub the purée through a sieve to remove the pips.
2   Heat the water and sugar over low heat, stirring frequently until the sugar has dissolved. Increase the heat, bring to the boil and fast-boil for 5 minutes. Stir in the lemon juice.
3   Stir the syrup into the fig purée and mix well. Set aside to become completely cold.
4   Pour the mixture into a container, cover and freeze for 2-3 hours, until the mixture is half frozen. At the same time chill a bowl.
5   Turn the partly frozen mixture into the chilled bowl and whisk well to break down the ice crystals. Whisk in the egg white.
6   Return the mixture to the container, cover and freeze for 2-3 hours until set.
7   Transfer the sorbet to the refrigerator for 10 minutes before serving to soften slightly. Serve it, crushed, in chilled glasses. Halved or quartered fresh figs make a lovely decoration for this dish.

SERVES 4-6

Serving know-how

Sorbets and ice creams look pretty served in folds rather than scoops. Use a large tablespoon to take out shallow, rounded ovals of the dessert.

GREEN FRUIT SALAD

4 kiwi fruits
1 small melon
250g (9oz) grapes, peeled and seeded
100g (4oz) Cape gooseberries
1 green dessert apple, cored and thinly sliced

DRESSING
150ml (¼ pint) apple juice
75g (3oz) caster sugar flavoured with bay
(see p. 33)
1 × 15ml spoon (1tbls) lemon juice
3 × 15ml spoons (3tbls) brandy

1   To make the dressing, put the apple juice, sugar and lemon juice into a pan over low heat and stir occasionally until the sugar has dissolved. Increase the heat, bring to the boil and boil for 5 minutes. Add the brandy to the dressing and set aside to cool.
2   Peel the kiwi fruits and slice them into thin rings. Peel, halve and seed the melon and cut the flesh into large dice.
3   Mix all the fruit together in a serving bowl and pour on the syrup. Serve chilled.

SERVES 4-6

Variation Green or black figs, sliced into rings, are a good alternative to kiwi fruits. They, too, have an attractive seed pattern.

CAPE GOOSEBERRIES WITH CREME FRAICHE

24-30 Cape gooseberries
150ml (¼ pint) water
4-6 cardamom seeds
2 × 5ml spoons (2tsp) lemon juice
50g (2oz) caster sugar
2 × 15ml spoons (2tbls) clear honey

CREME FRAICHE
300ml (½ pint) double cream
1 × 15ml spoon (1tbls) buttermilk

1   If the cream and buttermilk have been stored in the refrigerator, take them out and bring them to room temperature. Stir the buttermilk into the cream. Cover and leave in a warm room overnight. Then chill before serving.
2   Cut open the calyces (covering leaves) of all but one of the Cape gooseberries. Twist out the fruits.

3   Put the water, cardamom seeds, lemon juice, sugar and honey into a pan over low heat and stir occasionally until the sugar has dissolved. Increase the heat and boil for 5 minutes. Strain the syrup and pour it, while it is still hot, over the fruit. Leave to cool, then chill.
4   Serve the Cape gooseberries in a bowl. Decorate it with the reserved fruit, the calyx cut and opened out like the petals of a flower. Serve the crème fraîche separately.

SERVES 4

Scoops of Apricot sorbet decorated with lemon leaves, Cape gooseberries and crushed Black fig sorbet, a cool trio of glasshouse fruit desserts.

Crème fraîche

This is a French farmhouse speciality which tastes a little like soured cream. It will keep for up to two weeks in a covered container.

STONE CREAM WITH PEACHES

Stone cream is a traditional old English dessert, which usually has a layer of jam beneath the 'set' cream. This more luxurious version uses peaches from the glasshouse.

1 × 15ml spoon (1tbls) powdered gelatine
3 × 15ml spoons (3tbls) water
300ml (½ pint) milk
15g (½oz) caster sugar
150ml (¼ pint) double cream, whipped
1 egg white, stiffly whisked
2 ripe peaches, skinned and sliced
1 × 15ml spoon (1tbls) lemon juice
50g (2oz) ratafia biscuits, broken
4 ratafia biscuits, to decorate

1 Dissolve the gelatine in the water. Heat the milk and sugar over low heat, stirring now and again until the sugar has dissolved. Stir in the gelatine liquid. Chill for about 30 minutes until the mixture is cold and starting to set.
2 Fold the cream into the milk. Fold in the whisked egg white.
3 Toss the peaches in the lemon juice and divide them between 4 individual serving dishes. Scatter the broken-up ratafia biscuits over the fruit.
4 Pour the cream over the peaches and biscuits. Chill for at least 1 hour until the dessert is set. Decorate with the remaining ratafias.

SERVES 4

GRAPE FLAN

Alternating rings of green and black grapes look particularly striking in this flan, but you can use either type.

100g (4oz) flour
salt
75g (3oz) butter
1 × 5ml spoon (1tsp) caster sugar
1 egg, beaten

FILLING
300ml (½ pint) milk
50g (2oz) caster sugar
25g (1oz) flour
2 × 5ml spoons (2tsp) cornflour
1 egg
1 × 5ml spoon (1tsp) grated orange rind
2 × 5ml spoons (2tsp) orange liqueur
350g (12oz) grapes, halved and seeded
2 × 15ml spoons (2tbls) redcurrant jelly
1 × 15ml spoon (1tbls) water

1 Sift together the flour and salt. Rub in the butter until the mixture is like fine crumbs. Mix in the sugar. Stir in the egg and form the mixture into a dough. Knead very lightly until the dough is smooth.
2 Roll out the dough and use it to line a 20cm (8in) flan tin.
3 Line the pastry case with foil and fill it with 'baking beans'. Bake it 'blind' in the oven, preheated to 200°C, 400°F, gas 6, for 20 minutes. Remove the beans and foil and continue baking the pastry for 5 minutes. Stand the tin on a wire rack to cool.
4 To make the filling, heat the milk just to simmering point. Beat the sugar, flour, cornflour and egg and stir in enough of the hot milk to make a smooth paste. Stir the paste into the milk. Bring to the boil over low heat until the custard boils, then simmer for 3 minutes, stirring constantly. Stir in the orange rind and liqueur. Cover the surface closely with a piece of wetted greaseproof paper and set aside to cool.
5 Pour the custard into the pastry case.
6 Arrange the grapes, round side up, in rings over the custard filling.
7 Heat the fruit jelly and water. Brush the glaze over the fruit.

SERVES 4-6

PASSION FRUIT SOUFFLE

350g (12oz) passion fruits
4 eggs, separated
100g (4oz) caster sugar
2 × 15ml spoons (2tbls) lemon juice
300ml (½ pint) double cream, whipped
candied angelica, to decorate

1 Cut the tops from the passion fruits and scoop out the flesh and seeds. Press it through a sieve and reserve some of the seeds.
2 Beat the egg yolks and caster sugar in a bowl fitted over a pan of simmering water, or the top of a double boiler. Do not allow the water to boil, or to touch the upper container. When the mixture is thick and creamy, remove it from the heat and set aside to cool.
3 Stir the lemon juice into the fruit purée. Stir the fruit purée and cream into the beaten egg.
4 Whisk the egg whites until they are stiff. Fold them into the cream.
5 Pour the mixture into a serving bowl. Chill in the refrigerator for 2-3 hours to set.
6 Decorate the top with a few of the passion fruit seeds and 'leaves' cut from Candied angelica (see page 105). A bunch of grapes pattern is most effective.

SERVES 4-6

MIXED FRUIT SAVARIN

25g (1oz) fresh yeast
5 × 15ml spoons (5tbls) warm milk
50g (2oz) caster sugar
25g (1oz) butter
2 eggs, beaten
3 egg yolks, beaten
250g (9oz) flour
½ × 5ml spoon (½tsp) ground cinnamon
200g (7oz) granulated sugar
300ml (½ pint) water
1 × 15ml spoon (1tbls) lemon juice
4 × 15ml spoons (4tbls) kirsch
4 × 15ml spoons (4tbls) redcurrant jelly
2 × 15ml spoons (2tbls) water

FILLING
100g (4oz) grapes, seeded
4 apricots, peeled, stoned and sliced
2 nectarines, peeled, stoned and sliced
2 peaches, peeled, stoned and sliced
1 small banana, sliced

1   Crumble the yeast on to the warm milk, stir well and set aside in a warm place for 20 minutes, until it becomes frothy.
2   Add the sugar, butter, eggs, egg yolks and the flour sifted with the cinnamon, and mix well. Form the mixture into a dough. Cover with cling film or foil and leave in a warm place for about 45 minutes to 1 hour, until the dough has doubled in size.
3   Knead the dough again for 1-2 minutes – this is called 'knocking back'.
4   Press the dough into an oiled 1.5 litre (2½ pint) ring mould. Cover with cling film and leave in a warm place again until the dough has risen to the rim of the mould.
5   Bake the mould in the oven, pre-heated to 170°C, 325°F, gas 3, for 40 minutes, until it is firm yet springy to the touch. Cool slightly in the tin then turn it out on to a folded cloth on a wire rack to become cold.
6   Heat the sugar, water and lemon juice over low heat, stirring occasionally until the sugar has dissolved. Increase the heat and boil for 5 minutes. Stir in the kirsch.
7   Return the savarin to the tin, prick holes in it with a fine skewer and pour on all but 8 × 15ml spoons (8tbls) of the syrup.
8   Toss the prepared fruit in the reserved syrup.

9   Melt the redcurrant jelly with the water. Turn out the savarin on to a serving plate. Brush the surface with the glaze. Spoon the fruit in the centre. Serve with cream.

SERVES 6-8

GLACE FRUITS

Precious fruits you have grown in the glasshouse are well worth the care it takes to make exotic sweetmeats. Set aside a little time each day: in all, the process is completed after 13 days.

500g (1½lb) kumquats or tiny oranges
600ml (1 pint) water
about 625g (1¾lb) sugar
caster sugar, for glazing

1   Prick the fruit all over with a sterilized darning needle. Poach it in the water for 25-30 minutes until tender. Drain the fruit and measure out 300ml (½ pint) of the water.
2   Put the water and 175g (6oz) of the sugar in a pan over low heat and stir occasionally until the sugar has dissolved. Bring to the boil, then pour over the fruit. Set aside for 24 hours.
3   Pour the syrup into a pan and dissolve 50g (2oz) of the remaining sugar. Bring to the boil, pour over the fruit and leave for 24 hours.
4   Repeat Step 3 every day for 5 days, adding another 50g (2oz) sugar each time.
5   Repeat the process, this time adding 75g (3oz) sugar and leaving to soak for 48 hours.
6   Repeat Step 5, then leave the fruit to soak in the syrup for 4 days.
7   Remove the fruit from the syrup with a draining spoon. Spread it on a wire rack to dry.
8   To glaze the dried and candied fruits, hold each one on a skewer, dip it in boiling water, shake off any excess and then dip it into caster sugar to coat it thoroughly on all sides. Leave the fruit in a warm, dry room for 5-6 hours to dry.
9   Store the fruits, individually wrapped in waxed paper or placed in sweet-paper cases, in an airtight container.

MAKES 500G (1¼LB) GLACE FRUITS

CANDIED ANGELICA
You can candy angelica shoots by the same process, to make the 'leaves'. Cut the young, green shoots in April or May and drop them at once into a brine made with 1 × 15ml spoon (1tbls) salt to each 600ml (1 pint) water to preserve the bright colour. Soak for 15 minutes, then rinse.

Cook them in boiling water for 7-10 minutes until they are tender, then plunge them straight into cold water. Drain the shoots and scrape off the outer skin. Weigh them and use sugar in the proportion given for glacé fruits.

FIG PUFFS

40g (1½oz) caster sugar
1 × 15ml spoon (1tbls) lemon juice
4 × 15ml spoons (4tbls) water
12 fresh figs
oil, for deep frying
6 × 15ml spoons (6tbls) sesame seeds

BATTER
75g (3oz) flour
salt
2 × 15ml spoons (2tbls) caster sugar
2 eggs, separated
1 × 15ml spoon (1tbls) vegetable oil
4 × 15ml spoons (4tbls) orange juice
5 × 15ml spoons (5tbls) milk
1 × 5ml spoon (1tsp) grated orange rind

1   Heat the sugar, lemon juice and water over low heat, stirring occasionally, until the sugar has dissolved. Poach the figs in the syrup for 8-10 minutes, stirring them frequently. Lift them out with a draining spoon.
2   To make the batter, sift the flour and salt, stir in the sugar and beat in the eggs, oil, orange juice, milk and orange rind. Beat until the batter is smooth.
3   Hold each fig on a skewer, dip into the batter and drain off any excess. Deep-fry the figs in batches for 2-3 minutes, until they are puffed up and golden. Lift them out with a draining spoon, dry them on kitchen paper and toss them in sesame seeds. Keep the cooked figs warm while you fry the remainder. Serve hot.

SERVES 4

THE SALAD GARDEN

I t's a tempting and colourful world in the salad garden: frilly hummocks of bright green loose-leaved lettuce and corn salad; tall, stately, tightly packed heads of pale and delicate Chinese cabbage and deep deep green cos lettuce; intriguing untidy flowering stalks of pak choi; slim-as-a-reed leaves of bunching onions; and deep vivid red chicory.

It's also a surprisingly long season. Plant breeders are constantly developing seeds with ever earlier and ever later harvesting times. You can help things along still further with the simplest of protective cover – glass or plastic cloches, for example – and cut crisp saladings almost the year round; indeed, right through the year, if you have a heated glasshouse.

Many salads are quick-growing crops – which is why they are such a favourite with children eager to devour the first of their home-grown seedlings. This makes them eminently suitable to raise in ground well manured from a winter crop and waiting for a summer one – catch the space with a row of lettuce or radish – called catch crops – and achieve the gardener's dream, three yields from the same ground in the course of a year.

Salads are decorative crops, too, ideally suited for a small formal garden plan, planted in concentric circles or diminishing squares, perhaps, with tall decorative herbs in the centre. Lettuce come in all shapes and sizes, some short and plump to plant as edging for the front rows, others impressively tall to take their place in the ranks nearer the back. Radish seed can be planted where harvesting leaves gaps – and a tight cluster of the dense green leaves, in this context, can be more attractive than a row.

If you opt for a defined salad patch, work it into your overall garden scheme – here one year, there the next – rotating salad crops as you do brassicas and legumes. That's the way to get the best from the soil and to fool the resident pests that are lying in wait for the same diet to be served up year after year.

The Romans knew a thing or two about salad gardening, and how to get the best from the soil wherever they went. A favourite way to serve raw lettuce was to toss it with dandelion leaves and elderflowers – the combination of saladings and flowers has a well-documented parentage – but the Romans didn't often serve them raw. They had a weakness for *salades tièdes*, so popular still in France, and cooked chopped lettuce with eggs in a kind of leafy scramble to serve as an appetizer and intensify hunger. They also braised lettuce leaves with onion, oil, vinegar and honey. Endive crops up in many a Roman recipe, raw or cooked,

A truly satisfying sight – a wealth of crisp and shiny salad vegetables, culled from the garden.

with a couple of spoonfuls of honey to offset the bitterness – an idea that is still worth copying, centuries later.

When is a salad not a salad? To many, the answer to this is when it doesn't have a dressing. No matter how simple the dressing may be – just olive oil and orange or lemon juice perhaps – it forms an important link, bringing together different ingredients with contrasting flavours into one happy culinary family. Not only that, but a dressing can completely alter the character of a dish, accentuating or minimizing flavours just as you wish. It pays to experiment with different types of oil, each of which brings its own individual flavour to the sauce; with apple, pineapple and other juices; apple, apricot and any number of fruit purées; and with a ring-the-changes list of dairy products from low-

fat yoghurt to double cream, a particularly good choice for saladings with a slight edge of bitterness.

Vegetables that are served raw or partly cooked as salads – mushrooms, cauliflower florets, courgettes, peppers and so on – may benefit from marinating in a dressing for an hour or two. Indeed, marinating can substitute for cooking in those (such as mushrooms, cucumbers and courgettes) with a high water content.

But for salad leaves the maxim is, toss as you serve. Mix the salad ingredients, cover and leave them in the refrigerator to chill. Mix the dressing and have it ready. Turn the salad into a chilled bowl, lightly sprinkle the dressing over it, toss it quickly with two spoons and take it to the table, cool, crisp and sparkling.

SALAD FOR ALL SEASONS

Bunching onions Similar to spring onions, with a mild flavour and the added bonus that they grow in clusters of 5 or 6. The onions are easily grown from seed, to harvest in spring or summer. Long white Tokyo (about 45cm (18in) long actually) are like slim leeks; Multi-stalk 5 (60cm (2ft) long) are as slender as chives and delicious both raw and lightly braised.

Sow in April and thin to 25cm (10in) apart, and by the next year you will have a considerable number of scallions from each bulb. They can be divided to produce further clumps, and in fact it is best to do this in later years, replanting only the younger bulbs and eating the rest. You won't have to worry about pests and diseases with this hardy plant.

Chicory This unusual salad crop can be grown for harvest in two ways: the leaves cut in autumn, or the roots dug up and stored in a warm, dark place until they produce the tightly closed clusters of white stalks called chicons.

To harvest as for lettuce, sow seed in shallow drills from mid June until mid July and thin the plants to 30cm (12in) apart. They will be ready to cut in October and can then be stored in a cool place or refrigerator for up to 3 months.

To produce winter chicons, sow seed from April to June, thinning to 23cm (9in) apart. Lift the parsnip-like roots in October and November, cut off the foliage and 'replant' them upright in a seed box of damp sand or loamy soil.

Cover with another box and store at a temperature no lower than 10°C, 50°F. In 4 weeks the chicons should be 15-20cm (6-8in) long. Cut them off carefully as you need them, recover the box to exclude the light and another crop should grow.

Winter Fare and Snowflake are 'leafy' varieties which can produce heads of up to 1.25kg (2¾lb) each. Witloof (Brussels chicory) is grown for its much smaller blanched chicons.

Chinese cabbage In culinary terms somewhere between cos lettuce and cabbage, the leaves can be eaten either raw or lightly cooked. Some varieties – the kind now readily available in shops – form thick tight hearts, while others do not 'heart up' at all. Sow seed outdoors in May, June and July – it can be ready to harvest after only 10 weeks.

F₁ hybrid seeds, bred to improve cropping, disease resistance and uniformity of size, include Tip Top, an early variety producing heads of up to 2kg (4½lb) and China King, up to 2.5kg (5¾lb). Che-Foo, a mid-season variety, has cannonball-shaped heads; Shantung is semi-heading with a spreading habit; and both Round Leaved Santo and Serrated Leaved Santo are less bulky and have a loose-leaf formation.

It is also called Chinese leaf, Nappa cabbage and celery cabbage – and its Chinese name of pe-tsai.

Corn salad A cut-and-come-again plant, also known as lamb's lettuce and found in the wild. Corn salad is a useful winter standby. Sow seed in 2.5cm (1in) drills in August and September, thinning seedlings to 10-15cm (4-6in). Harvest in winter or early spring, pulling a few leaves from each plant.

Broad-leaved English, a hardy variety, has long, wide oval leaves. Although it is most valuable when there is a shortage of salad greens in winter, you can sow it in the spring for a summer crop.

Cress Every child knows how to grow cress on the kitchen windowsill on a piece of damp flannel or several layers of white kitchen tissue. You can also sprinkle the seed on the surface of seed compost in pots or boxes outdoors in summer, or on very fine loamy soil.

Varieties include Mega, Curled, Extra Curled, Super Salad and American or Land cress, which is a good substitute for watercress. These minute mustard-flavoured leaves are superb for garnish and decoration and almost an institution in egg sandwiches.

Endive Curly endive, confusingly called chicory in the US, is like an attractively frilled plump lettuce. Sow seed outdoors from April to July to harvest in autumn and winter – the plant can withstand a few degrees of frost. Transplant when 5-7.5cm (2-3in) high or thin out to 38cm (15in) apart.

When the plants are nearly fully grown, blanch 3 or 4 at a time to exclude the light, either by gathering the leaves together and tying them round or by covering the plants with boards or pots.

Two varieties to try are Moss Curled and Batavian Broad Leaved.

Lettuce If you have a cool or slightly heated glasshouse it is possible to harvest lettuce all the year round. Sowing in open ground under cloches provides fresh crisp leaves from May to November; without such protection for seedlings in spring and plants in winter, you shorten that span by some 2 months. Lettuce grows quickly and will perform best in moist, well-drained soil. It is an ideal 'catch crop' to grow between, say, a long-term winter crop of brassicas and a summer crop of peas or beans.

It's a busy schedule in the world of lettuce cultivation. For an early spring harvest, sow in a warm greenhouse or frame in January or February, prick off into boxes and plant out under cloches in March. This is when you can make the first outdoor sowings, then sow at fortnightly intervals (unless you *want* a deluge) until July.

Some varieties, such as Arctic King and Winter Density, may be sown outdoors in late August and early September for harvesting later in the year. If you have cloches or a frame, sow seed of Magiola, for example, in early October and grow on under glass until February. You can leave the crops (well protected from birds) to mature under glass, or transplant them out in March.

Summer-cropping cabbage lettuce are divided into butterhead types, with large well-folded heads and creamy yellow hearts, and crisphead types, which have white-blanched hearts.

The long-leaved cos lettuce, with either white or green hearts, also crops in summer. Salad Bowl, with delicately frilled 'loose leaves' and Great Lakes, a red-tinged equivalent, can be harvested leaf by leaf.

Winter-cropping varieties tend to have firm, solid hearts – Valdor and May King are just two examples. Flip through the seed packets in the garden shop, check the dates, and make your choice.

Mustard The traditional partner to salad cress and grown in similar ways, mustard has rounded, figure of eight-shaped leaves, while cress leaves are longer and thinner.

Pak choi A Chinese vegetable well suited to the salad garden, it is grown for both leaves and stalks. Sow seed in boxes or straight into the ground, thinning to 40cm (16in) apart for harvest about 8 weeks later.

Japanese White Celery Mustard and Chinese pak choi have deep green leaves like the bowls of spoons on long white stems. Chinese Tsai Shim, which grows well from late spring to early autumn, and Hon Tsai Tai, which can be grown for both summer and an over-wintered harvest, are flowering stalks, delicious for use in *salades tièdes*.

Radishes The tastiest radishes are those grown quickly in a light, fairly rich soil and, in the case of summer crops, harvested as soon as they 'plump up' about 6 weeks after sowing. Sow thinly in drills 5mm-1cm (¼-½in) deep and 15cm (6in) apart in a warm sheltered position, at intervals from February through spring and summer. (Sow the whole packet at once and you'll have an 18m (20ft) row of peppery roots to munch!) Winter radishes are sown in moist soil in July and August and seedlings thinned to 20cm (8in) apart. Leave in the ground, or lift in autumn and store in a clump of dry sand.

Radishes come in all sizes, shapes and colours. Among the summer-cropping varieties, choose from Cherry Belle and Prinz Rotin, both round; Inca, globe-shaped, and French Breakfast, cylindrical – all four are bright red. Then there's Long White Icicle, tap-

ered, and Minowase Summer No. 2, long and slim – both white; Pink Beauty, globe-shaped and pink, and Sparkler, globe-shaped and scarlet tipped with white. Winter-cropping radishes include Black Spanish Round, which should be grated or sliced; China Rose, 13-15cm (5-6in) long and deep rose with a white tip, and Mino Early, a large Japanese variety 38cm (15in) long, for salads and soup.

Red chicory (radicchio) A most worthwhile autumn and winter crop, because its beetroot-red leaves contrast so strikingly with salad greens. The plants are reasonably hardy and their growing season can be extended by the use of cloches.

There are 2 types, ones which bulk up and form hearts, and ones which stay 'loose-leaved', and are referred to as a cutting crop. The leaves are green initially, but turn spectacular red and bronze shades in cold weather.

Sow the first, hearted, category from May to July, transplanting to 20-30cm (8-12in) apart, and the cutting crop from March to September. For over-wintering, cover plants with glass or straw, or pile earth around them to blanch the stalks. To force heads, lift the roots as for chicory chicons.

Sprouted seeds The perfect crop for both the impatient and the indoor gardener. All you need is a wide-necked glass jar, a piece of muslin or cheesecloth and an elastic band. Pea and bean seeds will sprout within 2-6 days and can yield up to 10 times their original weight in a crop which is rich in Vitamin C.

Put 1-2 × 15ml spoons (1-2tbls) into the jar, half-fill with warm water, cover with muslin and tip out the water. Place the jar on its side in a drawer, half-fill and drain twice a day until the shoots are about 2.5-5cm (1-2in) long. Give them a final rinse and drain them well. If you have to store them, cover them with cold water in a lidded container. Keep them in the refrigerator for up to 2 days.

All salad shoots are delicious raw in salads, stir-fried or steamed for about 3 minutes. They should always be served crisp.

Alfalfa shoots, crisp and sweet, taste of green peas and sprout in 5 days. Harvest when 2.5cm (1in) long. *Adzuki beans* have a nutty flavour. *Fenugreek* shoots are hot and spicy and are harvested in 3-4 days when they are just over 1cm (½in) long. *Mung beans*, the familiar Chinese beansprouts, germinate best if soaked overnight in water. *Chick peas* and *soya beans*, both candidates for overnight soaking, are ready to eat after 6 days. Others to try include non-roasted sunflower seeds and whole lentils.

Watercress Not everyone has a sparkling, tinkling, running stream, but you can grow watercress in any ground that can be kept constantly moist. It's a profitable crop to grow in a damp, shady site.

Dig a trench 60cm (2ft) wide and 30cm (12in) deep, make a layer of manure under a layer of soil, firm it down well and saturate it. Plant rooted cuttings – there are plenty in every bunch of watercress you buy – 10cm (4in) apart. Pinch out leading shoots to make the plants bushy and cut them back when the white flowers appear. Or sow seed in boxes in the spring and transplant strong seedlings in the way described.

SALAD BUFFET

From the earliest crops nurtured under glass through the profusion of salad vegetables in summer, there's an almost bewildering choice of colour, texture and flavour. Mix and match these crisp garden ingredients to make an appetizing and attractive buffet, or choose one or two dishes for a simple meal. Serve the salads lightly cooked or refreshingly chilled.

SALAD BOWL SOUP

2 × 15ml spoons (2tbls) tomato purée
2 × 15ml spoons (2tbls) lemon juice
300ml (½ pint) chicken stock, chilled
300ml (½ pint) tomato juice, chilled
2 hard-boiled eggs
2 garlic cloves, peeled and crushed
3 × 15ml spoons (3tbls) olive oil
salt
freshly ground black pepper
2 × 15ml spoons (2tbls) chopped chervil
2 × 15ml spoons (2tbls) finely snipped chives

GARNISH
4 × 15ml spoons (4tbls) chopped
Chinese cabbage
1 small green pepper, seeded and chopped
1 small red pepper, seeded and chopped
2 spring onions, peeled and thinly sliced
100g (4oz) peeled prawns

1   Mix together the tomato purée, lemon juice, chicken stock and tomato juice.
2   Separate the yolks and the whites of the hard-boiled eggs and mash the yolks. Stir in the garlic and oil. Stir the paste into the tomato mixture and season with salt and pepper. Cover and then chill in the refrigerator for about 1 hour.
3   Stir the herbs into the chilled soup. Taste and adjust the seasoning if needed. Chop the egg whites.
4   Serve the soup in bowls with the chopped egg white, Chinese leaves, peppers, onions and prawns handed separately.

SERVES 4-6

Salad bowl soup

This soup has an oriental air to it. Try serving it in small Chinese porcelain bowls, with porcelain spoons. These are easily available from ethnic shops.

TOSSED FISH SALAD

500g (1¼lb) squid, cleaned
3 × 15ml spoons (3tbls) olive oil
250g (9oz) haddock fillet, skinned and flaked
2 × 15ml spoons (2tbls) lemon juice
100g (4oz) peeled shrimps
50g (2oz) seedless raisins
100g (4oz) blackberries
3 spring onions, trimmed and sliced
16-20 corn salad leaves
1 dessert apple, cored and thinly sliced
½ small cucumber, thinly sliced
1 green pepper, seeded and thinly sliced
1 × 15ml spoon (1tbls) chopped tarragon
1 lemon, cut in wedges, to serve

DRESSING
4 × 15ml spoons (4tbls) olive oil
2 × 15ml spoons (2tbls) apple juice
2 × 5ml spoons (2tsp) clear honey
salt
freshly ground black pepper

1   Slice the squid into thin rings. Heat the oil and fry the squid over moderate heat for 10 minutes, stirring once or twice. Add the haddock and cook for a further 10 minutes. Stir in the lemon juice, set aside and cool, then stir in the shrimps, raisins and blackberries.
2   Mix the dressing ingredients.
3   Toss together the spring onions, corn salad, apple, cucumber and pepper. Pour over the dressing and toss.
4   Arrange the green salad on a serving plate. Pile the tossed fish on top. Garnish with the chopped tarragon and lemon wedges.

SERVES 4-6

COS LETTUCE WITH BACON DRESSING

Crisp salad leaves such as cos lettuce and Chinese cabbage take well to being tossed in a hot dressing moments before serving.

1 small cos lettuce, separated
4 spring onions, trimmed and sliced
4 large tomatoes, sliced
3 × 15ml spoons (3tbls) grated
Emmenthal cheese

DRESSING
1 × 15ml spoon (1tbls) olive oil
6 slices bacon, rinded and chopped
3 × 15ml spoons (3tbls) red wine vinegar
1 × 5ml spoon (1tsp) sugar
½ × 5ml spoon (½tsp) paprika
salt
freshly ground black pepper

1   To make the dressing, heat the oil and fry the bacon over moderate heat for 3-4 minutes, stirring once or twice. Lift out the bacon with a draining spoon.
2   Add the vinegar, sugar and paprika and season with salt and pepper. Heat the dressing.
3   Preheat the grill to moderate. Sprinkle the tomatoes with the cheese and grill until it melts.
4   Toss together the lettuce, spring onions and bacon. Pour on the dressing and toss. Arrange the tomatoes for colour contrast around the outside. Serve at once.

SERVES 4-6

Poached salmon, served with Strawberry salad, Red, white and green salad, and Tossed fish salad – with a light hedgerow wine.

ORIENTAL SALAD

2 eggs
1 × 15ml spoon (1tbls) water
salt
freshly ground black pepper
25g (1oz) butter
½ small Chinese cabbage, sliced
150g (6oz) fresh beansprouts, washed
and drained
6 bunching onions, trimmed and sliced
12 radish roses

DRESSING
2.5cm (1in) piece fresh root ginger, peeled
and chopped
4 × 15ml spoons (4tbls) sesame oil
1 × 15ml spoon (1tbls) dry sherry
2 × 5ml spoons (2tsp) soy sauce
1 × 15ml spoon (1tbls) sesame seeds
a pinch of cayenne

1   Beat the eggs with the water and
season with salt and pepper. Melt the
butter in a small omelette pan, tip in
the mixture when the fat is hot and fry
over moderate heat until the omelette
is just set. Slide it on to a plate and set
aside to cool.
2   Mix the dressing ingredients.
3   Toss together the sliced Chinese
leaves, beansprouts and onions.
4   Line a serving plate with the salad.
Strain on the dressing.
5   Cut the omelette into thin strips
and arrange them over the salad in a
trellis pattern.
6   Garnish the dish with the radish
roses for a pretty finish.

SERVES 4-6

POACHED SALMON

1kg (2¼lb) piece of fresh salmon
2 bay leaves
3-4 parsley stalks
6 black peppercorns
salt
12-18 leaves corn salad
250g (9oz) cooked shelled broad beans
2 × 15ml spoons (2tbls) chopped savory
1 × 15ml spoon (1tbls) olive oil
½ × 5ml spoon (½tsp) lemon juice
½ cucumber, thinly sliced
4 cucumber spirals (see p.112)

DRESSING
6 × 15ml spoons (6tbls) mayonnaise
1 × 15ml spoon (1tbls) olive oil
1 × 15ml spoon (1tbls) double cream
1 × 5ml spoon (1tsp) Dijon mustard
freshly ground black pepper

1   Put the salmon in a pan with the
bay leaves, parsley and peppercorns.
Cover with salted water, cover the pan
and bring to the boil. Simmer for 18-20
minutes, until the fish is just tender.
2   Let the salmon cool in the stock.
3   Skin the fish and cut it into 4 slices.
4   Cover a serving plate with the corn
salad leaves. Arrange the salmon.
5   Toss the broad beans with the
savory, oil and lemon juice and
arrange them in mounds between the
salmon slices. Arrange the sliced
cucumber around the dish. Cover each
piece of salmon with a cucumber
spiral.
6   Mix together the mayonnaise, oil,
cream and mustard and season with
pepper.
Serve the mayonnaise separately.

SERVES 4

SALAD TERRINE

350g (12oz) young carrots, trimmed
250g (9oz) young French beans, topped
and tailed
350g (12oz) young asparagus spears, trimmed
175g (6oz) pak choi stalks, trimmed
salt
450ml (¾ pint) chicken stock
6 × 15ml spoons (6tbls) aspic crystals
3 × 15ml spoons (3tbls) sherry
6 × 15ml spoons (6tbls) full-fat cream cheese
6 × 15ml spoons (6tbls) mayonnaise
1 × 5ml spoon (1tsp) lemon juice
freshly ground black pepper
a pinch of cayenne pepper
salad leaves, to serve

SAUCE
½ bunch watercress sprigs, trimmed
about 12 young sorrel leaves
2 × 5ml spoons (2tsp) lemon juice
300ml (½ pint) mayonnaise

1 Cut the carrots into matchstick strips. Halve the French beans. Discard any tough white lower stalk of the asparagus.
2 Steam the carrots, beans, asparagus and pak choi over boiling salted water for 4-5 minutes, or until all the vegetables are just tender. Drain and dry the vegetables.
3 Heat the stock to boiling point and dissolve the aspic crystals. Stir in the sherry and cool slightly. Beat together the cream cheese, mayonnaise and lemon juice. Gradually pour on the aspic, beating constantly. Season with black pepper and cayenne. Cool, then put in the refrigerator until the mixture is thick and syrupy.
4 Pour a little of the aspic mixture into a wetted 1.2 litre (2 pint) rectangular mould. Arrange a layer of half the beans in strips. Spoon over a little more aspic. Arrange half the asparagus, aspic, half the pak choi and more aspic. Repeat the strips until all the vegetables and aspic are used.
5 Cover the mould with foil. Chill in the refrigerator for 3-4 hours.
6 To make the sauce, boil the watercress and sorrel in salted water for 3 minutes. Drain, plunge the vegetables into cold water, drain again and dry thoroughly. Liquidize the vegetables in a blender or food processor with the lemon juice and a little of the mayonnaise. Cool, then beat in the remaining

mayonnaise. Season with salt and pepper.
7 Line a serving plate with salad leaves. Turn out the terrine. Serve the sauce separately.

SERVES 6-8

MAYONNAISE

2 egg yolks
½ × 5ml spoon (½tsp) Dijon mustard
salt
freshly ground black pepper
1 × 15ml spoon (1tbls) lemon juice
300ml (½ pint) olive oil

1 Beat the egg yolks and beat in the mustard, salt and pepper. Beat continuously while you add a few drops of lemon juice.
2 Pour on about 3 × 15ml spoons (3tbls) of the oil, drop by drop, and beat so that it is immediately taken into the sauce. Gradually add the remaining oil and lemon juice in a thin, steady stream, still beating. Taste the sauce and add more salt and pepper if needed.

MAKES 300ML (½ PINT)

Variation You can make mayonnaise very quickly in a blender or food processor. Put in the egg yolk, mustard, salt, pepper and lemon juice and add 2 × 15ml spoons (2tbls) cold water. Blend until the mixture is smooth. Pour on the oil in a thin, steady stream and blend with the motor running until all the oil is incorporated and the sauce is smooth.

TOMATO ROUNDABOUTS

4 large tomatoes
2 × 15ml spoons (2tbls) cooked peas
2 × 15ml spoons (2tbls) sweetcorn
25g (1oz) goat's cheese, finely chopped
1 × 15ml spoon (1tbls) chopped mint
salt
freshly ground black pepper
2-3 × 15ml spoons (2-3tbls) mayonnaise
1 small curly endive, separated
3 spring onions, trimmed and sliced
5cm (2in) piece cucumber, thinly sliced
1 bunch salad cress

DRESSING
3 × 15ml spoons (3tbls) olive oil
2 × 15ml spoons (2tbls) tomato juice
½ × 5ml spoon (½tsp) sugar
salt
freshly ground black pepper
2-3 drops hot pepper sauce

1 Cut the tomatoes into 'cups' (see opposite).
2 Mix together the peas, sweetcorn, cheese and mint. Season with salt and pepper and stir in enough mayonnaise to blend the ingredients together.
3 Fill the tomato cases with the salad.
4 Mix the dressing ingredients.
5 Cover a serving plate with the endive leaves and scatter the spring onions over. Arrange the tomato cases.
6 Wrap the cucumber slices into cones and fill each one with a small bunch of salad cress, the stalks cut suitably short.
7 Arrange the cucumber cones. Sprinkle the dressing over the salad.

SERVES 4

> ### CUCUMBER SPIRALS
> *Cut the very thinnest strips of cucumber skin, and you can shape them into spirals, hearts, rings or even letters of the alphabet.*
>
> *Use a cannelle knife and, with the notch, remove a continuous spiral of skin, working round and round the cucumber. You can make a not-quite-so-narrow strip, using a small, sharp knife.*
>
> *Strips of orange, lemon and grapefruit rind are pretty decorations for desserts.*

TOMATO CUPS

To make tomato cups, choose large, ripe, firm tomatoes. If necessary, cut a thin slice from the base so that the tomatoes stand firm.

Using a small, sharp knife cut out a lid by making zig-zag cuts just below the top. Carefully remove the lid. Scoop out the flesh, leaving the base intact and taking care not to pierce it. A small teaspoon or a vegetable baller is ideal.

Sprinkle inside with salt and turn the cases upside down on a plate. Leave them to drain for 15-20 minutes. Rinse the tomato cases in water, then dry them thoroughly.

STRAWBERRY SALAD

1 small curly endive, separated
2 heads chicory, trimmed and separated
8-12 young nasturtium leaves
3 × 15ml spoons (3tbls) mint leaves
250g (9oz) strawberries, hulled

DRESSING
4 × 15ml spoons (4tbls) olive oil
1 × 15ml spoon (1tbls) clear honey
2 × 15ml spoons (2tbls) red wine vinegar
1 × 5ml spoon (1tsp) finely snipped chives
salt
freshly ground black pepper

1   First make the dressing. Beat the oil into the honey until it has dissolved, then whisk in all the other ingredients.
2   Toss together the salad leaves.
3   Just before serving, pour on the dressing and toss to coat the leaves thoroughly. Toss in the strawberries, sliced if they are large and reserving a few to decorate the top.

SERVES 4-6

Variation When the strawberry season is over, make this salad with blackberries instead.

LETTUCE HEARTS

This is a version of a dish which originated in the south of France, in which the lettuce is served with a spicy, creamy topping

2 lettuce hearts
2 hard-boiled eggs
1½ × 15ml spoons (1½tbls) finely snipped chives
1½ × 15ml spoons (1½tbls) chopped chervil

DRESSING
100ml (3½fl oz) olive oil
3 × 15ml spoons (3tbls) red wine vinegar
1 × 5ml spoon (1tsp) paprika
100ml (3½fl oz) double cream
salt
freshly ground black pepper

1   Discard any damaged and discoloured outer leaves of the lettuce. Cut each lettuce heart into 4 wedges. Wrap in a polythene bag and chill.
2   To make the dressing, whisk the oil, vinegar and paprika and gradually whisk in the cream. Season with salt and pepper.
3   Separate the yolks and the whites of the hard-boiled eggs and chop them separately.
4   Arrange the lettuce wedges on a serving dish. Spoon over the paprika dressing so that it virtually covers each piece. Make lines of the chopped egg yolk, chives, chopped egg white and chervil over each lettuce slice.

Serve chilled to accompany cold meat or fish, or as a salad course in its own right.

SERVES 4

SALAD STALK CURLS

Make garnish frills with the stalks of salad leaves such as Chinese cabbage, spinach, perpetual spinach (Swiss chard), pak choi and celery. Use them to garnish salads and savoury dishes of all kinds. They are especially effective with simple egg dishes such as omelettes and scrambled eggs and, being easy to eat with the fingers, they are good to take on picnics.

Cut pencil-thin strips about 10cm (4in) long. Make 7.5cm (3in) deep cuts, close together from one end. Soak the strips for 2-3 hours in ice-cold water, then drain them. The slits will have opened out and the strips curled over.

RED, WHITE & GREEN SALAD

12-16 leaves lettuce
1 small head red chicory, separated
1 small bulb Florence fennel, trimmed
1 small courgette, trimmed
100g (4oz) French beans, cooked
3 × 15ml spoons (3tbls) hazelnuts

DRESSING
4 × 15ml spoons (4tbls) sesame oil
2 × 15ml spoons (2tbls) hazelnuts
1 × 15ml spoon (1tbls) cider vinegar
1 × 5ml spoon (1tsp) lemon juice
1 egg yolk
a pinch of sugar
salt
freshly ground black pepper

1   Liquidize the dressing ingredients in a blender or food processor. Taste the dressing and adjust the seasoning if needed.
2   Arrange the salad leaves on 4 or 6 serving plates.
3   Thinly slice the fennel into rings. Thinly slice the courgette.
4   Arrange the fennel, courgette slices and beans over the leaves. Just before serving, pour over the dressing.

SERVES 4-6

PICNIC SALADS

Fresh leaves and vegetables from the salad garden make a highly portable feast – crisp home-grown lettuce, chicory, corn salad, endives, radishes, onions are all perfect picnic fare. Thread them as kebabs, pack them in individual pots and moulds, layer them in oven-fresh bread, wrap them in pancakes, fill flans with them, enjoy them in chilled or steaming soups – a picnic from the garden is a feast indeed.

RED CHICORY SOUP

50g (2oz) butter
1 medium onion, peeled and sliced
12-16 large leaves red chicory
2 small beetroots, peeled and diced
2 medium potatoes, peeled and diced
900ml (1½ pints) chicken stock
salt
freshly ground black pepper
a pinch of grated nutmeg
300ml (½ pint) single cream
4 × 15ml spoons (4tbls) soured cream
2 × 15ml spoons (2tbls) finely snipped chives

1   Melt the butter and fry the onion over moderate heat for 4 minutes, stirring once or twice. Add all but 2 of the chicory leaves and cook until they collapse. Add the beetroots, potatoes and stock and season with salt and pepper.
2   Cover the pan, bring to the boil and simmer for 20 minutes, or until all the vegetables are tender.
3   Liquidize the soup in a blender to make a smooth purée. Add the nutmeg and single cream. Taste and adjust seasoning if needed.
4   Cool, then chill the soup.

5   Finely chop the remaining chicory leaves and stir them into the soup. To serve, swirl the soured cream on top and sprinkle with the chives. Serve chilled.

SERVES 4-6

RADISH SOUP

40g (1½oz) butter
1 medium onion, peeled and sliced
8 large Chinese cabbage leaves, sliced
½ × 5ml spoon (½tsp) curry powder
350g (12oz) radishes, trimmed and halved
900ml (1½ pints) chicken stock
300ml (½ pint) buttermilk
salt
freshly ground black pepper
2 × 15ml spoons (2tbls) chopped tarragon
4 radishes, thinly sliced

1   Melt the butter and fry the onion over moderate heat for 4 minutes, stirring once or twice. Add the Chinese leaves and cook for 3 minutes. Stir in the curry powder and cook for 1 minute. Add the radishes and stock.
2   Cover, bring to the boil and simmer for 15-20 minutes, or until the radishes are tender.
3   Liquidize the soup in a blender. Return to the pan, stir in the buttermilk and season with salt and pepper.
4   Heat gently without boiling.
5   To serve, sprinkle a ring of chopped tarragon over each serving and float sliced radishes in the centre.

SERVES 4-6

Left Red chicory soup, served chilled with a swirl of soured cream and chopped chives, looks almost too good to eat.
Facing page Leaf-green pancakes and Roquefort moulds, topped with parsley and sliced radishes for a splash of colour.

ROQUEFORT MOULDS

15g (½oz) powdered gelatine
3 × 15ml spoons (3tbls) hot water
2 eggs, separated
6 × 15ml spoons (6tbls) chopped watercress
75g (3oz) Roquefort cheese, crumbled
2 spring onions, trimmed and chopped
300ml (½ pint) double cream, whipped
½ red pepper, seeded
10cm (4in) piece cucumber, thinly sliced
salad leaves, to serve

1   Dissolve the gelatine in the water and leave to cool.
2   Beat the egg yolks until they are creamy. Whisk the whites until they are stiff.
3   Stir together the egg yolks, watercress, cheese and spring onions. Stir in the cooled gelatine and whipped cream. Fold in the egg whites.
4   Brush 4 × 225g (8oz) margarine tubs with oil. Cut the pepper into small diamond shapes and arrange them in a pattern in the tubs.
5   Spoon in the mousse and chill in the refrigerator for a minimum of 1½ hours to set.

6   Arrange the cucumber slices over the mousse and put on the lids for travelling.
7   Run a knife around the inside of the tubs. Line 4 picnic plates with salad leaves and turn out the mousse. Serve with crusty wholewheat rolls.

SERVES 4

SALAD KEBABS

4 mini Swiss cheeses
4 young sorrel or spinach leaves
10cm (4in) piece cucumber
½ small green pepper
½ small red pepper
50g (2oz) smoked salmon, thinly sliced
4 corn salad leaves
8 radishes or radish roses
4 small gherkins
salad leaves, to serve

DIP
150ml (¼ pint) plain yoghurt
4 × 5ml spoons (4tsp) finely snipped chives
salt
freshly ground black pepper
1 × 15ml spoon (1tbls) mayonnaise

1   Wrap the cheeses in the sorrel or spinach leaves. Cut the cucumber into 8 slices. Trim the green and red pepper halves, remove the seeds and chop each one into 4 pieces. Cut the smoked salmon and corn salad leaves and wrap them into 8 rolls.
2   Thread each of 4 cocktail sticks with 1 cheese, 2 slices of cucumber, 2 slices of red pepper, 1 radish, alternating the colours.
3   Thread each of another 4 cocktail sticks with 2 slices of cucumber, 1 gherkin, 2 slices of green pepper, 1 radish and 2 salmon rolls, again alternating the colours.
4   Line a lidded polythene box with salad leaves, arrange the kebabs and cover the box.
5   Mix together the ingredients for the dip and take them in a yoghurt pot. Serve the kebabs with the yoghurt dip.

SERVES 4

Variation You can vary the kebabs according to the season. Firm, ripe strawberries, grapes, small button mushrooms and scoops of melon are all suitable.

GLAZED LAMB

8 lamb cutlets
freshly ground black pepper
1 × 5ml spoon (1tsp) paprika
40g (1½oz) aspic crystals
175ml (6fl oz) condensed consommé, hot
3 × 15ml spoons (3tbls) dry sherry
1 cooked carrot, thinly sliced
10cm (4in) piece of cucumber
1 small curly endive
1 red pepper, seeded and cut into rings
1 small onion, peeled and cut into rings
2 × 15ml spoons (2tbls) chopped mint leaves
4 tomato cups (see p.113)
2 × 5ml spoons (2tsp) finely snipped chives
4 mint sprigs

DRESSING

4 × 15ml spoons (4tbls) olive oil
1 × 15ml spoon (1tbls) orange juice
1 × 5ml spoon (1tsp) grated orange rind
salt
freshly ground black pepper
¼ × 5ml spoon (¼tsp) mustard powder

1   Sprinkle the meat with pepper and paprika and cook in the oven, pre-heated to 180°C, 350°F, gas 4, for 25-30 minutes. Cool on a wire rack.
2   Dissolve the aspic crystals in the hot consommé, stir in the sherry and season with pepper. Set it aside until it is beginning to set, and is syrupy.
3   Using aspic cutters, cut the carrot slices into decorative shapes.
4   Arrange the carrot shapes over the cutlets to represent flowers. Thinly pare the skin from the cucumber, cut it into the shapes of stalks and leaves and arrange them on the cutlets.
5   Spoon the aspic over the cutlets to cover them completely. Chill in the refrigerator for 1 hour until set.
6   Thickly slice the cucumber and cut each slice into 4. Set aside 8 of the outside leaves of the endive. Slice the rest. Mix together cucumber, endive, pepper, onion and mint leaves.
7   Line 4 polystyrene or waxed paper plates with the endive leaves. Arrange the lamb chops on one side and the mixed salad on the other. Place 2 tomato halves and sprinkle them with chives. Garnish with mint sprigs. Cover the plates with cling film and chill until needed.
8   Mix the dressing ingredients and take separately.

SERVES 4

SALAD IN RYE

6 slices black rye bread
6 slices light rye bread
butter, for spreading
350g (12oz) full-fat cream cheese
1 × 15ml spoon (1tbls) chopped marjoram
150g (5oz) shelled raw shrimps
3 small peaches, skinned, stoned and thinly sliced
1 × 15ml spoon (1tbls) lemon juice
1 small lettuce heart, shredded
4 × 5ml spoons (4tsp) chopped mint
lettuce leaves

1   Spread the black bread slices with butter. Mix together the cheese, marjoram and shrimps and spread on the bread. Toss the peaches in lemon juice.
2   Scatter half the shredded lettuce on the bread, sprinkle with half the mint, arrange the peach slices over it, cover with the remaining lettuce and mint and the light rye bread.
3   Cut off the crusts and cut the sandwiches into triangles. Wrap the sandwiches in lettuce leaves to keep them moist, and then in foil.

MAKES 6 SANDWICHES

ASPARAGUS ROLLS

8 small lettuce leaves
8 red chicory leaves
8 young sorrel leaves
8 cooked asparagus tips
100g (4oz) lean ham, chopped
2 × 15ml spoons (2tbls) pine kernels
2 × 15ml spoons (2tbls) stuffed olives
2 × 15ml spoons (2tbls) chopped cucumber
8 long thin strips cucumber peel

1   Cut away any tough stalks from the salad leaves. Place a lettuce, chicory and sorrel leaf on top of each other and an asparagus spear along the centre – 8 times.
2   Sprinkle the ham, pine kernels, olives and cucumber over the leaves and roll them to enclose the filling.
3   Tie up the rolls with a length of cucumber peel and tie it into a bow.
4   Pack the rolls in a lidded box for travelling.
    Serve them with tomato salad and a soured cream dressing.

SERVES 4

LEAF-GREEN PANCAKES

75g (3oz) flour
salt
2 eggs
200ml (7fl oz) milk
25g (1oz) butter, melted
225g (8oz) cooked spinach
a pinch of grated nutmeg
freshly ground black pepper
oil, for frying

FILLING

225g (8oz) cottage cheese
4 × 15ml spoons (4tbls) double cream
175g (6oz) shelled prawns, chopped
a pinch of cayenne pepper
2 × 15ml spoons (2tbls) grated
Parmesan cheese
10cm (4in) piece cucumber, peeled and chopped
2 large tomatoes, skinned, seeded and chopped

1   Sift the flour and salt into a bowl. Beat in the eggs and gradually pour on the milk, still beating. Stir in the melted butter.
2   Liquidize the spinach in a blender or food processor. Beat it into the batter and season with nutmeg and pepper. Cover and set aside for 1 hour.
3   Heat the oil in a small omelette pan. Pour in about 3 × 15ml spoons (3tbls) of the batter and tip the pan so that it covers the base completely. Cook over moderate heat for about 3 minutes or until bubbles appear on the surface. Flip or toss the pancake and cook on the other side for 2-3 minutes.
4   As each pancake is cooked, slide it on to a wire rack to cool. Cook the remaining batter in the same way.
5   To make the filling, beat together the cottage cheese and cream. Stir in the prawns, cayenne, Parmesan, cucumber and tomato and season with salt and pepper.
6   Divide the filling between the pancakes and roll them up.
7   Pack the pancakes in a lidded box for travelling.
    These pancake rolls are good with Red, white and green salad (see p.113) and crunchy crudités of spring onion and celery.

MAKES 8 PANCAKES

BRIOCHE SURPRISE

4 brioches
175g (6oz) boneless chicken, cooked and
chopped
1 stalk celery, finely chopped
50g (2oz) button mushrooms, finely chopped
1 spring onion, trimmed and chopped
1 small lettuce heart, very finely chopped
1 hard-boiled egg, chopped
1 × 15ml spoon (1tbls) chopped chervil
6 × 15ml spoons (6tbls) mayonnaise
2 × 5ml spoons (2tsp) mango chutney,
chopped
salt
freshly ground black pepper
salad cress, to garnish

1   Cut the top from each brioche.
Using a teaspoon, scoop out the
crumbs in the centre, leaving a bread
container with firm 'walls'.
2   Mix together the chicken, celery,
mushrooms, onion and lettuce.
3   Mix together the chopped egg,
chervil, mayonnaise and chutney and
season with salt and pepper. Stir the
mayonnaise mixture into the salad and
mix well.
4   Pile the salad into the brioche
cases and garnish the tops with salad
cress. Take the lids separately and
perch them on at a jaunty angle, to
serve.
  Serve with a crisp green salad.

SERVES 4

BAGUETTE LAYER

1 long French stick loaf
butter, for spreading
175g (6oz) liver pâté
6-8 cos lettuce leaves, shredded
2 large tomatoes, thinly sliced
2 × 15ml spoons (2tbls) chopped
nasturtium leaves
1 small onion, peeled and finely chopped
175g (6oz) full-fat cream cheese
2 hard-boiled eggs, chopped
2 × 15ml spoons (2tbls) finely snipped chives
salt
freshly ground black pepper
1 dessert pear, peeled, cored and thinly sliced
1 × 15ml spoon (1tbls) lemon juice
6-8 red chicory leaves, shredded

1   Split the loaf into 3 slices lengthways. Spread 2 sides of the bread with
butter and then with pâté.
2   Cover the bottom slice of bread
with the cos lettuce and tomato slices
and sprinkle on the chopped nasturtium leaves and half the onion.
3   Mix together the cheese, egg and
chives and season with salt and
pepper.
4   Spread the cheese mixture over
the remaining 2 sides of the bread.
Toss the pear in lemon juice.
5   Cover with the red chicory leaves
and pear slices and sprinkle with the
remaining onion.
6   Sandwich the loaf together and
wrap it in foil for travelling. Serve the
loaf cut into 4 slices.

SERVES 4

YOGHURT SALAD

2 × 15ml spoons (2tbls) alfalfa shoots
4 × 15ml spoons (4tbls) chopped red cabbage
1 small green pepper, seeded and chopped
1 × 15ml spoon (1tbls) sultanas
1 × 15ml spoon (1tbls) chopped dried dates
1 × 15ml spoon (1tbls) sunflower seeds
1 dessert apple, peeled, cored and chopped
salad cress, to garnish
4 radishes, thinly sliced

DRESSING
150ml (¼ pint) Greek-style yoghurt
2 × 15ml spoons (2tbls) soured cream
1 × 15ml spoon (1tbls) olive oil
salt
freshly ground black pepper

1   Mix the dressing ingredients.
2   Mix together the alfalfa shoots,
cabbage, green pepper, sultanas,
dates, sunflower seeds and apple.
3   Pour on the dressing and mix well.
4   Spoon the salad into yoghurt pots.
Make a ring of salad cress on top,
stalks to the middle. Cover the stalks
with a ring of radish slices. Put on the
lids for travelling.
  Serve with crudités.

SERVES 4

Home-made yoghurt

*Heat some milk to boiling point, allow it
to cool, and stir in a tablespoonful of
commercial live yoghurt. Cover with muslin
and leave in a warm place for twelve
hours or more until set.*

THE WILD GARDEN

L ooked at from the imaginative cook's point of view, the whole world is a wild garden, a paradise of fruits, flowers, leaves, roots and shoots to discover and enjoy. Yet how many of us do? A ritual afternoon in October spent blackberrying in the hedges and a rapid return a month or so later to collect enough blue-black fruits for sloe gin – and for most of us that's about the sum total of our wild food gathering for the year.

Perhaps we have been so seduced by the thrill of growing our own produce, the sheer magic of producing abundant and tasty crops from minute seed, that we don't consider any other harvest worth having. But where's our spirit of adventure? For adventure it certainly is, 'beachcombing' for tonight's supper or tomorrow's preserves, when you're not quite sure what new experience awaits you.

What you will discover as you explore the realms of the wild is a choice so bewildering that you scarcely know where to begin. That is just the problem we encountered when compiling the recipes for this section: which ingredients to include and which ones to leave out, when the world is your oyster? We had to settle for a representative selection of the foods you can find in reasonable quantity, and of the many ways in which you can prepare and serve them. Let these be a stepping stone to your own experiments.

The wild food year begins, as it does in the garden, in early spring, with the first young bright green shoots and leaves. There'll be no salads to compare later on with those you can gather in April, May and early June: garlic mustard, hawthorn, dandelion, clover, deadnettle, sowthistle and ground elder. Fill your basket with a few shoots of each and serve a salad course that is a feast of contrasting flavours – some subtle, some fiery – textures and colours.

Wild flowers don't, in general, have exceptional qualities of aroma and flavour, but when they are good they are very good, as country dishes, wines, beer and tisanes have testified for generations. Elderflower fritters, broom salad, clover wine, camomile tea – there's an incomparable link with our heritage in the ritual of gathering, preparing and enjoying these and other wild flower delights.

As the seasons progress, leaves toughen, flowers fade and the fruits – hips, haws, nuts and berries – take over. And why stop at old favourites when there are cloudberries for liqueur or tartlets; rowanberries for jelly to serve with pheasant; bullace to make a creamy meringue filling (not all wild food lacks sophistication!); and elderberries for warm winter drinking?

As for mushrooms and other fungi, damp meadows and fieldsides can be fruitful hunting ground from April, when the

Facing page *The dog rose, flowering charmingly in a hedgerow. Use its petals for jam or sorbet and its hips for marmalade. Left Bright rowanberries for picking.*

first species – St George's mushrooms – are to be found, through to late autumn when the unfriendly weather becomes destructive. The delights of fungi are many and varied – and so are the species. If this is an aspect of food for free that interests you, arm yourself with a comprehensive field guide, check each specimen carefully, and only then be prepared to taste it. Some species – a very few – are poisonous and you mustn't take chances.

The same goes for all wild foods. (There is a note about some poisonous berries and flowers on page 132.) If you are not sure that any part of the plant is edible, don't eat it.

Be discriminating about where you pick wild foods. Avoid those that grow near busy roads and all the exhaust fumes;

those that might have been recently sprayed with agricultural chemicals; and those that are particularly rare in your area. The law prohibits digging up any wild plant without the landowner's permission and gives special protection to some 60 plant species which are particularly endangered and under threat of extinction.

Be discriminating about how you pick, too. Never strip any plant of all, or even most, of its leaves, fruits or seeds – you'd be taking away its life support system.

All that being said, there are thousands of native wild plants, many of them rampant weeds, growing abundantly throughout the countryside – a cook's treasure trove and yours for the finding.

WILD GARDEN TREASURY

Blackberry or bramble, *Rubus fruticosus* One of the most delightful things about the wild blackberry is the wealth of imaginative country names it enjoys – brumblekite, lawyer, gartenberry and mush among them. The fruits turn from pale green to brick red and then, from August almost to November, to purplish black. The first berries to ripen are sweet enough to eat raw, later they have the makings of pies, puddings and preserves. The very young tips of the shoots are used to make a country 'bramble top' wine.

Bullace, *Prunus domestica* The autumn-ripening fruits are one of the treasures of the hedgerows. They are like firm cherry-sized plums and can be blue-black or green. Both kinds are good for preserving, stewing and purée – think of fruit fools, ice creams and sauces to serve with meat.

Cloudberry, *Rubus chamaemorus* The small, low-growing shrub – it's a hands-and-knees task to harvest – grows on moors and high ground in Scotland and northern England. The small burnt orange-coloured fruits reveal its relationship to the blackberry, for which they can be substituted.

Elder, *Sambucus nigra* It would be difficult to decide, if supplies were limited, between gathering the pale greeny yellow and highly scented flowers in spring or the heavy umbrella heads of tiny, round, juicy-black berries in autumn. Luckily, however, there are enough to do both.

Gather the flowers before they start to turn brown – a slight bitterness spoils the flavour then – and infuse them in milk, cream, sugar, oil or vinegar. Cook them with gooseberries, make a non-alcoholic lemony drink, or use them as the basis for wine.

Cut the thick stems with the multitudes of berries and strip them off with a fork. You probably won't enjoy them raw but they are superb cooked (as are blackberries) with apples, for pies, jams and jellies, cordial, liqueur and, perhaps the all-time country favourite, a burgundy-coloured wine.

The young fresh green leaves of this versatile plant can be eaten raw in salad and cooked like spinach.

Hawthorn, *Crataegus monogyna* From August the hedgerow bushes are covered with clusters of round, deep red berries. You can reward your harvest endeavour by eating some straight from the bush, but the dryish berries are best used to make jelly, liqueur or a mixed-fruit jam.

The small fan-shaped leaves, picked in their prime in the spring, are attractive and tasty in salads.

Rosehip, *Rosa canina* In the West Country the fruit of the wild rose or dog rose is – because of its shape – aptly called 'pixie pears'. It is used commercially to make a highly nutritious syrup – rosehips have 20 times as much Vitamin C as oranges.

You can easily make the delicious syrup at home; use the fruit to make liqueur; and add the hips to orchard fruits for jam and chutney. But in this case they need to be halved and seeded – and it's a laborious task to remove the prickly hairs surrounding the seeds.

Rowan or Mountain ash, *Sorbus aucuparia* You find these tall trees with their bright green, toothed leaves in woods, on hillsides, and in not-so-wild places – they are frequently planted to line urban areas.

The tiny round vivid orange fruits hang in clusters, like elderberries. Cut the stem and strip off the berries with a fork. They make superb jelly to serve with game or to glaze flans.

Sloe or Blackthorn, *Prunus spinosa* The minute white flowers appear on the 4m (13ft) high spiky bushes before the leaves. The small round blue-black fruits, greyish with 'bloom', are well known for their ability to turn a bottle of colourless gin into a deep rose-coloured liqueur, and can also be made into a jelly preserve. Gather them after the first frost, when the skins will be softer, but don't attempt to eat one raw.

Wild strawberry, *Fragraria vesca* Woods, heathland and old railway banks are good hunting grounds for these creeping plants, their huge clover-like leaves hiding minute red fruits speckled with white seeds. Small as they are, the fruits are sweet, juicy and full of the flavour most commercially grown strawberries lack. In Australia, wild strawberry tarts are a pastry-shop delicacy. The plants can be cultivated – when they are known as the Alpine strawberry.

FLOWERS AND LEAVES

Broom, *Sarothamnus scoparius* The brilliant yellow, pea-shaped flowers of this tall bush shine like a beacon on dry heathland in May and June. You can pickle the buds, make beer and wine from the tips of the slender branches and fritter, candy, infuse or just enjoy the flowers 'neat'.

Camomile, *Anthemis nobilis* The perky yellow and white daisy-like flowers brighten the meadows and roadsides in summer. Distinguish them from similar composites by their apple scent and feathery leaves – these do not have downy undersides. Cut long stems, hang bunches upside-down and dry the flowers for tisane. Camomile tea is said to act as a sedative.

Clover, *Trifolium pratense* Both the red and white flowers can be added to salads, used as a garnish and made into wine. The three-leaved (four if you're lucky) clover foliage is also good in salad and can be lightly cooked as spinach.

Comfrey, *Symphytum officinale* The dark green, spear-shaped and hairy leaves, not an attractive addition to a herb garden, can be found in the wild, mainly in ditches. Chop them into pancakes, scrambled eggs or wild ratatouille. The clusters of pink, white, blue or cream bell-shaped flowers wilt as soon as they are cut.

Dandelion, *Taraxacum officinale* Everyone knows the brilliant yellow, multi-petalled flowers, which make a delightful wine. The roots can be dried and ground as a coffee substitute and the leaves, picked when young, used in salad or cooked as greens.

Deadnettle, *Lamium purpureum* (red) and *L. album* (white) The flowers are carried in rings round the stems just above pairs of small heart-shaped leaves. Lightly cook the whole stems – 3 minutes is enough – and toss them in butter, or serve the leaves in salad.

Garlic mustard, *Alliaria petiolata* Alias hedge garlic and Jack-by-the-hedge, these tall (1m (3ft)) plants have exceptionally brilliant green, slightly toothed leaves and, from April to June, small snow-white flowers. Use the leaves in salads, sandwiches and, cooked as spinach, in a sauce.

Meadowsweet or Meadwort, *Filipendula ulmaria* From June right through to October, watersides and waysides are the brighter for the fluffy clusters of cream flowers atop 1m (3ft) reddish stems. The flowers, with their scent of new-mown hay, make delightful infusions and wine. In Victorian times the dried leaves were infused in mead and wine.

Sowthistle, *Sonchus oleraceus* Among the most attractive of wild leaves, they have fleshy stems, are heavily veined, deeply cut and a bright bluish green. They were a regular 'pot herb' used to flavour broths and stews. Serve young leaves in salads and sandwiches, or cook them gently, with no added water, in a little butter and lemon juice.

Stinging nettle, *Urtica dioica* Roadsides look gloomy towards August with the ageing leaves of shoulder-high stinging nettles. Put on strong gloves and gather the young shoots in early spring. They make very good soup, can be cooked and served as spinach, infused for a tisane or – the farmworkers' traditional thirst-quencher – brewed to make 'small beer'.

NUTS

Sweet chestnut, *Castanea sativa* The tall, upright trees have long, pointed, oval serrated leaves, and fruits enclosed in round bright green spiky cases. The nuts ripen in October and November and this is the time to go a-squirrelling, gathering them from the ground. Prize the nuts from the husks, then slit the shiny brown shells (to prevent them from exploding) before you cook them by boiling, roasting or grilling. You can then more easily shell them, peel off the inner brown skins (three layers to get through!) and eat them hot – fabulous straight from the embers – or cook them in casseroles, as soup, purée or, that most luxurious of sweetmeats, candied as marrons glacés.

Hazel, *Corylus avellana* Hedgerows throughout Britain are thick with this 4m (13ft) high shrub, noticeable in spring for its bright yellow catkins. The nuts, borne in clusters of two or three and enclosed in green lobed husks, ripen from late August to October and are variously known as cobnuts, filberts and woodnuts.

You can eat the nuts fresh and raw – they're a lovely snack mixed with raisins – or store them in their shells in a dry, warm room. Toast them under a grill and chop or grind them to use in meringues, confectionery, pastry and as a topping for milk drinks and desserts.

Walnut, *Juglans regia* Because of the very long time it takes a tree to mature, it is said that you plant a walnut for your grandchildren. Gather the nuts in the wild in July if you want to pickle them, in October and November if you want to enjoy them in the traditional way with a glass of port at Christmas, or in desserts and confectionery.

The leaves, carried in 'sets' of five on a stalk, can be used to make a liqueur called noyau.

LUNCH IN THE GARDEN

A table set for lunch on the terrace, a cloth spread on the grass for an impromptu meal on a sunny day – no matter how you arrange it, the garden is the perfect place to enjoy a menu of foods brought in from the wild. Salad leaves, flowers, fruits, nuts and berries all combine to create a selection of dishes that is distinctly different and decidedly delicious.

NETTLE SOUP

You can play guessing games with your friends – most people will say this soup is made with spinach.

1 large onion, peeled and sliced
1 garlic clove, peeled and chopped
2 medium potatoes, peeled and chopped
40g (1½oz) butter
500g (1¼lb) young stinging nettle tops

1 litre (1¾ pints) chicken stock
salt
freshly ground black pepper
150ml (¼ pint) soured cream
a pinch of grated nutmeg

1   Fry the onion, garlic and potatoes in the butter over low heat for 7-10 minutes, stirring once or twice. Add the nettle tops, stir well and then pour on the stock.

2   Cover the pan and boil for 15-20 minutes, until the potatoes are tender.
3   Liquidize the soup in a blender or food processor until it is smooth.
4   Return the purée to the pan, season with salt and pepper and stir in half the cream. Reheat gently.
5   To serve, stir on the rest of the cream and grate a little nutmeg on top. Serve hot.

SERVES 4-6

WILD RATATOUILLE BAKE

*This dish makes a lovely light lunch
with baskets of crusty rolls and a
flowery wine.*

750g (1½lb) mixed wild leaves and shoots
40g (1½oz) butter
1 large onion, peeled and sliced
2 garlic cloves, peeled and finely chopped
1 × 15ml spoon (1tbls) lemon juice

SAUCE
25g (1oz) butter
25g (1oz) flour
300ml (½ pint) buttermilk
50g (2oz) feta cheese, crumbled
1 × 5ml spoon (1tsp) Dijon mustard
a pinch of grated nutmeg
salt
freshly ground black pepper
50g (2oz) Cheddar cheese, grated

1   Wash the leaves and shoots, discarding any damaged ones and tough
stems.
2   Melt the butter in a large pan and
fry the onion and garlic over moderate
heat for 3-4 minutes, stirring once or
twice.
3   Add the leaves and lemon juice,
stir well and sauté over low heat for
10-12 minutes, until they collapse.
4   To make the sauce, melt the butter
in a small pan and stir in the flour.
When the mixture is smooth, gradually
pour on the buttermilk, stirring constantly. Strain on the liquid from the
vegetables and stir until the sauce
boils. Simmer for 3 minutes. Stir in the
feta cheese and mustard and season
with the nutmeg, salt and pepper.
5   Transfer the leaves to a heatproof
dish. Pour the sauce over and scatter
the cheese on top.
6   Preheat the grill to moderate. Grill
the dish until the sauce is golden
brown and bubbling. Serve at once.

SERVES 4-6

*A meal from the wild, but fit for a king.
Gather mushrooms, chestnuts and nettles
and make, left to right, Montpazier veal,
Rowanberry castle and Nettle soup. Serve
with sparkling elderflower 'champagne'
and enjoy the double pleasure of eating
delicious food that you have neither had to
grow nor buy!*

CHESTNUT SOUP

450g (1lb) chestnuts
25g (1oz) butter
1 large onion, peeled and finely chopped
450ml (¾ pint) chicken stock
450ml (¾ pint) milk
1 bouquet garni
salt
freshly ground black pepper
a pinch of ground mace
150ml (¼ pint) single cream
2 × 15ml spoons (2tbls) chopped sowthistle,
or mint
a pinch of grated nutmeg

1   Prick the skins of the chestnuts
and boil them for 30 minutes. Peel off
the skins and the inner brown skins.
Chop the nuts.
2   Melt the butter and fry the onions
and chestnuts over moderate heat for
4-5 minutes, stirring once or twice.
3   Stir in the stock and milk and add
the bouquet garni. Simmer for 20
minutes. Discard the herbs.
4   Liquidize the soup in a blender or
food processor. Season with salt and
pepper and stir in the mace and most
of the cream. Reheat gently. Stir in the
chopped leaves.
5   Swirl on the remaining cream and
sprinkle with the nutmeg. Serve hot.

SERVES 4-6

MONTPAZIER VEAL

350g (12oz) chestnuts
1kg (2¼lb) lean shoulder of veal
40g (1½oz) butter
1 × 15ml spoon (1tbls) olive oil
1 medium onion, peeled and sliced
1 garlic clove, peeled and chopped
1 × 15ml spoon (1tbls) flour
150ml (¼ pint) chicken stock
300ml (½ pint) soured cream
1 × 5ml spoon (1tsp) grated lemon rind
4 × 5ml spoons (4tsp) lemon juice
salt
freshly ground black pepper
100g (4oz) mushrooms, sliced
2 × 15ml spoons (2tbls) chopped mint
1 lemon, cut into 6 wedges, to garnish

1   Prick the skins of the chestnuts
and boil them for 30 minutes. Peel off
the skins and the inner brown skins.
Halve the nuts.

2   Trim any excess fat from the veal
and cut the meat into approximately
4cm (1½in) cubes.
3   Heat half the butter and the oil in a
flameproof casserole and fry the meat,
in several batches, over moderate
heat. Stir it often to seal and brown it
evenly on all sides. Lift out the meat
with a draining spoon.
4   Fry the onion and garlic for 3
minutes. Stir in the flour, then the
stock and cook for 3 minutes. Stir in
the chestnuts, soured cream, lemon
rind and lemon juice. Return the meat
to the casserole and season with salt
and pepper.
5   Cook the casserole in the oven,
preheated to 170°C, 325°F, gas 3, for
1¼ hours.
6   Fry the mushrooms in the remaining butter for 2-3 minutes. Stir them
into the casserole. Taste the sauce and
adjust the seasoning if needed.
7   Sprinkle the mint over the casserole and serve with the lemon wedges.

SERVES 6

JEWELLED SALAD

*You'll find these leaves contrast well
not only for flavour but for shape, with
the hawthorn leaves looking like tiny
green fans.*

2 large handfuls young hawthorn leaves
1 handful young dandelion leaves
1 handful young hedge garlic leaves
1 cup broom buds
2 spring onions, thinly sliced

DRESSING
4 × 15ml spoons (4tbls) olive oil
1 × 15ml spoon (1tbls) orange juice
2 × 5ml spoons (2tsp) clear honey
salt
freshly ground black pepper
2-3 drops soy sauce

1   Mix the dressing ingredients.
2   Toss together the salad leaves.
Pour on the dressing and toss to coat
the leaves thoroughly. Scatter on the
broom buds – the golden jewels on the
wild leaves – and the spring onions.

SERVES 4-6

POT HERB QUICHE

175g (6oz) wholewheat flour
salt
2 × 5ml spoons (2tsp) baking powder
50g (2oz) butter
25g (1oz) white vegetable fat
1 × 5ml spoon (1tsp) grated lemon rind
about 2½-3 × 15ml spoons (2½-3tbls) water

FILLING
about 250g (9oz) young ground elder leaves
50g (2oz) butter
1 medium onion, peeled and finely chopped
2 eggs
150ml (¼ pint) single cream
¼ × 5ml spoon (¼ tsp) mustard powder
salt
freshly ground black pepper
75g (3oz) Cheddar cheese, grated

1 Sift the flour, salt and baking powder and tip in the bran remaining in the sieve. Rub in the fats until the mixture is like fine crumbs. Stir in the lemon rind and sprinkle on just enough water to make a firm dough. Wrap in cling film or foil and chill in the refrigerator for about 30 minutes.
2 To make the filling, cook the leaves in half the butter in a covered pan over low heat for 10 minutes, stirring once or twice. Increase the heat and cook, uncovered, until all the moisture has evaporated. Remove from the heat.
3 Roll out the pastry and line a 23cm (9in) greased flan ring on a baking sheet. Trim the edges and prick the base all over with a fork.
4 Sauté the onion in the remaining butter for 3 minutes over moderate heat. Stir into the leaves.
5 Beat the eggs and cream, season with mustard, salt and pepper and stir into the leaf mixture. Stir in half the cheese.
6 Pour the filling into the pastry case and sprinkle the remaining cheese on top. Bake in the oven, preheated to 190°C, 375°F, gas 5, for 25 minutes, or until the filling is set and the pastry well browned. Serve warm.

SERVES 4-6

ELDERFLOWER FRITTERS

12 elderflower heads
100g (4oz) flour
salt
2 × 15ml spoons (2tbls) caster sugar
1 egg, separated
150ml (¼ pint) orange juice
oil, for deep frying
sugar

1 Cut off the elderflower stalks.
2 Sift the flour and salt, stir in the sugar and beat in the egg yolk and orange juice until the batter is smooth. Whisk the egg white until it is stiff, then fold it into the batter.
3 Heat the oil to 180°C, 350°F, or until a cube of bread browns in 60 seconds.
4 Dip the elderflowers in the batter, shake off any excess and fry them a few at a time for about 3 minutes, until they are puffed up and golden. Lift them out with a draining spoon, toss them on kitchen paper to dry, and keep them warm while you fry the remaining flowers.
5 Toss the fritters in sugar and serve them straight away.

SERVES 4

HOP, SKIP, & A JUMP

This is a dish to serve in April or May, when the hop shoots are young and tender, the dandelion leaves are a pale, bright green colour, and you can find St George's mushrooms in the fields.

2 large handfuls of hop tops
2 large handfuls of dandelion leaves
salt
50g (2oz) butter
freshly ground black pepper
2 × 5ml spoons (2tsp) lemon juice
50g (2oz) bacon, rinded and chopped
about 300g (11oz) mushrooms, sliced

1 Wash the hop tops and dandelion leaves. Put them in a pan of boiling, salted water, cover and boil them for 5 minutes, until they are tender. Drain the vegetables and return them to the pan. Add half the butter, season with salt and pepper and sprinkle on the lemon juice. Keep the vegetables warm.
2 Grill the chopped bacon until crisp on both sides. Meanwhile melt the remaining butter and fry the mushrooms for 3-4 minutes.
3 Stir the cooked bacon and mushrooms into the vegetables and serve at once.

It's a delicious accompaniment to roast or grilled meat.

SERVES 4-6

HEDGEROW MERINGUE CAKE

The meringue layers are crunchy with hazelnuts and the filling is the rich, deep red colour of bullace, the wild plum. It's a perfect countryside combination.

75g (3oz) hazelnuts, shelled
3 egg whites
75g (3oz) caster sugar
75g (3oz) demerara sugar

FILLING
350g (12oz) bullace
1 × 15ml spoon (1tbls) water
1 × 15ml spoon (1tbls) lemon juice
50g (2oz) light Muscovado sugar
300ml (½ pint) double cream, whipped

1 Toast the nuts on a baking sheet in a low oven or under the grill until golden brown. Grind or chop them.
2 Whisk the egg whites until they are very stiff. Add the caster sugar and whisk again until the meringue is stiff and glossy. Fold in the demerara sugar and the toasted hazelnuts.
3 Spread the meringue mixture into 2 × 20cm (8in) circles, on baking sheets lined with non-stick silicone paper. Level the tops.
4 Bake the meringues in the oven, preheated to 110°C, 225°F, gas ¼, for 2 hours, or until they are dry.
5 Turn out the meringue layers on to a wire rack and peel off the paper.
6 To make the filling, put the fruit, water, lemon juice and sugar into a pan. Stir occasionally over low heat until the sugar has dissolved, then simmer for about 20 minutes, until the bullace are tender.
7 Rub the fruit and juice through a sieve. Cool the purée.
8 Fold the cold fruit purée into the cream. Sandwich the meringue layers with the filling.

SERVES 6

CLOUDBERRY TARTS

100g (4oz) flour
salt
50g (2oz) butter
1 × 5ml spoon (1tsp) caster sugar
about 2 × 15ml spoons (2tbls) orange juice

FILLING
150g (5oz) full-fat soft cheese
2 × 15ml spoons (2tbls) caster sugar
1 × 5ml spoon (1tsp) grated orange rind
1 × 5ml spoon (1tsp) orange juice
2 × 15ml spoons (2tbls) double cream
350g (12oz) cloudberries
2 × 15ml spoons (2tbls) red wine, or water
50g (2oz) sugar
1 × 5ml spoon (1tsp) arrowroot

1 Sift together the flour and salt, rub in the butter until the mixture is like fine crumbs, then stir in the sugar. Sprinkle on enough juice to make a firm dough. Knead the dough lightly.
2 Roll out the dough on a lightly floured board and use it to line 12 tartlet tins. Trim the edges and prick the bases all over with a fork.
3 Line the tartlets with circles of foil and fill them with baking beans. Bake them 'blind' in the oven, preheated to 190°C, 375°F, gas 5, for 15 minutes. Remove the foil and beans and return the pastry cases to the oven for 3-5 minutes until they are golden brown. Leave on a wire rack to cool.
4 To make the filling, beat the cheese and beat in the caster sugar, orange rind, orange juice and cream.
5 Put the cloudberries, wine or water and sugar into a pan. Stir occasionally over low heat until the sugar has dissolved, then increase the heat and simmer the fruit for 10-15 minutes, until it is tender. Stir a little of the juice into the arrowroot to make a smooth paste. Pour it into the pan and stir for about 3 minutes, until the sauce clears and thickens. Cool.
6 Line the tartlet cases with the cheese mixture. Spoon the fruit on top.

MAKES 12 TARTLETS

Variation If you cannot find the small, russet berries – their habitat is the northern moors and bogland – use blackberries instead. And if you can find any late, late borage flowers, they make the prettiest of decorations to these wild fruit tarts.

FILBERT SHORTCAKE

350g (12oz) flour
salt
100g (4oz) caster sugar
4 × 5ml spoons (4tsp) baking powder
2 × 5ml spoons (2tsp) mixed ground spice
175g (6oz) butter
100g (4oz) hazelnuts, shelled and chopped
2 egg yolks
120ml (4fl oz) milk

FILLING
50g (2oz) caster sugar
300g (½ pint) double cream, whipped
2 egg whites, whisked
450g (1lb) ripe blackberries

1 Sift the flour, salt, sugar, baking powder and spice. Rub in the butter until the mixture is like fine crumbs. Stir in the chopped nuts. Beat the egg yolks and milk, pour on to the dry ingredients and form into a dough. Knead the dough lightly until smooth.
2 Divide the dough into 3 equal pieces and press each one into a greased, floured 20cm (8in) sandwich or flan tin. Prick all over with a fork.
3 Bake the shortcake in the oven, preheated to 220°C, 425°F, gas 7, for 12-15 minutes, until it is firm and golden brown. Leave to cool in the tin for a few minutes, then turn out on to a wire rack to cool.
4 To make the filling, stir the sugar into the cream. Fold in the egg white.
5 Spread each layer with the cream filling. Divide the blackberries between the 3 layers, arranging them in a pattern on the top one. Sandwich the shortcake layers together.

SERVES 6

ROWANBERRY CASTLE

750g (1½lb) rowanberries
65g (2½oz) sugar
150ml (¼ pint) white wine
15g (½oz) powdered gelatine
3 × 15ml spoons (3tbls) water
candied herb leaves, to decorate

FILLING
150ml (¼ pint) double cream, whipped
1 × 20cm (8in) meringue round,
crushed

1 Strip the berries from the stalks by threading them through the tines of a large fork, then wash them.
2 Liquidize half the berries in a blender or food processor. Put the purée into a pan with the sugar and wine and stir occasionally over low heat until the sugar has dissolved. Add the berries and simmer for 10-15 minutes, until they are tender.
3 Soften the gelatine in the water and stir it into the fruit mixture.
4 Rinse a 750ml (1¼ pint) ring mould in water. Pour in the fruit mixture and leave to cool. Chill in the refrigerator for 3-4 hours, until set.
5 Stir together the double cream, crushed meringue and single cream.
6 Run a knife around the mould. Turn it out on to a serving plate and pile the meringue cream in the centre. Decorate with candied herb leaves.

SERVES 6

COUNTRY DRINKS

Wandering along the hedgerows in springtime gathering fragrant flowers, tender young shoots and bright green leaves; and returning in autumn to fill your baskets with rosy hips, haws and juicy berries: it's one of the most exciting ways of bringing home the harvest. And this is no ordinary harvest – it is your countryside treasure trove to turn into wines, liqueurs, tisanes, and cordials.

ELDERFLOWER MILK SHAKE

2 heads elderflowers
300ml (½ pint) milk
225g (8oz) vanilla ice cream
300ml (½ pint) Elderflower 'champagne'
(see right)
4 scented geranium leaves, to decorate

1   Prick off the flowers from the stalks. Put them in a sieve and run cold water through them.
2   Put the milk, ice cream, elderflower drink and flowers into a blender or food processor and blend to a foamy cream.
3   Pour into 4 chilled glasses and decorate each glass with a scented leaf. Serve chilled.

SERVES 4

WILD STRAWBERRY MILK SHAKE

225g (8oz) wild strawberries, hulled
300ml (½ pint) milk, chilled
300ml (½ pint) plain yoghurt
225g (8oz) vanilla ice cream
4 × 15ml spoons (4tbls) Rosehip syrup
(see p. 127)
4 mint sprigs, to decorate

1   Put the strawberries, milk, yoghurt, ice cream and syrup into a blender or food processor and blend to a foamy cream.
2   Pour the milk shake into 4 chilled glasses and decorate each one with a sprig of mint. Serve with straws.

SERVES 4

ELDERFLOWER 'CHAMPAGNE'

Delicately flavoured with spring flowers from the hedgerows, this non-alcoholic drink is refreshing served chilled with a slice of lemon and sprig of apple mint or lemon balm.

4 large heads elderflowers
500g (1¼lb) sugar
2 × 15ml spoons (2tbls) white distilled vinegar
4.5 litres (8 pints) water
2 lemons

1   Put the flowers, sugar, vinegar and water into a large jar or bowl. Halve the lemons, squeeze the juice and cut up the peel. Add the lemon juice and peel to the container.
2   Stir or shake well to dissolve the sugar. Cover and leave for 24 hours, stirring or shaking occasionally.
3   Strain into screw-topped bottles and screw on the caps. Label the bottles and store in a cool, dark place.

MAKES 4.5 LITRES (1 GALLON)

Variation Those who wish may add a dash of white rum, gin or vodka!

CAMOMILE TEA

5 × 5ml spoons (5tsp) dried camomile flowers
750ml (1¼ pints) boiling water
4 thin slices of orange
honey, if liked

1   Infuse the flowers in the boiling water for 3 minutes. Stir well.
2   Strain the tea, float a slice of orange in each cup and sweeten with honey, if liked.

MAKES 4 CUPS

LINDEN TEA

Linden tea is said to soothe the nerves and the digestion. In Edwardian times ladies drank a cup of the hot tea to induce sleep.

5 × 5ml spoons (5tsp) dried lime flowers
750ml (1¼ pints) boiling water
4 thin slices of lemon or lime
honey (optional)

1   Infuse the flowers in the boiling water for 5 minutes. Stir well.
2   Strain the tea and float a slice of lemon or lime in each cup. Sweeten with honey if you like.

MAKES 4 CUPS

MEADOWSWEET TISANE

Meadowsweet has a delicate almond-like flavour, and in medieval times it was used as a strewing herb, to scent rooms.

8 heads meadowsweet flowers
a handful of meadowsweet leaves
750ml (1¼ pints) boiling water
4 thin slices lemon
honey (optional)

1   Pick the flowers from the main stalk. Wash the flowers and leaves.
2   Infuse them in boiling water for 5 minutes. Stir well.
3   Strain the tea. Float a slice of lemon in each cup and sweeten with honey if wished. Serve hot.

MAKES 4 CUPS

Another delight from the garden – Blackberry vodka.

ELDERBERRY CORDIAL

750g (1½lb) elderberries
100g (4oz) sugar
juice of 1 lemon
2 × 15ml spoons (2tbls) water

1   Strip the elderberries from the stalks. Wash and drain them.
2   Put the berries, sugar, lemon juice and water into a pan and stir occasionally over low heat until the sugar has dissolved. Simmer for 15 minutes, mashing the fruit from time to time with a wooden spoon.
3   Liquidize the fruit in a blender, then cool. Pour it into a sterilized bottle and cover with a cap or cork.

To serve, pour about 3 × 15ml spoons (3tbls) of the cordial into a tumbler, fill it with chilled sparkling or still mineral water and float a slice of orange or lemon on top.

MAKES ABOUT 450ML (¾ PINT)

ROSEHIP SYRUP

Be sure to make enough of this delicious syrup: add a few drops to fruit salad dressing; drizzle a spoonful over ice cream; use it hot as a glowing sauce for steamed sponge pudding; and add it to the sauce for game and poultry.

1kg (2¼lb) rosehips
2.5 litres (4½ pints) water
500g (1¼lb) sugar

1   Wash the rosehips and remove the stalks. Mince the rosehips or chop them finely.
2   Put them into a pan with half the water, bring to the boil and boil for 20 minutes.
3   Tip the rosehips and liquid into a scalded jelly bag and leave it to drip into a bowl for about 2 hours, or overnight if it is more convenient. Pour the strained juice into a covered container and store it in the refrigerator.
4   Tip the rosehips into the pan and boil them with the remaining water for 15 minutes. Strain the liquid through a jelly bag.
5   Measure the two juice extracts, and boil together until they have been reduced to about 1 litre (1¾ pints).
6   Add the sugar and stir occasionally over low heat until it has dissolved. Increase the heat and boil for 10 minutes.
7   Pour the syrup into warmed sterilized bottles to within 2.5cm (1in) of the top and close them with corks tied in place.
8   Stand the bottles on a folded cloth in a deep pan with cold water to come up to the necks. Bring to the boil and boil for 10 minutes.
9   Press in the corks. Leave the syrup to cool. Label the bottles and store in a cool, dark place.

MAKES ABOUT 1.5 LITRES (2½ PINTS)

BRAMBLE TIP WINE

A West Country winemaker says that this wine, made with the green succulent tips of the young bramble shoots, tastes 'of old books'. But she must like old books – because she makes it every year!

4.5 litres (8 pints) young bramble tips
4.5 litres (8 pints) boiling water
a campden tablet
a little warm water
1.3kg (3lb) sugar
wine yeast
juice of 1 lemon

1 Wash the tips of the blackberry shoots and put them into a scrupulously clean bucket. Pour the boiling water over them and stir well. Dissolve the campden tablet in a little warm water and stir into the liquid. Cover and set aside for 24 hours.
2 Transfer the mixture to a large pan, bring to the boil and simmer for 20 minutes.
3 Strain the liquid, stir in the sugar, cover and leave to cool.
4 Add the yeast according to the manufacturer's instructions. Cover and keep in a warm place, such as an airing cupboard, for 10 days.
5 Pour off the liquid into a fermenting jar and fit an air lock. Leave to ferment until there is no more activity and the wine has cleared.
6 Siphon off the wine, bottle and close with corks. Label and store for 6-12 months before drinking.

MAKES 4.5 LITRES (1 GALLON)

CLOVER WINE

2 litres (3½ pints) clover flowers
2 cups lemon balm leaves
4.5 litres (1 gallon) boiling water
juice of 3 lemons and 3 oranges
1kg (2¼lb) sugar
wine yeast
6 × 15ml spoons (6tbls) Rosehip syrup (see p. 127)

1 Put the flowers and leaves in a scrupulously clean bucket and pour on the water. Stir in the lemon and orange juice.
2 Dissolve a little sugar in warm water and sprinkle on the yeast. Leave it in a warm place for 20 minutes until it becomes frothy.
3 Stir the yeast into the liquid, cover and leave for 5 days to ferment.
4 Strain off the liquid into a sterilized jar, close with an airlock and leave in a warm room until it has ceased bubbling.
5 Stir in the rosehip syrup.
6 Pour the wine through a filter into bottles and close with corks. Label the wine and store it for at least 4 weeks.

MAKES 4.5 LITRES (1 GALLON)

NETTLE BEER

Here's a drink the farmworkers used to quaff eagerly at the end of a thirsty day's work – long before the end, often!

1 bucket stinging nettle leaves
9 litres (16 pints) water
1.3kg (3lb) sugar
50g (2oz) cream of tartar
15g (½oz) brewer's yeast

1 Boil the nettle leaves in the water for 20 minutes.
2 Strain off the liquid, pressing the leaves against the sieve to extract the maximum moisture.
3 Add the sugar and cream of tartar and stir over low heat until the sugar has dissolved.
4 Leave the liquid to cool to blood heat, then sprinkle on the yeast and stir it well.
5 Cover and leave in a warm place for 3 days.
6 Skim off any foam from the top. Pour off the beer into sterilized bottles, without disturbing the sediment. Cork the bottles and it's ready to drink.
   Serve with a slice of lemon or lime and a sprig or two of herbs.

MAKES 9 LITRES (16 PINTS)

BROOM BEER

50g (2oz) young broom tips
4.5 litres (8 pints) water
500g (1¼lb) malt extract
250g (9oz) sugar, plus extra
15g (½oz) dried yeast

1 Wash the broom tips. Put them in a large pan with about one-third of the water, bring to the boil and boil for 15 minutes.
2 Put the malt and sugar in a pan with half the remaining water and dissolve it over low heat, stirring occasionally.
3 Strain off the broom tips. Pour the liquid into the malt mixture.
4 Boil the broom with the remaining water for 15 minutes. Strain and add that liquid to the malt mixture.
5 Pour the liquid into a scrupulously clean bucket or crock, cover and leave to cool to blood heat.
6 Sprinkle on the yeast, cover and leave in a warm place, such as an airing cupboard, for 3-4 days, or until fermentation stops.
7 Pour off the beer, taking care not to disturb any sediment. Pour it into 1.2 litre (2 pint) bottles and add 1 × 5ml spoon (1tsp) sugar to each. Screw on the lids. Leave the bottles undisturbed for 7-10 days, until the beer is clear. Serve chilled.

MAKES 4.5 LITRES (1 GALLON)

BLACKBERRY VODKA

When you have strained the liqueur, the blackberries, full of flavour, can be added to fruit salad or used to decorate a creamy dessert.

500g (1¼lb) blackberries
225g (8oz) sugar
700ml (1¼ pints) vodka
2 × 15ml spoons (2tbls) orange juice

1   Wash the blackberries and put them into a screw-topped jar, sprinkling the sugar between the layers.
2   Pour on the vodka and orange juice, cover the jar and shake well.
3   Put the jar into a cool, dark place for at least 10 weeks, shaking it occasionally.
4   Strain off the blackberries and pour the liqueur into a bottle. Close the bottle, label and store it, away from the light.

MAKES 900ML (1½ PINTS)

NOYAU

This is a French liqueur, particularly good served after dinner with sweetmeats such as marrons glacés.

1 litre (1¾ pints) young walnut or beech leaves
700ml (1¼ pints) gin
250g (9oz) sugar
300ml (½ pint) water
150ml (¼ pint) sweet sherry

1   Wash the leaves and dry them. Put them into a large, wide-necked jar and pour on the gin. Cover the jar and leave it for 3 weeks.
2   Strain off the leaves.
3   Put the sugar and water into a pan and heat over low heat, stirring occasionally until the sugar has dissolved. Increase the heat and boil the syrup for 5 minutes. Cool.
4   Stir together the gin, syrup and sherry. Pour into sterilized bottles, cover, label and store, away from the light.

MAKES 1.25 LITRES (1¼ PINTS)

SLOE GIN

Serve this sloe-flavoured liqueur in tiny glasses after a meal, with nuts or sweetmeats.

250g (9oz) sloes
150g (5oz) sugar
2 × 15ml spoons (2tbls) blanched almonds
450ml (¾ pint) gin

1   Pick the sloes from the stalks and wash them. Prick them all over with a sterilized darning needle and put them into a screw-topped jar. Add the sugar and almonds, pour on the gin, cover the jar and shake well.
2   Leave the jar in a cool, dark place for at least 3 months, shaking it occasionally.
3   Strain off the sloes, pressing them against the sieve to extract the maximum moisture and flavour.
4   Pour the liqueur into a bottle. Close the bottle, label and store it, away from the light.

MAKES 450ML (¾ PINT)

BLACKBERRY COCKTAIL

500g (1¼lb) blackberries
4 × 15ml spoons (4tbls) sugar
2 × 15ml spoons (2tbls) lemon juice
150ml (¼ pint) white rum
crushed ice, to serve
sparkling mineral water

1   Purée the blackberries thoroughly in a blender, then rub the purée through a sieve.
2   Stir together the sugar, lemon juice and rum and stir in the fruit purée.
3   Put crushed ice into tumblers, pour over the cocktail and fill the glasses with mineral water. Serve chilled.

MAKES 4-8 DRINKS

HEDGEROW RUM

500g (1¼lb) mixed rosehips, rowanberries and haws
250g (9oz) blackberries
750g (1½lb) sugar
700ml (1¼ pints) dark rum

1   Wash the rosehips, rowanberries, haws and blackberries. Halve the hips. Put them all into a screw-topped jar, sprinkling sugar between the layers. Pour over the rum and put the lid on the jar. Shake it well.
2   Set aside in a cool, dark place for 3 months, shaking the jar occasionally.
3   Strain off the fruits, pressing them against the sieve to extract the maximum moisture and flavour.
4   Pour the liqueur into a bottle and close the top. Label and store, away from the light.

MAKES 700ML (1¼ PINTS)

DANDELION 'COFFEE'

This has a slightly bitter flavour, like the French coffee and chicory mixture.

Dig up dandelion roots and strip off the hairy roots. Cut off the leaves – you can use them in salad. Wash and scrub the roots, then dry them thoroughly.

Place the roots on a wire rack in an airing cupboard, over a central heating boiler or on top of an all-night-burning cooker. Depending on the heat the roots will be dried in 3-4 days.

Chop the roots finely. Spread them on baking trays and roast them under the grill, stirring them frequently until they are deep brown. The length of roasting time affects the flavour.

Cool the roasted roots completely, then store them in an airtight container. Grind the dandelion root and use, as ground coffee, in either a percolator or a jug.

Sweeten it with sugar or honey. A pinch of ground cinnamon sprinkled over a blob of whipped cream is a delicious addition.

THE FLOWER GARDEN

ottage gardens – the old-fashioned kind that make city eyes go misty – had a way of muddling pretty flowering plants, such as pansies, border pinks, and primroses, with practical kitchen crops like peas and parsnips. It was almost as if our ancestral gardener hadn't grasped the distinction between the purely decorative and the simply delicious – or didn't care.

Actually, it was not like that at all. These roses-round-the-door gardeners were neither eccentric, nor guilty of paltry planning. It is rather the ones who came later who were at fault, drawing an entirely false line between those plants which are pretty and those which are practical – and oh, how much culinary joy we have been missing ever since.

In times past, if a plant was edible it was eaten, or used as a medicine or flavouring, or preserved. And as some part of almost all plants *is* edible, and in many cases that part is the flower (there's a word of warning about some which are not on page 132), there they were, higgledy-piggledy, all growing together.

Strangely enough, in an age when every plant was put, so to speak, under the culinary microscope, the potential of both runner beans and tomatoes was slow to dawn, and these crops were first grown for their attractive red flowers and fruit respectively. It's a topsy-turvy world. Imagine an old

farm kitchen with a great earthenware jug filled with stems of scarlet bean flowers and heavy trusses of tomatoes on the scrubbed pine dresser, while the cook is busy setting moon-faced pansy flowers in jelly and infusing confectioner's sugar with pinks!

In recent years, we have foolishly turned our backs on the culinary possibilities of so many of the flowers we grow. What a waste, to let scented rose petals flutter to the ground when we could strew them in custards, creams and ices, or to let proud gladiolus or nasturtium flowers fade away when they could make a spectacular showing in a salad buffet, their loud trumpets filled with some savoury concoction.

Cooking with flowers has its place in culinary history around the world and its roots are deep in every culture. In South America – Mexico especially – it is the hot, spicy flowers which find most favour; and in Turkish cooking, by contrast, it is the sweet pungency of the rose that rules – where would Turkish delight be without it? The Chinese – who have a saying for everything – put it neatly a long time ago in this proverb: 'If you have two loaves of bread, sell one and buy a lily.' And make lily sandwiches, of course.

To those who are not familiar with the gentle art of floral cuisine, exploring the flower garden – inhaling and assessing fragrances, sampling the flavour of petals and leaves, and

Facing page *Try bright red nasturtiums for a sandwich filling with a difference.* Left *You could make wine or syrup from these pansies – or decorate a salad with them.*

taking a fresh look at flower shapes and colours – has all the promise and excitement of a first visit to a spice market. Those flowers with the strongest scent – roses, carnations, pinks, jonquil, jasmine, orange blossom, broom and hyacinth – all make delightful decoctions. You can infuse the petals in sugar, oil, honey, vinegar, syrup, milk, cream or plain water.

Capture the scent, transform it into a flavour, and use it to give new personality to baking, desserts, salads, even cosmetics. A sponge cake made with carnation-flavoured sugar and fondant icing sugar; cookies made with jasmine honey; fresh fruits tossed in orange-blossom syrup; dried fruits soaked in rose-petal water: there are so many ways in which the memory of your flower garden can linger in your cooking all year round.

You really have to taste flowers for yourself to appreciate their subtle flavours – some are obvious once you know about them, others will surprise you. Sweet pea flowers, for example, taste of the freshest, youngest garden peas and are lovely in salads; golden yellow broom buds taste of almonds; marigolds are pleasantly spicy, and their petals have the added advantage that they can be used as a saffron colouring in both sweet and savoury dishes; gladioli and nasturtiums both taste peppery – and you can use nasturtium leaves in salads, and pickle the small green buds as pretend capers.

There's no need to overlook the fact that flowers, however tasty, are decorative too. You can candy or crystallize them in egg white and sugar and dry them to a crisp frostiness to store, for prettying up cakes and desserts, or to enjoy as sweetmeats. Borrow their lovely colours as a dramatic contrast to other foods – sweet pea or broom flowers nestling among salad leaves – and use them as simple garnishes. Edible flowers are both pretty and practical.

EDIBLE FLOWERS

Carnation, *Dianthus caryophyllus* The flower name derives from the word 'coronation', as carnations were a favourite flower for summer festivals. Some varieties are easy to grow from seed. The highly scented petals are good for infusions and in pot-pourri. For cooking, pull off the white base.

Chrysanthemum, *Chrysanthemum* In China, where chrysanthemums have been cultivated for over 2,000 years, the white flowers are used for soup, pickled with fish, stir-fried with chicken and vegetables, made into wine, and used as a garnish. Perhaps their culinary popularity stems not only from the slightly sharp flavour but from the belief that they will increase longevity and physical fitness.

Geranium, *Pelargonium spp* The flowers, especially the single ones, can be candied for decoration, but it is the leaves of, to be accurate, pelargonium which have such irresistible culinary uses. *Pelargonium odoratissimum* smells of apples: *P. variegatum fragrans* is scented with cinnamon; *P. tomentosum* with peppermint; the varieties Lady Plymouth and Mabel Grey smell of lemons; and Attar of Roses, well, of roses. Infuse the leaves in sugar, custard and so on, or use them, fresh or candied, for decoration.

Gladiolus, *Gladiolus* It is many years since gladioli grew in the cornfields, but that's where they got their popular name of corn flag. The flowers, which come in all colours, have a distinct pepperiness, and their trumpet shape just asks to be filled with a salad. They are good to infuse in oil or vinegar for use in salad dressing.

Honeysuckle, *Lonicera spp* The sweet-scented flowers make delightful influsions. Try one or two flowers cooked with apple jelly.

Hyacinth, *Hyacinthus spp* The flower perfume is almost too much of a good thing in cooking, but the flowers, neat, bright little trumpets, are excellent additions to pot-pourri.

Jasmine, *Jasminum spp* The yellow or white flowers of this climbing shrub are perfectly suited to flavouring syrup and sugar for use in desserts, confectionery and cakes.

Jonquil, *Narcissus jonquilla* This spring-flowering bulb has the strongest and sweetest scent of all the daffodil family. The flowers can be infused in sugar, syrup, dairy products and so on, and are delightful candied and used for Easter cake decorations.

Lavender, *Lavandula vera* You have only to wave a magic wand of lavender flowers over preserves, syrup, poached fruit, milk drinks, mulled wine, for it to weave its spell. Add the young leaves to herbal teas, use the flowers to make a sweet white wine and use them lavishly in pot-pourri.

Lily, *Lilium spp* Lilies of all kinds are prized for their form and flavour: in China the flowers are floated in wine; in Mexico they enliven hot-pepper sauces; in the United States they are fried in batter; and in France they are steeped in honey. The buds can be pickled, to cook with poultry or meat.

Mallow, *Malva sylvestris* The young mallow leaves make a spinach-like soup. The pink, cup-shaped flowers are beautiful decorations when candied. Fill the centres, just before serving, with cream whipped with sherry. Marshmallow tea, made with dried flowers, is said to relieve colds.

Marigold, *Calendula officinalis* The brilliant orange petals act as a golden colouring agent and have many culinary uses. A 'marigold meal' was suggested in an old herbal: mutton broth, marigold buns, braised beef, crab salad, marigold butter, cheese, tart, wine and (perhaps essential!) after-dinner *digestifs* were all said to benefit from their flavour.

Nasturtium, *Nasturtium* This plant is nothing if not versatile. The dried flower buds can be pickled in vinegar and used as capers; the dried seeds ground and used as pepper; and the flowers steeped in oil and vinegar for salad dressings, filled with savoury cream, or dipped in batter and fried. And then there is the Victorian delicacy – nasturtium sandwiches.

Pansy, *Viola tricolor* The flowers make a lovely light, flowery wine, and a good syrup, but are best used decoratively, set in jelly or for decorating salads.

Pinks, *Dianthus spp* Clove carnations, border pinks, gillyflowers, call them what you will, use them in cooking as for carnations; candy the delicate, flowers.

Primrose, *Primula vulgaris* Prettiest of all flowers to candy and store for decorating cakes and desserts, primroses make a wine with a lovely bouquet, and can be used in salads.

Rose, *Rosa spp* An ode should be written to the ways you can use rose petals in cakes, desserts, preserves, confections, sauces. We have attempted the task on pages 133 to 136.

Sweet pea, *Lathyrus odoratus* You can capture the unmistakable scent in infusions of sugar, syrup and so on. Toss the flowers in a light vinaigrette dressing for salad, fry them in batter, or candy them for decorations.

Violet, *Viola spp* If you can gather only a few of these dainty flowers, it's best to crystallize them and use more prolific flowers for flavourings.

THE ENGLISH ROSE

The scents of the rose garden, the very essence of summer, can be more than just a lovely, lingering memory. Don't let the petals flutter to the ground like fragrant confetti. Gather old-fashioned roses such as musk, moss and damask types and capture their perfume in sweetmeats, creams and ices. Later in the season, harvest the red hips. They make brilliant sauces and preserves.

ROSEHIP MARMALADE

1kg (2¼lb) rosehips
1.75 litres (3 pints) water
1 kg (2¼lb) cooking apples, peeled, cored and chopped
850g (1¾lb) sugar
2 × 15ml spoons (2tbls) lemon juice

1   Put the rosehips in a pan with all but 150ml (¼ pint) of the water. Bring to the boil and simmer for about 45 minutes, until the hips are soft. Squash them from time to time with a wooden spoon.
2   Pour the rosehips into a scalded jelly bag and leave to drip into a bowl for several hours, or overnight.
3   Put the apples in the pan with the remaining water and cook over low heat for about 30 minutes, or until they are soft.
4   Add the rosehip juice and sugar and stir over low heat until the sugar has dissolved.
5   Stir in lemon juice, bring to boil and fast-boil for 10-15 minutes, until setting point is reached (see page 34).
6   Pour the preserve into warmed, sterilized jars. Cover the surface with waxed paper discs and cover the jars with jam-pot covers or screw-on lids. Cool, label and store in a cool, dry place.

MAKES ABOUT 1.5KG (3¼LB)

*Who knows down what wild centuries
wanders back the rose?*

Some roses are so old that their origins are unknown — but you can still grow a variety that was mentioned in the Bible. A favourite of the Romans was the autumn damask (rosa damascena bifera).

EGLANTINE SAUCE

This is a Victorian recipe for rosehip sauce to serve with roast and boiled mutton. It is also good with ham, pork and duck.

2 oranges
2 lemons
225g (8oz) rosehips, halved
175g (6oz) redcurrant jelly
4 × 15ml spoons (4tbls) red wine

1   Grate the rind and squeeze the juice of the orange and lemon into a pan. Add the rosehips and bring slowly to the boil. Cover and simmer for 15 minutes.
2   Rub the rosehips through a fine sieve.
3   Return the purée to the pan. Add the redcurrant jelly and melt it over low heat, stirring occasionally. Stir in the wine and simmer for 5 minutes. Set aside to cool.
    You can store the sauce for up to 3-4 weeks in the refrigerator.

MAKES ABOUT 300ML (½ PINT)

ROSE GARDEN SORBET

This sorbet is well flavoured, with the very essence of the rose garden.

600ml (1 pint) water
½ cup scented rose petals
250g (9oz) loaf sugar
1 strip thinly pared lemon rind
3 × 15ml spoons (3tbls) lemon juice
2 egg whites

1   Boil the water and leave it to cool. Pick off the yellow ends of the rose petals and discard any damaged ones.
2   Bring the water and sugar slowly to the boil, stirring occasionally until the sugar has dissolved. Add the rose petals and lemon rind. Increase the heat and boil for 10 minutes. Cool.
3   Strain the syrup through a sieve, pressing the petals to extract the maximum moisture. Stir in the lemon juice. Cool.
4   When the syrup is cool, pour it into a container, such as an ice-cube tray. Cover and freeze for 1 hour. Chill a bowl at the same time.
5   Turn the partly frozen mixture into the chilled bowl and whisk to break down the crystals.
6   Stiffly whisk the egg whites and lightly whisk them into the sorbet.
7   Return the mixture to the container. Cover and freeze for about 2-3 hours, until it is set.
8   Transfer the sorbet to the refrigerator for 10 minutes before serving, to soften it slightly.
    Serve in folds, or in small scoops tossed with chilled watermelon balls. You can make them both with a vegetable scoop or melon baller. Decorate with small sprigs of pineapple mint or lemon balm.

SERVES 4

ROSE PETAL JAM

This preserve makes a very tasty spread, used sparingly on toast and teacakes. It is also delicious spooned over ice cream or as a filling for sponge cakes.

450g (1lb) scented rose petals
750g (1½lb) sugar
300ml (½ pint) water
2 × 15ml spoons (2tbls) lemon juice

1   Pick the yellow bases from the petals and discard any damaged ones. Tear each petal into 2 or 3 pieces and put them in a bowl.
2   Pour on half the sugar, stir well, cover and leave for 2 days.
3   Put the remaining sugar, water and lemon juice into a pan and stir occasionally over low heat until the sugar has dissolved.
4   Tip in the rose petals and sugar and again stir over low heat. Bring to the boil and fast-boil for 20 minutes, or until the jam reaches setting point (see page 34).
5   Pour the preserve into warmed, sterilized jars, cover the surface with waxed discs and cover the jars with jam-pot covers or screw-on lids. Cool, label and store in a cool, dark place.
   This jam has a very pronounced flavour, so a little goes a long way.

MAKES ABOUT 1KG (2¼LB)

PICKLED ROSEBUDS

You can enjoy these rosebuds as a pickle, to serve with cold poultry or salads, or drain and dry them and use them to garnish or decorate savoury and sweet dishes.

600ml (1 pint) small scented rosebuds
175g (6oz) caster sugar
about 600ml (1 pint) white wine vinegar
2 strips thinly pared lemon rind

1   Pull off any damaged leaves from the rosebuds. Trim them level with the calyx. Wash and drain them if necessary.
2   Put the sugar, vinegar and lemon rind into a small pan and stir occasionally over low heat until the sugar has dissolved. Increase the heat, bring to the boil and boil for 5 minutes. Strain and cool.
3   Pack the rosebuds into sterilized jars. Pour on the cooled vinegar and close the jars with vinegar-proof lids.

FILLS 2 × 450G (1LB) JARS

OLD-FASHIONED ROSE POSSET

12 scented rose petals
450ml (¾ pint) double cream
50g (2oz) Rose sugar (see page 136)
8 × 15ml spoons (8tbls) Rose petal water (see page 136)
2 × 5ml spoons (2tsp) grated orange rind
1 × 15ml spoon (1tbls) orange juice
12 candied rose petals (see right)
4 candied rose leaves (see right)

1   Pick off the yellow bases from the rose petals. Put the petals in a pan with the cream and slowly bring to the boil. Cool and strain.
2   Whip the cream with the sugar until it is stiff. Stir in the rose petal water, a little at a time, the orange rind and the orange juice.
3   Divide the dessert between 4 individual glasses. Decorate the top with the candied rose petals and leaves. Serve chilled.

SERVES 4

CANDIED ROSE PETALS, FLOWERS AND LEAVES

Dip rose petals first in beaten egg white and then in sugar. Stand them on a wire rack in a warm, dry place for 2 hours to dry. Store them in an airtight container between greaseproof or waxed paper.

You can make sugar-frosted rose leaves in the same way. And then candy and crystallize your way through the flower garden – treat primroses, violets, border pinks, sprays of broom, hyacinth, sprigs of herbs in the same way. Use a camel hair paintbrush to 'paint' the egg white into the flower crevices and cover every part of every surface with sugar.

SUGAR-ROSE FUDGE

1kg (2¼lb) Rose sugar (see page 136)
300ml (½ pint) evaporated milk
100g (4oz) butter
4 × 15ml spoons (4tbls) Rose petal water
(see page 136)

1   Put the sugar, milk and butter into a large pan over low heat, stirring occasionally until the sugar has dissolved. Add the rose petal water.
2   Increase the heat, bring to the boil and boil, stirring frequently, until the temperature reaches 115°C, 240°F. At this point a little of the syrup dropped into cold water forms a soft ball.
3   Remove from the heat and beat until the mixture is thick and creamy and begins to form grains.
4   Pour the mixture into a greased 20cm (8in) square tin and leave until it is nearly cold. Mark it into small squares. Cut into squares when set and store in an airtight container.

MAKES ABOUT 1.25KG (2½LB)

ROSE PINK ICE CREAM

2 cups scented rose petals
300ml (½ pint) single cream
50g (2oz) icing sugar, sifted
4 scented geranium leaves
2 × 15ml spoons (2tbls) Rose petal water
(see page 136)
2 drops red food colouring (optional)

1   Pick off the yellow ends of the rose petals and discard any damaged ones.
2   Put the rose petals, cream, sugar and leaves into a pan and bring slowly to the boil.
3   Strain the cream through a sieve, pressing the petals to extract the maximum moisture.
4   Stir in the rose petal water and food colouring, if you like to use it. Set aside to cool.
5   Pour the mixture into a container such as an ice-cube tray, cover and freeze for 1 hour. Chill a bowl at the same time.
6   Turn the mixture into the bowl and

Above Rose-scented fondants wrapped in candied rose petals and decorated with crystallized violets; Old-fashioned rose posset with candied rose leaves; and Rose pink ice cream, decorated with tiny crystallized roses.

Facing page Make Rose petal jam and Rose-hip marmalade and put them into pretty jars. You will be able to liven your breakfast and tea table with these inventive preserves. Try them with a tisane of cowslip or strawberry leaves.

beat it thoroughly. Return the mixture to the container, cover and freeze for 2-3 hours until set.
7   Transfer the ice cream to the refrigerator for 30 minutes to soften slightly before serving.
Serve in 'folds' made with a tablespoon, or in tiny scoops made with a melon baller. Scented geranium leaves or tiny crystallized roses are perfect decoration for this delicately coloured dessert.

SERVES 4

ROSE-SCENTED FONDANTS

16-20 scented rose petals
500g (1¼lb) icing sugar
½ × 5ml spoon (½tsp) cream of tartar
½ × 5ml spoon (½tsp) Rose petal water (see this page)
1-2 drops red food colouring (optional)
1 small egg white

1   One or two days before making the sweets, pick the rose petals. Pick off the yellow bases and cover the petals with the sugar. Leave the sugar in a covered jar.
2   Sift the sugar with the cream of tartar. Stir in the rose petal water and, if you like to use it, the food colouring. Use just enough of the egg white to form a pliable paste.
3   Knead the paste on a board lightly dusted with sifted icing sugar.
4   Roll out the paste to a thickness of 6mm (¼in). Cut it into shapes, using aspic or pastry cutters. Re-roll the trimmings and cut more shapes.

You can store the fondants in an airtight tin for a few days. A decorative way to serve them is to wrap each one in rose petals.

MAKES 500G (1¼LB)

ROSE SUGAR

Caster or granulated sugar flavoured with rose petals makes delicious desserts, cakes and biscuits.

Gather scented rose petals – old-fashioned musk and moss roses are ideal – on a dry day around lunchtime, when there is no dew on them. Pull off the yellow fleshy part at the base and discard any damaged petals. Pack them lightly into a cup, then measure 2 cups of sugar and toss them together on a baking tray.

Put in the oven at 110°C, 225°F, gas ¼ for 1½-2 hours, stirring occasionally. The sugar will have drawn the moisture from the petals, then dried.

Pour the sugar through a sieve, discard the petals and store the sugar in a covered container.

Variation You can use many other scented petals in the same way – try carnations, border pinks, jasmine, mock orange and violets.

PICKING THE ROSES

Some of the most romantic and pretty of old roses are the ones that give your confections and preserves the sweetest flavour. The damask roses Quatre Saisons and Kazanlik; the Rosa gallica Cardinal de Richelieu, which dates back to 1840; the centifolia rose Chapeau de Napoléon (1826); the hybrid rugosa Roseraie de l'Hay (1901); and the hybrid perpetuals Souvenir du Docteur Jamain (1865) and Gloire de Ducher (1865) have all been delighting cooks for generations.

ROSE PETAL CREAM

3 eggs, separated
100g (4oz) Rose sugar (see this page)
1 × 15ml spoon (1tbls) powdered gelatine
3 × 15ml spoons (3tbls) water
1 × 15ml spoons (1tbls) Rose petal water (see this page)
300ml (½ pint) double cream, whipped
12 pink candied rose petals (see page 134)
candied angelica (see page 134)

1   Whisk the egg yolks and caster sugar in a bowl fitted over a pan of hot water or the top of a double boiler until they are thick and creamy. Do not let the water boil or touch the upper container, or the egg yolks might scramble.
2   Dissolve the gelatine in the water and whisk it into the egg yolks. Stir in the rose petal water. Set aside to cool.
3   Stiffly whisk the egg whites. Fold the cream and the egg whites into the mixture.
4   Pour the dessert into a serving dish and leave in the refrigerator for at least 2 hours to set.
5   Cut leaf shapes from the angelica. Arrange the rose petals and 'leaves', just before serving, to decorate the dessert.

SERVES 4

ROSE PETAL WATER

This can be used, in much the same way as the bought product (which is distilled), in Turkish and other Middle-Eastern dishes. It can also be added to fondant icing or butter cream and makes lovely toppings and fillings for cakes.

8 cups scented rose petals
600ml (1 pint) water

1   Pick off the yellow fleshy bases from the petals – they give the water a rather bitter flavour.
2   Put half the petals in a pan with the water and bring slowly to the boil. Cover and simmer for 1 hour.
3   Strain off the petals, pressing them firmly against the sieve to extract the most moisture and flavour.
4   Repeat the process with the remaining petals, strain and discard them.
5   Pour the water into a sterilized bottle and put on the lid.
6   Stand it on a folded cloth in a pan with warm water to cover. Bring it to the boil and boil for 20 minutes. Remove from the water and cool.
7   Label the bottle and store it in a cool place. It should keep well for up to 2 months.

MAKES ABOUT 300ML (½ PINT)

ROSE VINEGAR

French women used to sprinkle a few drops on to their handkerchief and press it to their foreheads to relieve headaches.

1   Pick off the yellow fleshy base of the rose petals, and discard any damaged ones. Spread them out on a baking tray and dry them in the sun (be careful of any breeze!) or an airing cupboard until they rustle like paper.
2   Put the dried petals into a jar, cover with vinegar and put on the lid or cork.
3   Leave the jar on a sunny window-sill or in a warm place for several days, shaking it occasionally.

As you use the vinegar throughout the season you can add more dried petals and more vinegar.

DELECTABLE FLOWERS

A garden border busy with sweetly scented flowers has all the makings of the colourful and decorative dishes of times past. Beef with marigolds, pansy jelly, nasturtium fritters, gladiolus salad, violet honey, gillyflower rice cream – they all evoke the nostalgic era of the Victorians, make a delicious talking point today, and inspire fresh ideas for cooking with flowers.

GILLYFLOWER RICE CREAM

Gillyflower is the old country name for those delightfully scented cottage garden flowers, single border pinks.

100g (4oz) caster sugar
12-16 heads scented border pinks
1.25 litres (2¼ pints) milk
250g (9oz) short-grain rice, washed
250g (9oz) strawberries, hulled and chopped
450ml (¾ pint) double cream, whipped

1   Put the sugar and pinks into a jar, cover and leave for 1-2 days to infuse. Sieve the sugar carefully. The flowers will by then be dried, and can be used to decorate the dessert.
2   Put the milk and sugar into a pan and bring slowly to the boil. Stir in the rice and simmer for about 30 minutes, or until it is soft. Set aside to cool.
3   Fold the chopped strawberries and 300ml (½ pint) of the cream into the cooled rice.
4   Rinse a 1.2 litre (2 pint) mould with cold water. Pour in the rice mixture and chill for 2 hours, until the mould is set.
5   Run a knife around the mould and turn it out on to a serving plate. Pipe the remaining cream around the top and base and decorate the mould with the flowers.

SERVES 4-6

Variation The mould can be decorated with sliced strawberries in place of the dried flowers. In that case, the sweet-scented flavour of the dessert would come as even more of a surprise!

VIOLET HONEY

It's almost like taking a step back into Victorian times, spreading scones, teacakes or dainty sandwiches with flower-scented honey.

½ cup violet petals
250g (9oz) clear honey

1   Stir the violet petals into the honey in a jar and cover the jar.
2   Stand the jar on a folded cloth in a pan of water. Bring it to the boil and simmer for 30 minutes. Remove the jar from the pan and set it aside to cool.
3   Leave the petals to infuse in the honey for 7 days. Strain off the petals and pour the honey back into the jar – this is easier and less wasteful if you reheat the honey. Cover and keep it in a cool, dark place.
    It can also be stirred into syrup for fruit salad, and into Greek-style yoghurt.

MAKES 250G (9OZ)

PANSY TOWERS

25g (1oz) powdered gelatine
350ml (12fl oz) water
2 lemons
100g (4oz) sugar
2 eggs
4 × 15ml spoons (4tbls) sweet sherry
150ml (¼ pint) sweet white wine
4 pansy flowers, washed and dried
scented geranium leaves, to garnish

1   Dissolve the gelatine in a little of the water.
2   Thinly pare the lemon rind and squeeze the juice.
3   Put the water, lemon rind, lemon juice and sugar in a pan and stir occasionally over low heat until the sugar has dissolved. Stir in the gelatine mixture.
4   Separate the eggs. Reserve the yolks for another dish. Beat the whites and crush the shells. Stir them into the pan, add the sherry and wine and whisk over moderate heat until the mixture boils. Remove the pan from the heat and set aside for 10 minutes.
5   Repeat this boiling and cooling process twice more.
6   Line a sieve with a double layer of muslin or cheesecloth and pour the jelly through.
7   Rinse 4 small decorative moulds in cold water. Place 2 × 15ml spoons (2tbls) of jelly into each. Place a pansy head face down in the jelly and chill in the refrigerator for 15 minutes.
8   Spoon on the remainder of the jelly (you may have to heat it very slightly to melt it). Chill in the refrigerator for 1-1½ hours until set.
9   Turn out the jelly moulds on to individual serving plates. Decorate with the scented leaves.

SERVES 4

MARIGOLD & APPLE TART

100g (4oz) butter, softened
50g (2oz) lard, softened
25g (1oz) icing sugar, sifted
250g (9oz) flour
1 egg, beaten
1 × 5ml spoon (1tsp) grated orange rind
2 × 15ml spoons (2tbls) orange juice

FILLING
300ml (½ pint) milk
4 × 15ml spoons (4tbls) marigold petals
2 egg yolks
50g (2oz) caster sugar
40g (1½oz) flour
25g (1oz) semolina
350g (12oz) dessert apples
25g (1oz) butter, melted
4 × 15ml spoons (4tbls) redcurrant jelly
2 × 15ml spoons (2tbls) water

1   Using a fork, mix together the butter and lard and mix in the icing sugar. Sift in the flour, work it into the mixture, then stir in the egg, orange rind and juice. Form a dough and knead until smooth. Wrap in cling film and chill for at least 1 hour.
2   Put the milk and half the marigold petals into a pan and bring slowly to the boil. Beat the egg yolks, sugar, flour and semolina in a bowl to fit over a pan of simmering water, or the top of a double boiler. Strain the milk on to the egg mixture, beating constantly. Stir over low heat until the custard thickens. Do not allow the water to boil or touch the upper container.
3   Stand the custard container in a bowl of cold water and leave it to cool.
4   Roll out the pastry on a lightly floured board and use it to line a greased 23cm (9in) flan ring on a baking sheet. Trim the pastry edges and prick the base all over with a fork.
5   Pour the cooled custard into the pastry case and level the top. Arrange the apples in neat, overlapping circles over the custard. Brush the apples with the melted butter.
6   Bake the tart in the oven, preheated to 200°C, 400°F, gas 6, for 45 minutes. Cool on a wire rack.
7   Melt the redcurrant jelly with the water. Brush it over the apples to cover completely and scatter the remaining petals in the glaze.

SERVES 8

NASTURTIUM FRITTERS

These fritters, light as air, crisply golden and tasting rather peppery, make a stunning first course.

20 orange and yellow nasturtium flowers
75g (3oz) flour
salt
1 × 5ml spoon (1tsp) grated lemon rind
3 × 15ml spoons (3tbls) vegetable oil
175 ml (6fl oz) water
1 egg white, stiffly whisked
oil, for deep frying
nasturtium leaves, to serve
1 lemon, quartered

SAUCE
1 × 5ml spoon (1tsp) lemon juice
1 × 5ml spoon (1tsp) grated lemon rind
6 × 15ml spoon (6tbls) mayonnaise
2 × 15ml spoons (2tbls) double cream
salt
freshly ground black pepper

1   Wash and dry the flowers.
2   Sift the flour and salt. Stir in the lemon rind and oil and beat in the water. Whisk to make a smooth batter. Just before you cook the fritters, fold in the egg white.
3   Heat the oil in a deep frying pan to 180°C, 350°F. At this temperature a cube of bread will brown in 60 seconds.
4   Dip 16 of the nasturtium flowers in the batter. Drain off any excess. Fry the flowers a few at a time in the hot oil until they are crisp and golden brown. Lift out the fritters with a draining spoon and dry them on kitchen paper. Keep the first batch warm while you fry the remainder.
5   To make the sauce, beat the lemon juice and lemon rind into the mayonnaise. Stir in the cream and season with salt and pepper.
6   Arrange the fritters on a dish lined with the nasturtium leaves. Garnish the dish with the fresh flowers and serve them with the lemon wedges. Serve the sauce separately.

SERVES 4

GLADIOLUS SALAD

The Victorians had a flair for dramatic presentation – witness this eye-catching first course.

250g (9oz) full-fat soft cheese
6 × 15ml spoons (6tbls) double cream
40g (1½oz) red lumpfish roe
2 × 5ml spoons (2tsp) grated lemon rind
1 × 15ml spoon (1tbls) lemon juice
2 × 15ml spoons (2tbls) chopped lemon balm
1 × 15ml spoon (1tbls) finely snipped chives
12 gladiolus flowers, washed and drained
salad leaves, to serve

1   Beat the cheese and cream and stir in the lumpfish roe, lemon rind, lemon juice and herbs.
2   Spoon the filling into the flower trumpets.
3   Cover 4 individual plates with salad leaves and arrange the flowers.

SERVES 4

Variation For a salad buffet you could arrange the filled flowers to garnish a plate of cold meats or a green salad, allowing just one or two per person.

JASMINE SYRUP

Use a little of this syrup when making bon-bons, creamy desserts, fruit salads, or fruit pies and crumbles.

250g (9oz) caster sugar
1 cup jasmine petals
200ml (7fl oz) water

1   Sprinkle a layer of sugar over a dish, cover with a layer of petals and continue, finishing with sugar. Cover the dish and leave for 2 days.
2   Tip the sugar and petals into a pan, add the water and stir occasionally over low heat until the sugar has dissolved. Increase the heat, bring to the boil and boil for 10 minutes.
3   Cool the syrup, then strain it, pressing the petals against the sieve.
4   Pour the syrup into a sterilized bottle and cover it with a cap or cork. The syrup will keep in the refrigerator for about 2 weeks. For longer-term keeping, stand the bottle on a folded cloth in a pan with water up to the neck. Boil for 20 minutes.

MAKES ABOUT 300ML (½ PINT)

BEEF OLIVES WITH MARIGOLDS

Marigolds always had a place in the medieval English herb garden and were often used to flavour and garnish meat dishes such as this.

4 thin slices beef topside, about
100g (4oz) each
50g (2oz) shredded suet
25g (1oz) fresh white breadcrumbs
2 rashers streaky bacon, rinded and diced
½ × 5ml spoon (½tsp) grated orange rind
2 × 15ml spoons (2tbls) chopped
fresh parsley
2 × 15ml spoons (2tbls) marigold petals
salt
freshly ground black pepper
1 egg, beaten
40g (1½oz) butter
1 medium onion, peeled and thinly sliced
1 medium carrot, trimmed and thinly sliced
1 small leek, trimmed and thinly sliced
1 celery stalk, thinly sliced
½ × 15ml spoon (½tbls) flour
300ml (½ pint) beef stock, hot

1   Lay the beef slices on a sheet of cling film on a board, cover with another sheet of cling film and beat them out with a mallet or rolling pin until very thin. Trim each beef slice to a neat rectangular shape, reserving the trimmings.
2   To make the stuffing, finely chop the beef trimmings and put them in a bowl with the suet, breadcrumbs, bacon, orange rind, half the parsley and half the marigold petals. Stir well to mix and season to taste with salt and pepper. Stir in the egg to bind, then spread a portion of the stuffing on each beef slice, dividing it equally between them. Roll up and tie securely in 2 or 3 places with fine string.
3   Melt the butter in a flameproof casserole, add the onion, carrot, leek and celery and fry over a gentle heat, stirring from time to time, until very lightly coloured.
4   Using a slotted spoon, remove and reserve the vegetables, and add the beef olives to the casserole. Fry over a brisk heat for 3-4 minutes, turning often, until browned all over.
5   Remove the beef olives from the casserole and stir the flour into the juices. Pour in the stock and stir well. Season to taste with salt and pepper.

6   Return the vegetables to the casserole and arrange the beef olives on top. Cover the casserole and cook in the oven preheated to 160°C, 325°F, gas 3 for 1½ hours, or until the beef olives are tender.
7   Discard the string from the beef olives, sprinkle with the remaining parsley and marigold petals and serve immediately with the vegetables.
   Serve straight from the casserole on a bed of mashed potatoes, with the vegetables spooned round them in a ring, and the sauce served separately in a heated sauceboat.

SERVES 4

Gladiolus salad, garnished with rocket leaves, makes a light and delicate side dish to go with Beef olives with marigolds, served with vegetables straight from the garden.

FLOWERCRAFT

*Bowls of sweet-smelling pot-pourri and circlets of dried flowers to
scent a room, perfumed oil, water and bath preparations to give
you that special pampered feeling – all these are possible with
flowers from your garden. Try making these, and the scents of
your flower and herb garden will be more than just a happy
memory; in these romantic ways they will give lasting pleasure.*

LAVENDER RING

Ring-a-ring of lavender flowers to hang
in a bedroom or wardrobe, or to place
in a drawer to scent clothes. It's
one-up on lavender bags – you can
enjoy the flowers and you don't even
have to thread a needle!

Make a ring from about 35cm (14in)
of coat-hanger wire and bind the join
with sticky tape.

Cut small bunches of lavender flowers and bind them on with a roll of fine
silver wire, first on one side and then
the other. Arrange the bunches so that
the heads face away from the top, and
each cluster of flowers covers the
stalks of the next. Make a bunch with
longer stalks and bind it to the top of
the ring (where it was joined), to hang
into the centre.

Tie a ribbon and make trailing bows
if the ring is to be hung.

ROSE HEART SOAP

12 × 15ml spoons (12tbls) grated Castile soap
2 × 15ml spoons (2tbls) home-made rose oil
(see p. 141)
1 × 15ml spoon (1tbls) clear honey

1   Put the soap in a bowl fitted over a
pan of simmering water, or in the top
of a double boiler. Stir the soap until it
has melted, then add the oil and honey
– and stir continuously for 5 minutes.
2   Pour the soap into oiled moulds
and set aside for about 2 weeks until it
is completely hard.
3   Unmould the soap and polish it
with a cloth soaked with a few drops of
oil until it has a smooth finish.

LAVENDER FLOWER BATH FOAM

4 × 15ml spoons (4tbls) dried lavender
flowers
12 × 15ml spoons (12tbls) grated Castile soap
10 × 15ml spoons (10tbls) boiling water
2 × 5ml spoons (2tsp) home-made lavender
oil (see p. 141)

1   Crush the lavender flowers to a
powder in a mortar, which is the
old-fashioned way, or with light taps
with a hammer, which is less romantic
but effective.
2   Dissolve the soap in the water and
stir in the crushed lavender and the
oil. Stir until the mixture is well
blended.
3   Pour into a bottle, cool and then
cover. Decorate with a pretty label.

MAKES 350ML (12FL OZ)

Variation Dried camomile flowers and
elderflowers are among the delightful
alternatives.

DRYING FLOWERS, PETALS AND LEAVES

*You can gather the materials you
need for pot-pourri over several
weeks. Add the rose petals a handful
at a time to the desiccant (see
Country cottage pot-pourri step 1,
opposite). Spread a selection of
flowers, petals and leaves on baking
trays and dry them in a warm place.*

*As each batch dries and rustles like
cornflakes, put it into a lidded
container. When you have enough to
complete the mixture, just stir it all
together lightly.*

SPICED ROSE POT-POURRI

4 cups dried rose petals
4 cups dried border pinks
2 cups dried rosebuds
2 cups dried basil or scented geranium leaves
4 × 15ml spoons (4tbls) ground coriander
2 × 5ml spoons (2tsp) ground cloves
50g (2oz) orris root powder
25g (1oz) gum benzoin
1 × 5ml spoon (1tsp) home-made rose oil
(see p. 141)

1   Put the petals, flowers and leaves
into a large jar. Mix together the
coriander, cloves and orris root, add
them to the jar and stir to blend
thoroughly. Stir in the gum benzoin.
then add the oil drop by drop.
2   Cover the jar and store in a warm,
dark place for 6 weeks, stirring occasionally, before filling bowls, sachets,
pillows and so on.

Variation If you use the commercially
prepared rose oil, which is much more
highly scented than one you can make
at home, you will only need 2-3 drops.

ELDERFLOWER LOTION

*This body lotion soothes as it
nourishes and softens the skin and is
safe to use on the face as well.*

12 × 15ml spoons (12tbls) elderflower water
4 × 15ml spoons (4tbls) glycerine

1   Whisk the flower water and
glycerine until they are well blended.
2   Pour into a bottle, cover and label.

MAKES ABOUT 250ML (8FL OZ)

JASMINE BODY LOTION

This is very refreshing to splash on after a shower, and is soothing to the skin.

1 × 5ml spoon (1tsp) borax powder
300ml (½ pint) jasmine flower water
3 × 15ml spoons (3tbls) home-made jasmine
oil (see below)

1 Dissolve the borax in the flower water.
2 Warm the oil (by measuring it in a heated spoon) and stir it into the liquid. Whisk until well blended.
3 Pour into a bottle, cover and label.

MAKES ABOUT 300ML (½ PINT)

FLOWER OILS AND WATER
You can make your own delicately scented oils from fragrant flowers and leaves in the garden. Add them to cosmetics, soap and candles, or, just for the joy of it, burn them in an oil lamp. Of course, they do not have the strength of commercial ones.

Put 150ml (¼ pint) sunflower oil into the top of a double boiler or a small bowl fitted over a pan of gently simmering water. Warm the oil and then add 1 cup of scented petals or leaves: jasmine, lavender, carnation, border pink, hyacinth and rose petals, scented geranium and herb leaves – they are all delightful.

Cover the pan with a lid or foil and simmer gently for 2 hours. Then strain off the petals or leaves and keep them in a covered container.

Add more fragrant material, and repeat the process two or three times.

Finally, tip the oil into a pan with all the petals or leaves. Bring slowly to the boil and simmer for about 30 minutes. Strain off the petals or foliage, pressing them to remove every last drop of natural oil.

Pour the fragrant oil into a bottle, cool and then cover. Add a decorative label marked with the fragrance.

Flower water *Gather 1 cup of flower petals, pour on 600ml (1 pint) boiling water, cool and then cover. Leave to infuse overnight, then strain, bottle and label.*

These gentle flower waters can be used in cosmetics and also make a soothing eye bath.

COUNTRY COTTAGE POT-POURRI

100g (4oz) coarse salt
100g (4oz) borax powder
25g (1oz) crushed cinnamon stick
8 cups fragrant rose petals
2 cups dried lavender flowers
1 cup dried carnation petals
1 cup dried larkspur flowers
1 cup dried marigold petals
1 cup dried scented geranium leaves
1 cup dried marjoram leaves
½ cup dried lemon balm leaves
½ cup dried bay leaves, crushed
thinly pared rind of 1 lemon, dried
thinly pared rind of 1 orange, dried
1 × 5ml spoon (1tsp) home-made rose oil
(see this page)

1 Mix together the salt, borax and cinnamon in a large jar. Add the rose petals, stir well, cover and leave for at least 10 days, stirring occasionally. The powders will act as a desiccant and draw out the moisture from the rose petals.
2 Stir in all the dried flowers, petals and leaves. Chop and add the lemon and orange rind and sprinkle on the rose oil. Mix all the ingredients together.
3 Cover the jar and set aside for 6-8 weeks, stirring occasionally. Keep it covered when not in use.

ROSEBUD POMANDER

The ancient practice of studding dried oranges with cloves to sweeten the atmosphere goes back to the 15th century. Now that the necessity for their odour-masking properties is a thing of the past, we can concentrate on the sheer good looks of scented pomanders.

First, dry your orange. Choose a large, thin-skinned type. Hang it in the airing cupboard for a couple of weeks until it looks rather wizened.

To hold it still while you work on the design, pierce the orange with a skewer held upright in a ball of playing clay. Mark out a design with a ball-point pen – up-and-over circles, rings round the orange, segments or whatever.

Draw outlines to the pattern by studding the lines with cloves. Make rings or blocks of dried rosebuds, the stems cut to 8mm (⅓in), or other dried flowers such as small helichrysum, santolina, tiny poppy or love-in-a-mist seedheads, statice or beechmast. This is mix and match time, using whatever you have in your collection.

Wrap the pomander in pot-pourri in several layers of tissue and leave for several weeks. Pierce the top with a U-shaped pin or staple, and hang from a ribbon.

GIFTS FROM THE GARDEN

Having a garden is a wonderful gift, and one which you can easily share with others. Whatever the time of year, there's always something – herbs, fruit, nuts, vegetables, fruits in store, dried flowers – that you can turn into gifts to give pleasure to friends or to raise money at a charity bazaar.

Think of not having a garden – horrible thought! – and what you would miss most. The scent of herbs and flowers on a summer's day; the satisfaction of stocking your shelves with jars of preserves; the chance to prepare a dish with that unmistakable straight-from-the-garden flavour? These are also the things that will give most pleasure to others.

Herbs and scented flowers have endless possibilities as gifts. Capture their flavour by infusing them in oil, vinegar, or sugar. Chop fresh herbs or soft fruits and mix them with butter: savoury butters are perfect to glaze grilled meat and fish, and sweet ones have many uses at tea-time.

Dry herbs and make little mixed bunches, or crumble the leaves and store them in tiny jars or sew them into dolly bags. Follow the instructions for the lavender ring on page 140, using evergreen herbs like bay and rosemary with seedheads – fennel or caraway – in between. Dry flowers – camomile, tansy, clover – or rosehips and give a collection for fragrant tisanes.

Make or search out pretty containers for pot-pourri – miniature baskets from ethnic shops, for example. Make small posies of dried flowers – pretty to place in a wine glass for each place setting – or a larger one with trailing ribbons. In medieval times flower and herb posies were called tussie mussies and carried by people going on a journey.

Candy flowers and herb leaves and arrange them in sweet-papers in a box: what a lovely surprise for someone who likes to make cakes and fancy desserts. Or make up a small but precious box of candied fruits.

Gather in the nut harvest: green walnuts for pickling, dried nuts for toffee, fudge, bread, cakes and biscuits, or offer them 'neat' with a bottle of home-made wine to enjoy on a winter afternoon.

Presentation is paramount in garden gifts. Labelling is a fine art: buy colour-printed ones, use stencils, or stretch your own artistic ability. Mix and match label and produce colours – deep pink-edged labels on rose petal jam, for example, deep green ones on berry-bright cranberry sauce.

Pack sets of flavourings, butters, preserves and sauces in boxes or baskets. Salvage everything that looks good – cardboard mushroom baskets, see-through plastic chocolate boxes, date boxes – and cover them with plain or candy-striped paper.

NATURE'S GIFTS

Share your delight in your own garden with friends, or turn home-grown and home-made produce into sure-fire money spinners for your favourite charity. Just to show how varied and versatile your harvest is, make up composite gifts of a loaf, a terrine and a jar of chutney; a pot of flower honey and a jar of biscuits, prettily packed in a box or basket. The possibilities – and the pleasures – are endless.

HAZELNUT TOFFEE

A couple of handfuls of nuts snatched from under the squirrels' noses and you can make melt-in-the-mouth toffee that looks good in a glass jar.

100g (4oz) shelled hazelnuts, chopped
500g (1¼lb) sugar
40g (1½oz) butter
2 × 5ml spoons (2tsp) white vinegar
150ml (¼ pint) water
salt
½ × 5ml spoon (½tsp) vanilla essence

1 Spread the nuts on a baking sheet and warm them in the oven at 110°C, 225°F, gas ¼.
2 Put the sugar, butter, vinegar, water and salt into a large, heavy-based pan and stir over low heat until the sugar has dissolved. Increase the heat and boil the mixture until the temperature reaches 150°C, 300°F. At this temperature, a little of the syrup dropped into cold water separates immediately into hard, brittle threads.
3 Stir in the essence. Pour half the toffee into a well-greased 18 × 13cm (7 × 5in) tin. Sprinkle the warmed nuts evenly over the surface and pour on the rest of the toffee.
4 When the toffee is almost set, mark it into squares. When it is completely set, break up the squares. Store it in an airtight container.

MAKES ABOUT 750G (1½LB)

Gift wrap Presented in a glass-lidded jar, this sparkly toffee is quite irresistible. For a pretty effect tie 3 bright narrow ribbons – red, green and white, or yellow, orange and brown – round the neck and leave long, curling trailers.

RHUBARB & ELDERFLOWER JAM

When the elderflowers hang low over plump, pinky stalks of rhubarb, put the two together for a store cupboard standby – a perfect gift for a country market stall.

3kg (7lb) rhubarb, trimmed
8 large heads elderflower
2.5kg (5¾lb) sugar
grated rind and juice of 2 lemons

1 Cut the rhubarb into 5cm (2in) pieces. Tie the elderflowers in a piece of muslin, otherwise they will 'drop'.
2 Put the fruit, flowers and sugar into a large mixing bowl (not a metal pan) and stir well. Cover and leave for several hours, or overnight.
3 Turn the fruit into a large pan and stir over low heat to dissolve the sugar. Increase the heat, add the lemon rind and juice, and bring to the boil. Fast-boil for 15 minutes, or until setting point is reached (see page 34).
4 Pour the jam into warmed, sterilized jars, cover the surface with waxed paper discs and cover the jars with jam-pot covers. Leave to cool.
5 Write pretty labels and store in a cool, dry place.

MAKES ABOUT 4KG (9LB)

Gift wrap The preserve is a delicate pink-sunset colour. Match it with a pretty cotton cover for a 'mob cap' top. To make the gift extra special, tie a wooden preserve spoon to each jar.

Facing page A spread of edible gifts. From right, Rhubarb and elderflower jam, Hazelnut toffee in a jar and a pretty package, Cranberry butter, Elderberry butter and Somerset apple cake.

SOMERSET APPLE CAKE

There's always a call for 'tray bakes' at tea parties, coffee mornings and bazaar stalls. Here's a way to turn your apple harvest to advantage.

150g (5oz) butter, softened
250g (9oz) flour
1 × 5ml spoon (1tsp) ground cinnamon
1 × 5ml spoon (1tsp) baking powder
2 × 15ml spoons (2tbls) caster sugar
1 egg yolk
4 × 15ml spoons (4tbls) milk
4 cooking apples, peeled, cored and thinly sliced
2 × 5ml spoons (2tsp) lemon juice

TOPPING
150g (5oz) caster sugar
½ × 5ml spoon (½tsp) ground cinnamon
2 × 15ml spoons (2tbls) medium oatmeal
50g (2oz) butter

1 Cream the butter until it is soft. Sift together the flour, cinnamon, baking powder and sugar and beat it a little at a time into the butter. Beat in the egg yolk and milk.
2 Turn the mixture into a greased 23 × 18cm (9 × 7in) tin. Arrange the apples in overlapping rows on the cake base and brush them with lemon juice.
3 To make the topping, stir together the sugar, cinnamon and oatmeal and rub in the butter.
4 Sprinkle the topping over the apples.
5 Bake in the oven, preheated to 180°C, 350°F, gas 4, for 50 minutes, or until the cake is firm and the topping golden brown. Cool on a wire rack. Cut into fingers.

MAKES 1 CAKE 23 × 18CM (9 × 7IN)

HERB MUSTARD SAUCE

Make a variety of mustards to give individually or as a set. Tarragon, in this recipe, chive, dill, chervil and basil are all suitable.

5 × 5ml spoons (5tsp) mustard powder
120ml (4fl oz) water
5 × 15ml spoons (5tbls) granulated sugar
1 × 15ml spoon (1tbls) light Muscovado sugar
8 × 15ml spoons (8tbls) tarragon oil
4 × 15ml spoons (4tbls) tarragon vinegar
8 × 15ml spoons (8tbls) chopped tarragon
salt
2 × 5ml spoons (2tsp) lemon juice

1   Mix the mustard powder to a smooth paste with the water. Stir in the sugars, oil, vinegar, herb, salt and lemon juice and mix until the sauce is well blended. Taste and adjust the seasoning if needed.
2   Pour into decorative jars, cover with vinegar-proof lids and label.

MAKES 250ML (8FL OZ)

Gift wrap Use salvaged glass jars – herb and spice ones, preserve, honey, mustard jars, whatever you have. Collect matching ones to give a set of mustards and finish them with paper caps with 'pinked' edges. To present a set, cover a long, narrow wooden date box with toning paper, stand the jars in it and cover them with cling film or transparent paper.

VEGETABLE TERRINE

Buy an earthenware baking dish, fill it with this herb garden pâté and you take a two-in-one gift.

1kg (2¼lb) courgettes
2 × 15ml spoons (2tbls) coarse salt
1 onion, sliced
50g (2oz) butter
4 eggs
300ml (½ pint) double cream
2 × 15ml spoons (2tbls) chopped mint
¼ × 5ml spoon (¼tsp) cayenne pepper
freshly ground black pepper
about 12 young spinach or sorrel leaves

1   Grate the courgettes into a colander, sprinkle them with salt and leave to drain for about 1 hour.
2   Rinse the courgettes thoroughly under cold, running water. Drain into a clean tea towel and wring to extract any excess moisture. Alternatively, put the rinsed and drained courgette into a salad spinner.
3   Cook the courgette and onion in the butter over low heat for 10 minutes, stirring occasionally. Leave to cool.
4   Beat the eggs and cream and beat in the vegetables and mint. Stir in the cayenne and pepper.
5   Grease a 1.5 litre (2½ pint) loaf tin or earthenware dish. Line the base and sides with overlapping leaves. Turn the mixture into the container, level the top and cover with foil.
6   Stand the container in a roasting pan with water to come halfway up the sides. Bake in the oven preheated to 180°C, 350°F, gas 4 for 1¼ hours, or until the terrine is firm.
7   Remove the container from the roasting pan and stand it on a wire rack to cool. Cover the top with cling film once it is thoroughly cold.

SERVES 4-6

Gift wrap The terrine is delicious served with soured cream stirred with a little lemon juice and snipped chives, so it is a nice idea to include the sauce in the gift.

FRUIT BUTTERS

You will find that small quantities of soft fruits, a precious harvest, go a long way in these unusual spreads to serve with scones, teacakes or toast. Cranberries make a tangy butter; try chopped strawberries and blueberries and sieved raspberries and blackberries for a tempting variety.

250g (9oz) unsalted butter, softened
about 3 × 15ml spoons (3tbls) sifted icing sugar
100g (4oz) cranberries, minced
1 × 5ml spoon (1tsp) lemon juice

1   Cream the butter and beat in the sugar. Stir in the minced berries and lemon juice. Taste and beat in a little more sugar if needed.
2   Spread the butter into small containers, cover with cling film and label. Store in the refrigerator, or freeze for up to 3 months.

MAKES ABOUT 250G (9OZ)

CHEESE HERB BAPS

Take them warm from the oven and wrapped in a napkin, for a bring and buy stall or when you go visiting.

500g (1¼lb) wholemeal flour
1 × 5ml spoon (1tsp) salt
2 × 5ml spoons (2tsp) bicarbonate of soda
½ × 5ml spoon (½tsp) mustard powder
75g (3oz) white vegetable fat
100g (4oz) Cheddar cheese, grated
2 × 15ml spoons (2tbls) chopped thyme
300ml (½ pint) buttermilk
milk, for brushing
2 × 15ml spoons (2tbls) cracked wheat or rolled oats, for topping

1   Sift together the flour, salt, soda and mustard powder and tip in the bran remaining in the sieve. Rub in the fat until the mixture is like fine breadcrumbs. Stir in the cheese and thyme. Pour on the buttermilk and mix well to form a dough.
2   Knead the dough until it is smooth.
3   Divide the dough into 8 equal-sized pieces and shape them into rounds. Place them on a greased and floured baking sheet and flatten the tops – the baps should be about 2.5cm (1in) high.
4   Brush the tops with milk and sprinkle on the wheat or oats.
5   Bake the baps in the oven, preheated to 200°C, 400°F, gas 6, for 25 minutes, until they are well risen and golden brown.
6   Transfer the baps to a wire rack. They are at their best served slightly warm.

MAKES 8 BAPS

Gift wrap Make a composite gift – perfect to take to a weekend hostess – of these tasty baps, a herb terrine and a jar of pickled walnuts. It's a sure way to be invited again!

Cook's tip
If you cannot find buttermilk in the shops, you can quite easily make your own — although in these days of treated milk you will need the help of a lemon! See page 30.

RASPBERRY VINEGAR

This spicy syrup is a jack-of-all-trades among flavourings. Present it with a label listing ideas for its use.

1kg (2¼lb) raspberries (see below)
2 dried red chillis
1.5 litres (2½ pints) red wine vinegar
1kg (2¼lb) sugar
2 or 3 raspberry leaves, optional

1   First of all, plan your raspberry picking in 3 stages – the amount given is the total you will need over a 12-day period.
2   Put 350g (12oz) raspberries into a wide-necked jar (not a metal pan) with the chillis and pour on the vinegar. Cover and set aside in a cool place for 4 days.
3   Strain off the vinegar, pressing the raspberries against the sieve to extract the maximum flavour.
4   Return the vinegar to the jar, add another 350g (12oz) raspberries, cover and leave for a further 4 days.
5   Repeat stage 4 with the remaining batch of raspberries.
6   Strain off the raspberries, but this time through a double thickness of muslin.
7   Put the flavoured vinegar into a pan with the sugar. Stir occasionally over low heat until the sugar has dissolved. Increase the heat and boil for 5 minutes, skimming off any foam as it rises to the surface.
8   Pour the vinegar into warmed, sterilized bottles. Cover and set aside to cool. Push a raspberry leaf into each bottle if you like.
9   Label the bottles and store in a cool, dry, dark place. The vinegar will keep well for up to 1 year.

MAKES ABOUT 1.5 LITRES (2½ PINTS)

Gift wrap Here are some ideas for your 'Uses' label. Serve a tot of the vinegar with hot water for a restoring tonic, or with sparkling mineral water for a refreshing 'pick-me-up'. Use it sparingly in salad dressings and syrup for fruit salads. Add a little to sauces and casseroles, particularly with game. Add a few drops to the braising sauce with stir-fried dishes, from prawns to pork.

HERB BISCUITS

These biscuits always seem to be extra tasty when they are made with herb seeds gathered from your garden.

50g (2oz) flour
salt
pinch of cayenne
25g (1oz) butter
50g (2oz) Cheddar cheese, grated
1 × 5ml spoon (1tsp) dried dill seed
½ × 5ml spoon (½tsp) Dijon mustard
1 egg yolk, lightly beaten
1 × 15ml spoon (1tbls) iced water

1   Sift the flour, salt and cayenne into a bowl. Rub in the butter until the mixture is like fine breadcrumbs. Stir in the grated cheese – a knife is best for this – and the dill seed.
2   Stir the mustard into the egg yolk, pour on the dry ingredients and mix well. Sprinkle on just enough water to mix to a firm dough.
3   Wrap the dough loosely in cling film or foil and chill in the refrigerator for about 1 hour.
4   Roll out the dough on a lightly floured board to a thickness of 3mm (⅛in). Cut the dough into 5cm (2in) rounds. Re-roll the trimmings and cut out more circles.
5   Place the biscuits well apart on a greased baking sheet. Bake in the oven, preheated to 200°C, 400°F, gas 6, for 7 minutes, or until they are golden brown and well risen. Leave them on the tray for 2-3 minutes to become crisp. Serve the biscuits warm, or transfer them to a wire rack to cool.

MAKES ABOUT 20 BISCUITS

Gift wrap For a Christmas gift, stack the biscuits, close-wrap them in cling film and then wrap them in tissue or crêpe paper to look like a party cracker. Or pack them into wide-necked glass jars and tie a small spray of fresh or dried herbs to the neck.

PICKLED WALNUTS

If you are lucky enough to have a walnut tree in your garden, or know where one is growing in the countryside, make this luxury pickle in the summer. It's a perfect Christmas gift, to serve with cold poultry.

750g (1½lb) young green walnuts
350g (12oz) coarse salt
about 3 litres (5½ pints) water
about 1 litre (1¾ pints) good quality malt vinegar
1 × 15ml spoon (1tbls) whole allspice
1 × 15ml spoon (1tbls) whole cloves
2.5cm (1in) piece cinnamon, crushed
8 black peppercorns
2 dried red chillis

1   Prick the walnuts all over with a sterilized darning needle so that the brine and the pickle can thoroughly penetrate the skins.
2   Place the walnuts in a glass or earthenware bowl (not a metal pan). Dissolve half the salt in half the water, pour over the walnuts and cover the bowl. Set aside for 7 days.
3   Drain off the brine and discard it. Rinse the walnuts in fresh water and return them to the bowl. Make a brine with the remaining salt and the water, pour over the walnuts, cover and leave for a further 14 days.
4   Drain, rinse and drain the walnuts again. Spread them on a wire rack and leave in the open for about 24 hours until they are completely black.
5   Put the vinegar in a stainless steel, enamel or non-stick pan and add all the spices. Bring the vinegar slowly to the boil and boil for 5 minutes.
6   Pack the walnuts into warmed, sterilized jars and cover them with the hot vinegar – you can strain off or leave in the spices, as you wish. Cover the jars with vinegar-proof lids (jam-pot covers are not sufficient) and leave to cool.
7   Label the jars and store them in a cool, dry place for at least 6 weeks before serving.

FILLS 3 × 450G (1LB) JARS

Gift wrap Cut out circles of black and white check gingham – or bright green and white – to cover the jars and secure them with narrow white ribbon.

ARRANGEMENTS

Forget about cooking just for once and you'll find that herbs, fruit and vegetables are as decorative as they are delicious. Aromatic leaves and flowers from the herb garden; vivid clusters of glistening hips and berries to arrange in autumn; boughs of tempting fruit, and baskets of shiny bright vegetables. You'll soon see that everything in the garden's lovely – to look at.

A jug on the kitchen windowsill spilling over with blue, soft pink and snowy white flowers cut from the herb garden; and a basket of fruit and vegetables – sweetcorn, courgettes, plums, quince and autumn berries and nuts – a study in colour contrasts: these two simple groups show just how decorative garden produce can be. An artist would even suggest that it's all much too attractive to eat!

Look around the garden with that in mind, recipes forgotten for the time being, and you will see that the natural materials for arrangements extend far beyond the flower garden.

Herbs are a natural. Many of them have the most decorative of leaves which blend perfectly in groups with summer border flowers. The palest cream of variegated pineapple mint, the acid yellow tinged with green of lemon balm and the sunshine shade of golden marjoram all add a sparkle, look fabulous with white flowers and contrast strikingly with dark ones. The deep velvety greens and purple of sage, absorbing as they do every shaft of light, are good towards the base of an arrangement to give visual weight and balance. And the fine-as-thread wayward leaves of fennel, dill and asparagus are effective placed in front of large flowers like dahlias to create a verdant veil and break up a solid colour patch.

Added to that, herb leaves have such a lovely scent! Use them in small sprays on the dining table or in a spare bedroom to welcome a guest. Or cut long sprays of angelica, comfrey, tarragon and other sky-scrapers to incorporate into a large flower design for a public room or church. Take posies or circlets of herb leaves and flowers when you go visiting – there are ideas on the next pages – or take a jar of herbs for a flat dweller both to use and enjoy.

Don't take no for an answer in the herb garden even when the flowering season is over. Make up your mind to dry the flowers at their peak and enjoy them in designs throughout the winter. All the composites, like tight little daisy cushions, camomile and feverfew; all the umbrella-shaped heads, both in flower and in seed, such as fennel, caraway, dill; and all the densely clustered flowers – lavender, chive, marjoram – dry like a dream. Tie them in bunches, hang them in a warm, dry room or a not-too-hot airing cupboard, and harvest them

Facing page *The gentle charm of flowering herbs is best offset by a plain vase or jug. The bolder statement of berries, hips, autumn leaves and cultivated roses* (left) *can take a more elaborate container.*

anew for decoration once they've become crisp and papery.

Another preserving method, in a solution of two parts glycerine to one of boiling water, greatly extends the scope of designs from the garden. By this simple means, sprays of herbs change their character completely. Bay leaves turn a shade of glowing leather brown, rosemary turns deep, deep green while still holding its aroma, and sage leaves are transformed into a rich range of hues. No matter how fierce the winter, these stocks won't fail you. The same method captures nuts, berries and hips on the branch – hazelnuts, blackberries, rosehips all hold their appeal and become virtually everlasting.

Sprays of blossom, fruit and berries – whether glycerine-preserved or not – take well to the floral art. Blackberry blossom, like miniature pink dog roses, hasn't the romantic appeal of apple, pear and cherry blossom but is just as pretty (thornless varieties preferred!). Partner the bramble flowers with others in the same colour range – such as border pinks, carnations, sweet william, clove and marjoram. Later in the season the sharp green and decidedly unripe blackberries look enchanting (if unappetizing) in a copper pot with green holly berries, bright orange honeysuckle and the even brighter asparagus berries.

Not every gardener wants to sacrifice boughs of tasty fruit, but if trees are getting out of hand, or encroaching over the neighbour's fence a branch or two of small red apples, crab-apples or tough old cooking pears look marvellous in a harvest design. Pick off the leaves – they'll soon wilt anyway – and leave the fruit to speak volumes.

Without going the whole way and using on-branch fruit, pierce individual fruits with florist's wire and arrange them among flowers and foliage. Tree fruits among evergreen leaves give a 'partridge in a pear tree' look at Christmas-time.

Leaving vegetables to go to seed – bad husbandry when it's crops you're after – needn't be the disaster it seems. Sorrel runs to long spires of soft red seeds like dock, brassicas blaze with long stems of mustard yellow flowers; parsnips sport jaunty yellow umbrellas and leeks thrust up huge mauve flower balls on stick-straight stems.

Some vegetables from the garden really do look too decorative to eat. Red and yellow peppers blend well with evergreen leaves – matt ones such as cypress and juniper – while button mushrooms and bulbs of garlic contrast strikingly with the shine of holly or ivy; aubergines have a depth of colour scarcely matched in the flower kingdom, and globe artichokes have a unique sculptured quality.

Herbs and flowers, hips and haws, fruit and vegetables – they all have their part to play in the decorative garden.

PRETTY AS A POSY

There's a long and evocative tradition of making posies from herbs and other scented cottage garden flowers. People used to carry them as a home-from-home air freshener whenever they went on a journey; children skipped along with posies in festive processions; and judges bore them with dignity on ceremonial occasions. Country brides carried flowers from the garden, and Victorian lovers conveyed their innermost thoughts with flowers chosen not for their beauty or perfume but for their age-old symbolic meaning – the original way to say it with flowers.

In this sentimental language, flowers plucked from the garden could speak volumes. A spray of broom flowers acknowledged in the recipient the virtues of neatness and humility; buttercups indicated childishness and candytuft indifference. Carnations given to and fro could conduct a conversation with never a word spoken: a pink one signified a woman's love, a red one that 'my heart is breaking'. Send back a striped carnation to signify the ultimate insult, refusal; or a yellow one to show disdain and a white one to admit to coyness.

A posy of herbs might look like a bunch of leaves to anyone not in the know, but to the romantics it had all the significance of a love letter. Mint was for virtue; rosemary for remembrance; sage for esteem; thyme for activity and courage; and sweet basil, best wishes. The story wouldn't have such a happy ending if there were rue (disdain), basil (hatred) or lavender (distrust). A marigold in the centre of the posy was a sign of uneasiness; a red rosebud, of young and joyous love; a ranunculus, an admission that 'you are very attractive'; and a stephanotis, an untentative invitation to 'come with me'.

Perhaps it is going too far to suggest that one should select posy material with this word code in mind. For one thing, you would have to be quite sure you were both using the same dictionary: Victorian books on the language of flowers did vary somewhat and must have caused the premature cessation of many a potentially perfect friendship. Nevertheless, the symbolic meaning of plants was important and is, after all, a part of our heritage – and it's fun to remember it now and again.

Victorian posies, meaning or no meaning, were formal little affairs, made up of concentric circles of small flowers and tidy leaves around a central bloom – usually a rosebud. More freedom of design crept in later, and arranged flowers nowadays tend to be not so much a posy, more a sheaf, the flowers placed in graduated height on a backing of foliage. Herbs lend themselves well to both of these styles and, formal or informal, an arranged posy is a thoughtful gift to take to a hostess. All she has to do is to stand it in water.

On the subject of water, it is important to give flowers and leaves a good long drink before you start to arrange them. Cut them in the morning or evening during a hot spell – never in the heat of the day. Stand the stems deep in tepid water and leave them in a cool place for several hours. Then, however you intend to arrange them and whether they have to endure a journey or not, they should be in fit condition.

That's what the floral art term, conditioning, means.

Plant material with woody stems – bay, rosemary, roses and even mature mints – will last rewardingly longer for a little pre-arrangement attention. Split the stems criss-cross with a sharp knife or lightly crush them with a small hammer. This enables them to take up water more easily and is a positive move against wilting.

Whether you are arranging stems in a posy or a container, remove all lower leaves and meticulously strip off thorns and spikes from any stems that are destined to be hand-held. As soon as a posy is completed, stand it in water, and, on a hot day, sprinkle the flowers with water from a spray.

VICTORIAN POSY

The selection of flowers is all-important. Choose just two colours – pale pink and white, yellow and cream, blue and pink, lime green and blue, whatever you have in the garden – or a kaleidoscope of colours which is not quite so traditional but certainly striking.

Flowers that are small and neat in form are especially suitable: rosebuds, border pinks, spray pinks, feverfew, camomile, blue alkanet, borage, tiny marguerites, campion, mouse-ear chickweed, buttercups, primroses, primula, pulmonaria – the list could go on and on.

Select the prize bloom for the centre and hold it in one hand. Let's say it's a tight pink rosebud. Arrange a ring of flowers – feverfew would be pretty – in a well-defined circle around it. Then arrange another circle – they're getting gradually bigger – of, for example, deep-coloured border pinks. A ring of yellow-centred camomile, similar to the feverfew but with attractive hummocky centres, could go next. Then choose slightly larger flowers for the outer ring – perhaps pink rosebuds or spray pinks. As you work, neaten each row carefully so that there are no gaps.

Protect the outer ring of flowers with a collar of leaves. Long-lasting evergreens do a good job such as small sprays of young bay shoots; green or purple sage; ivy, variegated or not according to your colour scheme; and magnolia. If the posy will have only a short spell out of water, then you can include a host of others, such as lemon balm, scented geranium, snippings of lovage, aquilegia – especially attractive in late summer when it turns nearly purple – violet and primrose.

Bind the stems round and round with soft twine – raffia is ideal – and cut them level at the ends. If the posy is to stand in a container as a table centrepiece, that's it. If it's to be presented – to a visiting speaker at a function perhaps – or carried by a bridesmaid or VIP, you will need to pretty it up with ribbons.

For the full Victorian flavour, cut a hole in the centre of a white, lacy paper doily, push through the stems and gather up the frilly collar so that it sits easily around the leaves. Sticky-tape it in place and bind the stems with all-concealing satin ribbon, leaving long curling trails.

INFORMAL POSY

Herbs make delightful free-style posies – as pretty as any you could order from the florist's and twice as scented! The leaves and flowers are arranged in graduating heights, tallest stems at the back and very short ones towards the grip – they can be as short as you like with the only reservation that they must be able to reach the water in the eventual container.

Now you are looking for 'backing' foliage, to form a firm foundation for the flowers, to protect them if they are to be carried, and also to frame them attractively. Again, evergreens get high marks for durability and strength, but beware of the deepest greens. They can make it look as if your lovely flowers are arranged on cardboard. Deeply-cut fern leaves are strong without looking solid. So are lovage, angelica, light-weight cupressus and sprays of grey-green eucalyptus.

First place a layer of foliage on the table in a narrow fan shape. That's the backing.

Next you need long, spiky flowers for height. Lavender, side shoots of delphinium, larkspur, clarkia, would all look well. Arrange these to come to a point at the top of the design and cut some shorter for the sides.

Then it's a question of placing the flowers in stepping-stones down the length of the foliage: marjoram, chive and clover flowers, antirrhinum, borage, cranesbill geranium, border pinks, wild marguerites, what you will. Finally make a little arc of flowers close to the grip, pansies perhaps or cornflowers.

Colour is a very personal thing – who's to say which scheme is preferable. If your fancy runs to the limited-colour theme, consider a posy with lime green cupressus and pale green lovage for the backing, sideways-trailing sprays of variegated lemon balm, and graduated stems of marguerites, lovely light fluffy green euphorbia, camomile, green or white nicotiana and yellow fennel.

Bind the stems and, if it's for presentation, conceal the binding with a twist or two of ribbon. The design can be stood upright in water, in a glass wine carafe for example, or laid at an angle in a basket, the stems just reaching water in an inner container.

The same arrangement looks just as lovely with dried flowers and, of course, has the advantage of lasting almost indefinitely. Use glycerined beech, lime or similar leaves for the backing, but not too many or they will dominate the delicate flowers. Then arrange the flowers in groups or clusters – single stems are fiddly to handle and don't make quite the impact. Golden rod, delphinium, larkspur and clarkia all have the height, then marjoram, statice, rosebuds, poppy and love-in-a-mist seedheads, and the daisy-like dried everlastings in serried ranks. A spray like this, subtly scented and in gentle colours, makes a delightful wall decoration that is as pretty as any picture.

RING-A-RING OF POSY

Posy rings have a hint of the 'thirties and 'forties, when pottery containers – the vase with the hole in the centre – were all the vogue. The present-day equivalent can be very pretty, a 30cm (12in) ring of green plastic filled with blocks of soaked foam and packed tightly with flower heads and single leaves.

Here's a way to put snippings from large arrangements to pretty effect. Think of a colour scheme – pink, cream and blue, maybe. Scatter the foam with a few ivy, bay and marjoram leaves to trail over the outside and inside of the ring and hide it completely. Then, cutting all the stems as short as 5cm (2in), arrange them so that the flower heads are close to the foam. Pink marjoram, thyme, chive and clover, cream feverfew, camomile and sweet peas, blue sage, borage, alkanet, snippings of lacy sheep's parsley or gypsophila. They look enchanting.

In the same mood, look out for pottery posy rings in junk shops and on curio stalls. They're so popular – and the chances of finding one admittedly correspondingly slim – that several firms are making them again. If you cut stems short enough the flower heads won't topple and you can create a close-packed design without foam. Primroses, snowdrops, celandine, even some deadnettles make pretty-as-a-picture posy rings.

HOME HARVEST

Bringing home the harvest is one of the most satisfying tasks a gardener performs. After all the digging and hoeing, raking and sowing, the anticipation of the first seed germination, then the battle against the elements and garden predators until the crops come to fruition – it seems a long and sometimes anxious haul. But now the crops are ripened, ready to pick and the moments of triumph are nigh.

Since the craft of gardening appeals to us in so many ways – as therapy, exercise, skill, thrift and good husbandry – the produce from the garden should appeal to more than just the taste buds. Straight-from-the-garden fruit and vegetables look good, too and a basket just brought into the kitchen has all the makings of a still-life painting.

Garden produce is usually at its best eaten as soon as possible after harvest. There's an old country saying that you shouldn't cut a head of corn until the pan of water is boiling and ready for it. And that the corn should never have been planted, anyway, more than a couple of paces from the kitchen door. Well, that's a counsel of perfection – typical of those self-righteous old sayings! Something has to be planted at the farther end of the plot, and it isn't always convenient to consume all the produce at the first sitting. That's just as well because it leaves some to put on show.

And for showing off the harvest, you can't beat baskets as containers. They have the right kind of rustic look, centuries of craft and tradition behind them, they come in all shapes and sizes – and they're cheap. Build up a collection from ethnic shops, charity sales and market stalls, and when they're not in use find somewhere to hang them. Baskets make a countrified feature hanging from a high kitchen or utility room ceiling, or can be similarly dealt with in a garage or shed.

Produce needs little preparation and no adornment before you put it on display. Simply wash orchard fruit such as apples and pears and polish with a dry cloth, but don't polish gages and plums, medlars or quinces – the 'bloom' is part of their charm.

Wash root vegetables and dry them thoroughly – mud is never a very appetizing feature – and wash and polish squashes like marrow and courgettes. Gather bean and pea pods into bundles of like sizes.

If several tomatoes ripen at the same time, cut off the tresses and even, for contrast, include some green ones. According to the season, green tomatoes continue ripening in the kitchen or, when they have had their few days of visual glory, you can pack them side by side in a box, keep them in a warm place and still be enjoying home-grown tomatoes in March.

Then how to arrange all this produce? A willow garden trug, a flat flower-gathering basket or even a clean wooden seed tray are aesthetically just the thing for a collection of fruit and vegetables. Group the produce as you would flowers in an arrangement, making a selection that contrasts well in form, shape, texture and colour.

Some vegetables and fruit are natural attention-getters (peppers, yellow courgettes and tomatoes, giant straw-berries). They often look even more spectacular when they are seen side by side with other less showy specimens.

Find a place in the kitchen for a basket of fruit and vegetables and immediately the room loses any 'workshop' tendency and looks homely. If surface space is scarce, hang a bowl or basket in a string macramé net, hang a flat-sided basket on a bracket, or hang a flat woven shopping basket on the wall. Partly fill it with crumpled newspaper, then have fruit and vegetables spilling out, cornucopia style.

Just one thing: don't resort to the windowsill and don't place a fruit and vegetable arrangement in full sun (at least not unless you are trying to stimulate the ripening process). Don't damage the skins or cut off the tops – once fruit and vegetable flesh is exposed to the air, it starts to lose valuable vitamins.

For an informal supper party, a flat basket of fruit and vegetables as a centrepiece sets the scene perfectly; guests get the appetizing message at one glance that all the produce on the menu is going to be home-grown. Use one of those flat round tray-like Chinese baskets, or beg a Brie cheese box from the grocer's. Line the base with vine leaves, ivy, fig, blackberry – whatever you have – and arrange the fruit and vegetables asymmetrically or in a pyramid. Small white golf-ball turnips, beetroot, apples, cherries, radishes and tomatoes arranged together in ever-decreasing circles are surprisingly effective.

For a festive occasion, you can make a not-to-be-eaten pyramid that won't tumble. Buy or carve a pyramid shape from a block of foam and arrange fruit and nuts round and round it. Keep the stalks on cherries, strawberries and beech-mast, make a hole in the foam with a skewer and press them in. Bind very fine wire round shiny nuts, almonds, hazelnuts and so on, twist the wire ends into a short 'stalk' and press them in. Push a florist's stub wire through plums, small apples and grapes, then twist it to give a firm grip. Arrange the fruits in concentric circles or helter-skelter spirals round the cone and stand the design on a dish of leaves.

In China, where they have remarkably nimble fingers, vegetable carving has become a fine art and 'sculptors' produce temples, towers, tulips, tortoises, exquisitely carved from roots such as carrots and radishes; one exotically shaped vegetable to garnish a dish. It's a pity about the Vitamin C – which will have died of exposure – but these vegetable sculptures can be delightful. Progress from radish roses and fans and chip away with a small craft knife to produce something a little more ambitious – letters of the alphabet, even. Gracing the cheeseboard or a cold dish, such a design would become not only the focal point but a talking point.

Less ambitious and almost as effective, crudités can be tied in bundles and served with cheese. Cut little matchsticks of crisp and crunchy carrots, celery and peppers, arrange them neatly like piles of wooden faggots and tie them with a long chive leaf or a string of thinly pared cucumber peel. It's an attractive way to serve cooked julienne strips of veg-etables, too.

A cornucopia of good things from the garden. This tempting arrangement of fruit, berries, vegetables and nuts looks almost too good to eat – but in a well-planned garden there will always be more delights to follow.

Fruit and cheese are perfect partners visually as well as gastronomically, but don't stop at a few token bunches of grapes or pairs of cherries. Pile soft fruits such as raspberries, loganberries, dessert gooseberries, fat and juicy blackcurrants into small ramekin dishes amongst the cheese and they'll shine like, well, berries.

Make an irresistibly attractive presentation of fruits to serve as dessert. A large flat plate brimful of grapes, peaches, figs, slices of melon, walnuts and hazelnuts – everybody loves to have a choice.

Line a dish – it could be a basket, plate or a pedestal cake stand – with scented geranium leaves and pack it with fruit of all kinds. Tuck a few leaves amongst the fruit and just before serving tuck in a few fresh flowers such as marigolds, zinnias, single chrysanthemums, pinks or other long-lastings. For a slightly more 'prepared' look make a small posy of flowers or a miniature arrangement in a piece of soaked foam and surround it with fruit and nuts. It's very French, and very tempting.

For the personal touch, the truly individual approach, arrange a one-portion selection of fruit on small leaf-lined dishes – peaches, kiwi fruit, grapes and nuts with a few silvered sugared almonds or foil-wrapped chocolates as petit-four surprises. The vegetable basket and the fruit bowl come in many guises.

INDEX

E

F

G

H

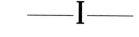
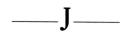

ACKNOWLEDGEMENTS

The publishers wish to thank the following organizations for their kind permission to reproduce the photographs in this book:

Ardea London (Liz & Tony Bomford) 118, (Bob Gibbons) 119, 120 centre; The Bridgeman Art Library 120 bel, 121 bel; Camerapix Hutchison Library Ltd 109; E T Archive Ltd (RHS) 43, 80, 81, 98, 102; Mary Evans Picture Library 51; The Harry Smith Horticultural Photographic Collection 10, 11, 55; Michael Warren/Photos Horticultural 14, 94, 95, 107, 130, (Louis Warren) 131.

Other photography: Bryce Attwell 75; Michael Boys 79; Laurie Evans 26, 90; Robert Golden 58; Jerry Harpur 54; Gina Harris 22; N Holmes 39, 78; Roger Phillips 127; Paul Williams 19, 59; George Wright 15, 38.

Designer Bob Gordon
Editor Camilla Simmons
Art Editor Jeremy Bratt
Production Controller Maryann Rogers

Special photography by James Jackson (pages 23, 27, 31, 35, 42, 46, 47, 50, 63, 67, 82, 86, 87, 91, 99, 103, 106, 111, 114, 115, 122, 134, 135, 139, 142, 146, 147, 151)

with Stylist Marie O Hara and Home economist Allyson Birch

Black-and-white line illustrations: David Lawrence

Black-and-white illustration page 36: Sandra Pond

Handwritten notes: Chris Sears